Crossing the Wasteland

and educational institutions and in the media—pleasure and instant gratification supplant all values. This is achieved by exploitation of the Western heritage which during the past three centuries has been turned into a wasteland. The result is a contamination of the character of a large part of the population. Under corporate tutelage desire becomes desire for pleasure and instant gratification. Desire is the fundamental raw material of corporate society. The corporations must control in order to gratify desire. When institutions other than the corporations influence desire, they limit the markets which are the life-blood of the corporations. Any restraint upon pleasure and instant gratification diminishes the markets. To the extent that corporations dominate society, a large part of the population undergoes moral degeneration. The progress of this culturally and spiritually debilitating process is sustained by a paradox.

The paradox is that the human beings who create and control the corporations do not undergo the same moral transformation which their institutions generate in general society. Theirs is a vocation demanding discipline and skill. Elements of puritanism were indeed essential to the rise of capitalism and are essential to sustaining corporate society. Pristine puritanism has all but disappeared from the Western world, but elements of it survive here and there in aristocratic families and can be regenerated in persons of superior talent in any social class by opportunity and the prospect of power. The paradox matures in the response of a substantial part of the population to the people of superior talent controlling corporations, which is to say, controlling the power and wealth of the nation.

The population forming solidarity with the corporate leaders has two sources. Most important are those of wealth–either great or relatively small—resulting directly from the power of the corporations. In times of great prosperity these are a large part of the population. For the most part they have undergone the moral transformation that corporate power generates in society generally, and, at the very best, are not inclined to argue with or inhibit successful corporate policies.

the most spectacular atrocities in the history of the West, witness episodes of the Crusades and the Inquisition. Through much of history, the Church has fostered anti-semitism. It has not successfully exonerated itself of charges that it inadequately opposed the Holocaust. All this can be said. And, despite all this—and part of the enormity, indeed—it will be maintained that the Church is a divine institution.

The facts relevant to many of these charges cannot be denied. In response to them here in the beginning of the argument, we can only offer cursory observations. During most of the centuries of the past, the Church has in large part constituted the world undergoing the processes of history. Its triumphs and failures have been those of Western humanity. The ethical evolution that has occurred in Western history has inevitably occurred also in the Church. Furthermore, the large and spectacular events that become conspicuous in the web of historical record are far from exhausting the life and function of the institution as an intimate and constant presence in human life within the Western world. And, while we are carping at the historical deficiencies of the Church, we will do well to compare them with successes and failure of modern Western society generally.

Inevitably secularized imaginations share an ambivalence toward Catholicism. On one hand there is unquestionably a fascination, but on the other a deep revulsion. My purpose is to attempt to dispel that revulsion by looking at its basis in history. Accordingly there is need for a pointed discrimination. The notion of religious conversion of secularized intellectuals is not to be associated with images of masses of people responding in sudden and emotional contrition to the passionate exhortation of a revivalist speaker. By stark contrast, the process, if it occurs, is assumed to involve assimilation of some equivalent of the large range of knowledge and understanding that makes up the following pages of this book.

Essentially the Church has been the history from which Modernism wished to escape. But in the progress of the divine spirit

in the world, history outgrows itself and is transformed. Roman Catholicism is the source of the faith outlined above. This formulation is inspired by and is an effort in a brief treatment to be true to the thought of the great Jesuit, Father Karl Rahner, the Church's most distinguished theologian.[7] The practice of Catholicism is more than this formulation, but whatever is contrary to these articles of faith is not Catholicism. To draw more nearly into accord with Catholic Christianity, it is necessary to add two discussions and their corresponding articles of faith. These are as follows:

We cannot love abstractions. The mystery and the power known in abstractions is inevitably conceived as less than human. Love of the infinite mystery and power insists that it be made known to us only in the highest form of which we can conceive—the form of a consciousness, the form of a person.

We participate in the divinity that is a person only if the person is also human, with a humanity that is authenticated only in the knowledge of death. Such a divinity is both divine and human, forming the prototype of reconciliation to death in the form of transcendence which we can share.

Summarized, the two paragraphs above become the following articles of faith:

[14] In so far as we can conceive of God, he exists within the reach of our power of love necessarily as a person, a mystery comprehending both the divine and the human. (For a formulation of this which does not make immortality imperative and which is harmonious with Judaism, see page 124.)

[15] The person that is divine is also human and is so to a depth that requires his dying and thus, in complete humanity, coming within the reach of our power of love.

These truths are the foundation of the refuge from the desert. They can become part of us. To the degree that this occurs the

social poison of corporate power will be neutralized. We must begin, however, by recognizing fully the character of the cultural wasteland which is the background against which corporate power shapes our lives..

Chapter Two

THE WASTELAND

T. S. Eliot's effort to distill the essence of his time is his great poem *The Waste Land:*

> What are the roots that clutch, what branches grow
> Out of this stony rubbish? Son of man,
> You cannot say, or guess, for you know only
> A heap of broken images, where the sun beats,
> And the dead tree gives no shelter, the cricket no relief.
> And the dry stone no sound of water. (19–24)

These are Eliot's basic images for the twentieth century. The "broken images" are the detritus of demolished faith, not only in religion, but in all values. Eliot's poem is one of the two greatest masterpieces of Modernism, that cultural wave that began with World War I and lasted until some time in the 1960's. The keynote of Modernism is the ending of Western civilization, especially as the embodiment of Christianity.[8] All Modernism is a register, in delight or despair, of this historical departure. The mood of lamentation or horrified recoil is persistent.

Nietzsche , the true father of Modernism, reveled in the declaration that "God is dead!"[9] but recognized that "the mythless man stands eternally hungry."[10] In Europe, he declared, "The wasteland grows." In 1920 William Butler Yeats wrote

Things fall apart; the center cannot hold
Mere Anarchy is loosed upon the world
The blood-dimmed tide is loosed, and everywhere
The ceremony of innocence is drowned

"Surely," it seemed, "some revelation is at hand; /Surely the Second Coming is at hand" and the Second Coming is imagined as "some rough beast" that "slouches toward Bethlehem to be born."[11] The world is "darkening," said Heidegger in 1935. "The essential episodes of this darkening, the flight of the gods, the destruction of the earth, the standardization of man, the preeminence of the mediocre."[12]

At the turn of the century the celebration of the failure may seem to us naive. And the disappearance of God may not touch us with a sense of tragic loss, but that is because we have become creatures of the desert. In our century, certainly, God did at least virtually disappear. In the civilization embodied in the steel, glass, and concrete of the city, there is no faint intimation of God. Here and there, occupying obscure corners, churches and temples are quaint anachronisms, attended presumably by mindless and totally insignificant people. Never mind the talk of a religious revival. It does not affect public life. Despite the persistence of certain antiquated and completely empty formalities, such as prayer at the opening of Congress, human affairs are conducted in total oblivion of the idea of God. In the general administration of basic human needs—for such as food and medicine—there is no slightest suggestion of a need for God. Most of the days of most lives and all of the days of many lives pass without the faintest occurrence of the idea of God. For many of those who take pride in thinking, the thought of God has become a preposterous notion, even quite contemptible. This despite the fact that something very different has also happened. With the waning of the century the circumstances eliminating God have lost their authority. We become more and more aware that, as

Nietzsche told us, if God is dead it is because we have killed him.

This suggests that the death of God may have been a dubious proclamation. If so, then we had better understand how it came about that we "killed God." For minimally thoughtful people in a secular society, the explanation may seem simple. It is a matter of what we now know. It is assumed that most people, now aware of modern science, have inevitably understood that God does not exist. This explanation is commonplace and universal. But it does not explain. It is true that from the Renaissance onward there have been individuals for whom the rejection of religious faith has followed from specific intellectual operations based on scientific knowledge. It is also true that for thinking people, once they are "liberated," scientific knowledge seems a virtually unmovable obstacle to faith.

We dare not attempt to approach the subject of God without having clearly in mind the cogent knowledge said to pose so awesome a prohibition of faith. A brief view of our cultural and intellectual history is therefore in order. Most of us need to remind ourselves of the real nature of the problem. A faith conceivable for modern minds can be built only on an understanding of the powerful difficulties to be overcome. No faith can survive that ignores these conditions.[13]

The History Tending to God's Death

In the thirteenth century Christianity had prevailed. Europe had been Christianized. European culture was in most respects a pervasive religious synthesis. The Papacy was the most powerful throne in the world. The now fully developed feudal structure was, in effect, integrated with the Church. As early, however, as the twelfth and thirteenth centuries there are evidences in the art and literature of Europe of a shift of human imagination. It drifts away from the Medieval preoccupation with God and the other world to a celebration of man and this world. This shift

climaxes in the profoundly humanized culture of the Renaissance of the fifteenth, sixteenth, and seventeenth centuries.

The first specific intellectual fracture in the Medieval religious synthesis came with the work of Copernicus in the first half of the sixteenth century (from 1512 to 1543). He questioned the Ptolemaic astronomy which, in accord with Christian pre-conceptions, had the earth at the center of the universe. Copernicus proposed a heliocentric system. In 1517 a more immediately fatal disruption of social and intellectual order occurred when Martin Luther nailed his theses to the door of the church of Wittenberg, inaugurating the Protestant Reformation. Then in the early seventeenth century what Copernicus had cautiously proposed as a "mathematical curiosity" became truly revolutionary. Subversion of the preconceptions of the past was enforced by the concrete observations of Galileo, who was the founder of modern physics. The implications for the entire structure of the Medieval world were now clear, and John Donne, Dean of St. Paul's in London, could lament the disappearance of cosmic order and the emergence of social chaos attending the rise of individualism:

> The new Philosophy calls all in doubt,
> The Element of fire is quite put out;
> The Sun is lost, and th'earth, and no man's wit
> Can well direct him where to look for it.
> And freely men confesse that this world's spent,
> When in the Planets, and the Firmament
> They seek so many new; then see that this
> Is crumbled out again to his Atomies.
> 'Tis all in peeces, all cohaerence gone;
> All just supply, and all Relation:
> Prince, Subject, Father, Sonne, are things forgot
> For every man alone thinks he hath got
> To be a Phoenix, and that then can be
> None of that kinde, of which he is, but hee.

—"The First Anniversary"

Of course, a great deal more was to come. In the first quarter of the seventeenth century two seminal thinkers separately proposed that all the thought of the past be abandoned and that the foundations of human knowledge be established wholly anew. Francis Bacon in England proposed a new beginning based on the empirical investigation of science. In France René Descartes proposed that every conception of the past should be discarded and that reason should seek foundations in absolute certainty. Bacon and Descartes respectively inaugurated modern empiricism (knowledge begins with observable facts) and rationalism (knowledge begins with reason). The spirit of these new beginnings underlay the explosion of scientific investigation and discovery during the seventeenth century. This development culminated in the work of Sir Isaac Newton at the end of the century.

The scientific revolution of the seventeenth was partly contemporary with a revolution that was very different but not less historically significant. In 1649 the Puritan armies of England overcame the royal forces and beheaded the anointed monarch Charles I. What happened in the Puritan theocracy that followed we will recall later. Under the eleven years of the dictatorship of the Puritan general Cromwell, religious sects multiplied at such a rate that efforts to count and keep track of them were frustrated. This points to part of the divisive conditions which meant the failure of the Puritan Interregnum and, after eleven years, the restoration of the Stuart dynasty placing Charles II on the throne.

If Puritanism and science seem strange cohorts, it should be remembered that they shared something fundamental. Both were centrally inspired by the craving for certainty. Science would build on direct observation of nature. Puritanism would know God directly, without the mediation of learning and the Church, by what was called inspiration. This craving for certainty, and

contemporaries—it leads eventually to a nihilism almost as complete as that informing postmodernism: no moral principle, no value, no meaning whatever, and certainly no God. Let us note for future reference that in this earlier version of nihilism, one thing remains intact: the processes of observation and reason that lead to this nihilism. For Hume in particular, however, this reservation did not stand; his nihilism is total.

We should note that underlying the empiricist argument there is a profoundly important assumption which is part of the heritage from the Cartesianism of the seventeenth century. This assumption is that the subject, the "knower," and the object, or that which is "known," exist in complete separation and independence. This implies that the knowing mind can stand apart from and observe the universe, objectively. In a naive way, it implies the possibility of absolute and complete knowledge (such as the religious must assume to be the prerogative of God). This separation of the knower from what he knows has been shown to be impossible by modern quantum mechanics. (On this point see Appendix A.)

Hume's most corrosive thought influenced very few people at the time. Virtually its only social consequence was that Hume, a kindly gentleman of mild temper and great sophistication, was despised by most of his intellectual contemporaries. By the last decades of the eighteenth century, however, the deadly implications of the combined traditions of empiricism and rationalism were widely recognized. A reaction set in that is called the Romantic movement.

Romanticism was a revolt against the implicit nihilism of the Age of Reason. Romanticism declared that the faculty of truth was not reason, by which was meant the critical intellect, that is, the faculty of division and analysis. This faculty is what Kant called the "understanding, which he contrasted with what he called "Reason." Reason in his sense was the basic impulse to unity which he took to be the motive force of all intellectual activity. Kant's was the major philosophical influence in the

development of Romanticism. The faculty for truth, the Romantics declared, was the imagination, which gives rise to truth in the form of poetry and religion. The affirmation of the imagination was the nineteenth century's defense against the eighteenth century heritage of rationalism and empiricism. It was one of a number of factors accounting for the vigor of religion in the nineteenth century. It is a tradition of permanent importance.

Both the mild common-sense religiosity of the Age of Reason and the more intense spirituality of the Romantic interlude shaped the general culture. But in the background and among a large part of the intellectual population, the seventeenth century heritage of rationalism and empiricism continued with great vigor. Empiricist assumptions informed nearly the entirety of the famous French Encyclopedia published between 1751 and 1766. In 1770 in France Baron D'Holbach could publish his *System of Nature*, declaring freedom of the will to be totally illusionary and demonstrating elaborately the total determinism supposedly controlling all human action. In 1798 the astronomer and mathematician Pierre Simon de Laplace published *The System of the World* asserting the applicability of Newtonian mechanics to the totality of the universe. He argued for cosmic determinism. A rational intellect with sufficient empirical information, Laplace argued, would be able on deterministic principles to predict the position at any time of any particle of the universe. Against Newton's protest, he maintained that total explanation was theoretically possible without any need of the hypothesis of God.

In the nineteenth century, scientific speculation and research moved more dramatically into conflict with religious faith. Developments in two fields were especially disturbing for literalist religion. In 1833 Sir Charles Lyle established the modern science of geology with publication of his *Principles of Geology*. Lyle was reticent about the implications of his work, but sophisticated readers understood that they destroyed the foundations of literalist Biblical faith. It was obvious from his work that the configurations of the surface of the earth resulted from geologi-

many of these belong among the soft-headed atheists, or we might call them "the virtual atheists." A debilitated God is the victim of this forgetfulness. In the environment of an abundantly favored population, God as a vital reality survives only by rigorous care. The complacently comfortable do not bestir themselves in the affirmation of life, which is an act. Faith is an act, the product of intellectual energy.

Technology insinuates intellectual absurdities. It also does something more insidious. It shapes the way the mind functions. This shaping and control amount to a conclusive censorship. As a practical matter in the workaday world, we tend to believe that authentic knowledge, the knowledge of ultimate reality, is achieved by a relatively rare and complex process. In order to become truly scientific, one attempts to becomes purely and exclusively an observer. One tries to set aside all that one knows, to make inactive all habits and preconceptions, to put in abeyance all preferences and desires. Perception must be unadulterated. You render yourself, your consciousness, utterly passive. Indeed, you act as though your body does not exist.

Then you, acting as scientist, expose yourself to the effects of laboratory manipulation, or its equivalent, and something happens to you. You are acted upon. Color, form, and movement register upon your perfectly translucent senses. What is thus recorded in your memory is a simulacrum of what exists external to your being. The external universe speaks to you. It acts upon you. But it can do so only if you become purely an observer, if you contrive to render yourself, your perceptions and condition of knowing, purely passive. If, in effect, you disappear. This is the presumed process of science; it gives us what we call objective knowledge. The result is a continental rift in human culture concerning the nature of truth. On one side truth is assumed to occur in a process that culminates in total passivity and the radical isolation of the single function of intellectual receptivity. On the other side of the rift, on an ever narrowing plateau, truth is taken to be a function of the entire human being. This is the total

energy that arrives at religious faith. It is justified ultimately by the assumption that we are the children, the descendants, of the stars. By radical contrast, the knowledge derived from the strategy of passivity, when we fully submit to it, tells us there is no God.

The objective posture we are taught to consider the key to truth, despite the notable fact that we can neither become totally passive nor disappear. It is the knowledge which, when we fully submit to it, tells us there is no God.

This posture of the mind has tended to be cultivated by educated people during most of the time since the scientific revolution of the seventeenth century that is associated with the name of Descartes. This conception of knowledge, which is a corollary of Cartesian objectivity, is a filter assuring that fundamentally religious ideas will be excluded. Cartesian objectivity, as noted above, meant that the human mind could stand apart from the universe and describe a totality of things in which it was, itself, not included. In the twentieth century we have come to understand, that although the conception of objectivity continues to prevail in the habits of mind of most literate people, it is valid, that is to say useful, only for limited superficial and practical purposes. Beyond that it is profoundly mistaken and deceptive. This point will be developed later when we consider a revision of our conceptions of reality.

The truth is that there is no belief and, contrary to scientistic faith, not even any positive knowledge that simply happens to us. It is only negative knowledge that just happens to us. What just happens to us are absences, failings, disappearances. With that in mind, we come to realize something else about the absence of religious faith from our ways of conceiving reality. For most people the death of God, the disappearance of God, was a matter of default, a kind of inattention. Faith was something that we did but for which we have lost the technique. In yet other, more particular ways, the loss was not first of all an intellectual achievement, but an effect of the environment.

As in all previous ages, the environment tends to shape thought. From the industrial revolution onward technology has increasingly saturated the environment. This enforces the predilections of the intelligentsia. Technology is a manipulation of material causation. It propagates the notion, as noted above, that material causation is the central principle of the universe and pervades it exhaustively. The obvious implication is that the universe is exclusively a range of matter. There is also the implication that the universe is rigorously determined, but this idea succumbs to the contradictory notion that man is capable of total control. Knowledge gained in total passivity gives rise to a delusionary dream of power. Implicit in the idea of total control, of course, is the idea of total knowledge. The idea of total knowledge–Godlike knowledge—is a powerful motivation among even the most distinguished scientists, who with extreme rarity acknowledge its absurdity.[14]

The Environment Where God Disappeared

Science, technology, and industrial development have created an environment providing for total gratification—or almost total. Most of us live in the world of the abundantly favored. In interiors of homes and businesses, we live in controlled climates, cool in summer, warm in winter. Food is abundant, varied, excellent, and cheap. Exquisite cuisine is available to most people at least some of the time. We move about daily in finely engineered machines, usually with speed and efficiency. The ache of distances has been eliminated by air travel and the long-distance telephone, and e-mail. The tedium, the boredom, otherwise inevitable in most lives, is immediately dispelled by electronic media. Modern medicine and pharmacology assure that most illnesses are prevented or quickly cured and that good health is virtually constant. Massive research efforts are directed at most of the remaining fatal diseases. Spectacular progress is being made in efforts to cure cancer and AIDS. Life expectancy has been radically extended.

Above all, pain and anguish have been expelled from the texture of life by taming of the two specters that were most constantly and universally their source—the spectres of death and of sex. Sex has been sanitized, rendered innocuous in every sense. Childbirth, always attended by the threat of death in the past, has been made essentially safe. Most momentously, sex has been rid of the grave social dangers. Sex in the past was always likely to result in conception. The result could be opprobrium or enslaving and permanent obligation and commitment.

Reproduction, once seemingly central to sex, has been made incidental, a completely controllable choice. This is the revolution wrought by the invention of oral contraception, one of the decisive events in human history. We are now on the verge of genetic interventions that can avert the horrors of abnormal births. The resulting transformation of social attitudes has divested sex of nearly every taboo. The universal rendering safe and sanitizing of contraception has, for perhaps a majority of people, transformed attitudes toward all forms of birth control. In depriving sex of all its aura of mystery and danger, birth control has softened and undermined attitudes that tended to restrict sexual activity in the past. Sex once hedged about with life-long patterns of expectation and excitement, defined by patterns of meaning, but charged with the pain of abstinence, of deferred pleasure, became a matter of indifference, hardly of more consequence than a daily routine.

But sex is not permitted to have so incidental and mild a role in our lives. It is as though sexuality is in critical condition and requires constant emergency resuscitation. Left to the solitude of human privacy, it will die. It must be made a constant presence in every waking moment of our lives. The motivation, however, is not really survival. The motivation is corporate profit. We discover a remarkable correspondence of corporate appetite and the cultivation of pleasure and instant gratification as a communal value. A headline in *The New York Times* reads: "Technology Sent Wall Street Into Market for Pornography."[15] In this article

ishing became intolerable. This was linked to the Faustian impulse to total power, to God-like autonomy. In the past, the Christian imagery of death in the Crucifixion was a presence in every public occasion. Protestantism banished the imagery of death. Even in secluded Catholic sanctuaries its power is symbolically restrained.

As Protestantism has waned with the waning of faith generally, the Faustian impulse travels on its own. Death becomes an object for "management," and its management has now a specific secular recourse in a psychological maneuver. Modern writer after modern writer has made the point: One cannot imagine his death. One can imagine dying but not the end result. This fosters a hygienic practice. The imagination is trained to stop always at the borders of life, and this subtly generates an assumption. There is only life. There is no death. It is quite true that we cannot imagine death. The point is that we obliterate its awful reality. We train our imaginations to eliminate the confrontation with what we cannot imagine but unquestionably exists. Quite deliberately we structure consciousness to consolidate the effects of technology. We welcome life in a technological cocoon that conceals from us the reality of the human condition. Our inherent metaphysical curiosity is repressed to become an itch of consciousness, a strain of endemic neurosis.

Massive powers offer to protect us. The environment says constantly to us that humanity is in charge. We are surrounded on all sides by the enormity of modern organization. We live near freeways. They obliterate communities, the small human congeries near to us. The massive lace-works of concrete and steel speak of extraordinary economic and technological resources. Corporations are larger than many nations. They thrust across national borders to become global forces. Their wealth is measured in billions. We are engaged continuously with electronic media that blanket the world. As workers we are employed by giant institutions and we serve, not individuals, but populations. As consumers we are deluged by a system of unlimited variety

and perpetual change moving in global dimensions. The human powers that saturate our world are of magnitudes we cannot imagine. Their enormity preempts the thought of God.

And yet, overwhelmed by human energies, we do not know human beings. And coming really to know human beings, becoming able to experience them as human beings, will bring us at least to the verge of salvation. Somewhere human beings are in control, but in their anonymity they are suspect. If they are responsible for the comforts which we presumably deserve, they are responsible for the pains their faceless agencies have described as unnecessary and avoidable. Saturating our environment with human efficiency and power, they have left us in solitude. We become human, we realize our being, only when we communicate with individual conscious beings. In the omnipresence of human power and its contrivance of universal solitude, we have the keys to contemporary discontent and protest as well as to what we call the religious revival, which stands not at the center but firmly on the periphery of our interests.

Most people have been shaped, to a large extent unconsciously, by living in the increasingly secularized atmosphere maintained in the West for over three centuries. Most people now living in this civilization have never known the experience of religious faith. This is no less true of the American masses who will say absent mindedly that they believe in God. (These are profoundly secularized human beings. They are the best evidence that the atmosphere, not an argument, has excluded religious faith.) The prevailing spiritual (non-spiritual) orientation results from the fact that we have created an entire culture which has excluded all vestiges of God. This is the most deeply pervasive culture in human record. That is to say, it is the culture which most exhaustively penetrates, shapes, and controls human life. It becomes an infection of blood and bone. The range and magnitude of history and circumstance occluding the thought of faith in the Western world is truly remarkable. We must feel a certain chill at the thought of what this culture does implant in

the human organism. This is why Cardinal Newman, observing the growth of modernism in the nineteenth century, could say, "And so I argue about the world—*if* there be a God, *since* there is God, the human race is implicated in some terrible aboriginal calamity."[16]

For so long as we can understand that, for so long as we are aware of the wasteland, we are in touch with civilization and remain within reach of potential spiritual resources. But by the processes of secularization we have been stranded in history. The greatest of dangers is that we are going to sleep. We may not be able to realize that the condition in which we live is an emergency. As a French critic says, the "ending of cultures is not perceptible from within."[17]

Only in historical perspective do we come to understand that the technological cocoon in which we languish has fostered an intellectual disease that results in the obliteration of reality.

The most obvious benefits of the modern world were gained at the price of religious faith. Yet, for those who think, as Modernism achieved its ultimate development in what we call Postmodernism, it became the revelation of radical religious need. It unveiled the ultimate abyss underlying the world as a secular experience. It is as authentic heirs of Modernism that we turn to faith, and ineradicably it conditions the faith of which we are capable.

Chapter Three

THE SPIRITUAL IMPERATIVE

In a statement published after his death in 1976 Heidegger said, "Only a god can save us."[18] For Pitrim A. Sorokin, at Harvard, one of the founders of sociology, Western culture even in 1941 simply faced an "ultimatum": change or "go to ruin, to a life uncreative, devoid of any genius, painful and inglorious." A "mild religious therapy," said Sorokin, would do no good. The main premises and values of the dominant culture had to be rejected. The necessary ordeal would go through a formula of conversion that always characterized recovery from such crises. The formula "crisis-ordeal-catharsis-charisma-resurrection" described the transformation in which Graeco-Roman culture was terminated by Christianity." "Purified and ennobled," said Sorokin, "society proceeded to erect a new house based on the Absolute, God, love, duty, sacrifice, grace and justice. Such was the invariable course of the great crises of the past. Such is the way out of our own crisis. There is no other possibility."[19]

In *Civilization on Trial*, Arnold Toynbee said, "The future of mankind in this world—if mankind is going to have a future in this world—lies, I believe, with the higher religions that have appeared within the last 4000 years."[20] Even the noble reviser of Marxism, Jürgen Habermas, who has devoted his intellectual life to resistance of postmodern nihilism, finds that to save ourselves we must again have faith, perhaps not in a specific or

literal religion, but in elements of religion: "Among modern societies, only those who can bring essential elements of their religious tradition, which points beyond the merely human, into the spheres of the profane will be able to save the substance of the human as well."[21]

Daniel Bell, the distinguished sociologist, says, "Despite the shambles of modern culture, some religious answer surely will be forthcoming." Bell considers religion a constitutive part of man's consciousness. He points out that all societies have "rites of incorporation and rites of release." In modern society, he says, "release itself has gone so far as to be without bounds." The need, then, is "for some new rite of incorporation, signifying membership in a community that has links with the past as well as the future."[22] For Vico in the eighteenth century the vital survivors of degenerate civilizations make new beginnings. They are able to do so because they are restored to "piety, faith, and truth which are the natural foundations of justice as well as the graces of beauties of the eternal order of God."[23]

Because we have a deep concern for the welfare of mankind, the wasteland must come to have a special meaning: Embracing religion is a social responsibility. Such a suggestion is not to be taken lightly. Emile Durkheim saw the idea of God as implicit in society.[24] For Durkheim the idea of God is a part of reality, and we may come to the opinion that there is in his analysis a deep truth about the truth of God. If so, then affirming God, coming to practice a religion as a social responsibility, is an authentically religious act.

Sociological arguments not withstanding, we are of distinctly secular mind. How can we be imagined to embrace religion? Concerning the proposal I intend here, I will from the start be quite blunt and—for many—unquestionably outrageous: We can believe because we want to. And we should. But coming to want to is not a simple matter. And what it is we would be wanting is not a simple matter. We may eventually be guided, and rewarded, by Kierkegaard: "To search for God is to have found Him."

Obstacles even to beginning the argument–the search—abound. How is it reasonable to expect spiritual change in entirely secularized minds? The answer is that we are prime products of modernist history, and history is sacred. Furthermore, writing from a religious point of view, one necessarily believes that we, especially as virtuous atheists, are unacknowledged and unknowing heirs of Christianity, perhaps the best of all its progeny. We have with fidelity and endurance gone through the crucible of time. We have been cleansed and purified of much of the dross of history.

In times past, it was evil in men that obstructed the call of faith. For us the obstacle to faith is our virtue. To believe because you want to? Isn't there something disgustingly corrupt about such a suggestion? When we are confronted with the proposal that we embrace religious faith, we are morally indignant. In fact one may rise to his highest capacity for moral indignation. He becomes more intensely moral than at any other time.

One is offended, first of all, by a suggestion that he should undergo a fundamental change. Being a secular person on principle, one, thinks of oneself as a highly moral person. He takes pride in the kind of person he is. He is above all a person of integrity. To suggest change may be to envision a violation of integrity. A suggestion of a change in the person is offensive and alarming. Furthermore, the means proposed for such a change is revolting. It is proposed that one may choose what he believes. A principle of fundamental loyalty is impugned, a violation of essential intellectual honesty.

One must ask: Honesty about what? Loyalty to *what*? Apparently the answer must be "scientific empiricism." Or in more practical terms, one says that he accepts nothing to be true that does not result from direct and independent reading of the world, of nature. This is the particular honesty on which the secular person prides himself. One accepts only what is established by controlled, scientifically disciplined observation. One believes only principles based on what can reliably and repeatedly be seen, heard, touched, smelled, or tasted.

questions. It is not unthinkable that, on occasion, you might read a treatise on ethics. In one way or another, various arguments and considerations may be brought to your attention, but what happens to them finally is that you submit them to your own supreme and unquestionable judgment. There is certainly no person or institution that you will permit to dictate to you on moral questions. You alone are the judge of your own morality and of the morality—all that will be recognized as morality— prevailing in your world.

The first consequence of this is that you are, logically and necessarily, a perfect being. Let us grant that you may now and then violate a moral canon which you have independently and autonomously certified, have decided it to be valid. However, you do not do that very often. For at a certain point the moral canon that you repeatedly violate changes. A particular article of morality loses its validity. Your moral code accommodates itself to your practice. Its failure to do so would be intolerable to your sense of dignity. So eventually your condition of moral perfection is restored.

The second consequence of your moral autonomy is that everyone becomes morally autonomous. This leads inevitably to the third consequence of your moral autonomy.

The third consequence of your moral autonomy is that morality disappears. This is because your autonomy leads you to recognize the moral autonomy of others. Once you accept the moral autonomy of others, you relinquish any basis for judging anything that anyone else does. Agreement between people on any element of morality is purely coincidental. The principle derives no special force from its being shared. Hence the strange phenomena of our time in which people living even by traditional standards refuse moral judgment on anyone. "Judgmentalism" is condemned. Even radical differences of behavior lose their significance. Morality as a regulative factor in society disappears. It is replaced by "a choice between lifestyles."

It is true that eventually there is general agreement on certain legal prohibitions. There are prohibitions of overt and dramatic deprivation of life and of property. There are prohibitions of certain forms and degrees of pollution of the environment. There are also public agreements to limit the degree of physical suffering that individuals within society may undergo. Agreement on these matters is undertaken essentially in self-defense. These agreements do not constitute morality. They are rather provisions for public safety.

Public policy takes on a strong tinge of moral quality in a single and very special preoccupation. There is a deeply felt concern to prevent the violation of any individual's moral autonomy. This is expressed in various legal restraints that apply to individuals, but especially to government. Various restraints are designed to assure that no one interferes in or limits the moral autonomy of anyone. This assures that no one is subject to any control other than his own values and judgment. And most especially, in the realms of intellect and sex.

Moral autonomy is eventually intellectual autonomy. Intellectual autonomy means human freedom that is virtually absolute. You are, and must remain, free to think absolutely anything. Any effort to control or limit the content of your thought must be considered unendurably oppressive. The only permissible restraint upon thought is the prohibition of restraints. We are outraged by the thought of "thought control." We come to recognize, then, that anyone may think or imagine anything whatever. It follows that anyone may express or communicate anything. We recognize that what one thinks or imagines is the prelude to what he may do, but we will limit expression only if it is of immediate danger to life and property. Within those restraints anything the individual may think or do is morally authorized by his moral autonomy. While we protect individuals from radical harm, general effects on the acts of the individual upon the community are assumed not to exist.

We recognize that the complete moral structure of the other

person, the total internal landscape of the other, may be radically different from our own, and we deny the existence of any basis for preferring one structure to the other. So I cannot in good faith hold my own set of values with a sense of deep conviction. There is no good or bad, no better or worse. There are only alternatives. The alternatives are not moral codes or moral principles. One does not judge!

Morality disappears. Absolute freedom becomes necessarily the only moral value.

We cannot ignore yet another perspective on moral autonomy. It may well be that while taking pride in your moral autonomy you are also aware that large areas of your behavior are in fact dictated by an extensive if informal moral code. If you now examine this code as product and evidence of your moral autonomy, you realize a certain failure. You recognize necessarily that yours is an inherited code, that by no means do you always behave autonomously, and that much of your behavior is controlled either by the past or by the opinions current around you. Such a discovery is inevitable, because a moral code cannot be produced by an autonomous intellect and will. You can produce a moral code only on the basis of a commitment to something larger than yourself. A moral code must serve a larger purpose. You can practice a moral code only by subordinating yourself—all your other interests in so far as they are relevant—to that purpose.

Consider the most abstract moral position we know about and the one most nearly representative, not of moral, but of intellectual autonomy: Kant's categorical imperative. It may be stated as follows: So act that you may will that the principle of your action be a law for all mankind.[25] This imperative can follow only upon assumption of the commitment of the individual to the welfare of mankind.

The idea of moral autonomy, implicit in the notion of spiritual equality, is morally bankrupt. You must decide to abandon morality deliberately and completely or you abandon the notion

of your moral autonomy. The very possibility of morality demands the capacity for subordination and humility. You must discover something larger than you are to which you can commit yourself.

As a civilized modern, you. have, in fact, committed yourself to something larger than you are. In this case, however, there is apparently no implication for traditional morality. Your commitment is involved with something very startling that happened to the conscience of modern intellectuals. In the democratic and revolutionary movements of the eighteenth century there came into being for the modern world what may be called "public morality." This morality governs opinions about the condition of the collectivity. It is a morality governing, voting, political alignment, and activism in forms as various as demonstrating, writing letters to the editor, and running for office. This morality can be distinguished from "private morality" or the norms governing ones personal behavior. Private morality governs behavior related to other individuals and ones own appetites. It may be essentially identified with traditional morality.

An extraordinary fact is that the growth and invigoration of public morality has contributed to the demise of private morality. Indeed, as widely conceived, the two moralities are incompatible. The usual assumption of public morality is that humans are naturally good and that undesirable personal behavior is the result of unsatisfactory conditions in the organization of the collectivity. To promote private morality is to obscure the social condition causing the evil, and thus to subvert the interests of public morality. In a satisfactorily organized society, there would be no need whatever for private morality. Ultimately the individual is not responsible for his behavior. Hence, harshly disapproving or condemnatory attitudes and expressions are seen as atavistic and in extremely bad taste. That would seem to leave a problem of explaining "public morality," which regularly gives rise to attitudes of harsh condemnation. Attitudes and measures opposed to the "politically incorrect" are characteristically unrelenting; often they are devastating.

an organic incompleteness and generates an incessant impulse to unify and to experience unity—which we call desire . All these— the impulse to narrative, desire as the impulse to unity, the generation of a stillness free of time—these fundamentals of consciousness combine to create myth, the materials in which we receive God. We must believe that an aptitude so deeply inherent is also a need. But consciousness also gives conscious urgency to the need.

Our deepest need is the constancy of desire arising from the incompleteness of our consciousness, the incompleteness of our soul. We gradually realize that each of us is a satellite in a system of which God is the Sun. Then there is a throat-catching awareness of our deep need. Impelled by unlimited desire, we strive for total knowledge. The effort of the intellect to take possession of all things is doomed to failure. We may acknowledge then that the missing totality is God, of whom we are a part. With this knowledge–and only with this knowledge—comes fulfillment and fundamental happiness.

Our intellectual and spiritual need for God is fundamental. The denials of modernity, however, have brought into being very special needs for God. We need not immortality, but something more urgent, the regeneration of life. The doctrine of immortality we can assign to the poetry of faith. Our great need is that life not be pervaded by death. We must have a direction of life. With the disintegration of community and its social support for standards of behavior, there must be a new spiritual invigoration of morality. We must have a foundation for social coherence. Reality has been absorbed into the technological elaboration of the environment. Reality must be awakened in the regeneration of the life-world, which has been debilitated by the science-world (See Chapter 6, "Reality Anew). We must restore the enchantment of the world. Only a religious faith can do these things. We must have religion because our allegiance to mankind is instinctively compelled in the passion called love.

the world in desolation. It meant that this world was unmistakably the scene where we were to attain salvation, but it was a salvation independent of the world. It could come only from within. Here was the centralizing value of the individual, standing essentially in isolation in this world but related to the beyond. The world of the here and now was affirmed in reality but diminished in its value. Separated from God, it was delivered into human hands. Here was a key to the enormous Western effort to master the world and of the history which turns in our time again to a search for God and a deepened conception of the relation of God to the world.[27]

Christ and his message stood between humanity and the all powerful and unintelligible God of monotheism. His message was in human terms understandable by human beings. Christ as a human figure was totally intelligible. His humanity represented God. As bearer of a message Christ was a mediator. As Man and God, He was an interpretation, but He was an interpretation that preserved the mystery. The one God remains beyond human comprehension, a mystery that is only preserved in the elaboration for partial intelligibility in the idea of the Trinity. As a mystery knowable only in the ambiguity of the soul's recesses, the relationship to God is profoundly an individual one. A relationship of the individual without regard for special localities and ethnic traditions, transcending the narrowness of special histories and circumstances, it is a relationship open equally to everyone. In Christianity, God becomes truly a universal God.

The Crucifixion is the consummation of the Incarnation. The completeness of Christ's being as a human requires his participation in mortality. The completeness of his being as God makes the mystery of his mortality conceivable only as a most terrible intensity. The paradox of God on the Cross is the psychological center of Christianity, the vision in which we perpetually know the catharsis of death, the image in which we know peace and love.

Eventually the need for God is the need for a Church. The

reason is that belief is not the result of an argument, but the will to believe strong enough to promote practice prior to believing. Practice is not the result of faith but of the desire for faith and the beginning of the search.

Chapter Four

THE INWARD CHANGE

In the diversity of a chaotic world, we either make choices or events will make them for us. We can, and must. choose between things that are beginning to happen. The physical environment has been changing during most of the century, but recently there have been conspicuous changes of another kind. These are changes within us–transformations of our souls. These changes are of two special and conflicting kinds. Suddenly, within a few decades, there has been an almost overwhelming surge toward total hedonism. But quietly and in diverse ways there has also been a movement toward meaning. Hedonism is one of the culminating effects of the Enlightenment. But for some the Enlightenment ends in disillusionment and despair. Despair gives rise to the search for meaning.

In 1935 Heidegger saw the "darkening of the world" in "the flight of the gods."[28] Thirty years later he predicted a "turning," a transformation in which modernity, the culture dominated by technology and scientism, would be supplanted by a culture rich with life-giving energies. He said, "Perhaps we stand already in the shadow cast ahead by the advent of this turning."[29] The change which Heidegger saw beginning, and which he helped to bring about, is now a dispersed and unorganized but powerful movement in contemporary culture.

A major aspect of the turning that is taking place is a harbin-

ger of cultural health. A proliferation of writers are reacting against and attempting to stem the tide of nihilism implicit in much modernism and unanimously explicit in postmodernism. These thinkers represent the creative thrust of the turning. They propose antitoxins for the postmodernist pestilence, which are also alternatives to the implications of scientism pervading academic education.

I will mention writers of very diverse points of view, ranging from Christianity, to Judaism, to Marxism, and to more consistently secular perspectives. A list in alphabetical order includes the following: Hannah Arendt, Mikhail Bakhtin, Richard J. Bernstein, Jerome Bruner, Martin Buber, Kenneth Burke, Hans-Georg Gadamer, Nelson Goodman, Jûrgen Habermas, Martin Heidegger, Gertrude Himmelfarb, Richard Kearney, Emmanuel Levinas, Alasdair MacIntyre, Iris Murdoch, Thomas Nagel, Michael Oakeshott, Walker Percy, Michael Polanyi, Hilary Putnam, Paul Ricoeur, Stanley Rosen, George Steiner, Charles Taylor, Stephen Toulmin.[30]

The list could easily be lengthened. We may call these writers of *affirmation*. Some of them embrace a religious faith; these include Mikhail Bakhtin, Martin Buber, Hans-Georg Gadamer, Gertrude Himmelfarb, Emmanuel Levinas, Alasdair MacIntyre, Iris Murdoch, Walker Percy, Michael Oakeshott, Michael Polanyi, Hilary Putnam, Paul Ricoeur, George Steiner, Charles Taylor. Fifty years ago such a list would not have been possible—religious people who are neither clerics nor theologians, but distinguished in secular professions and universally recognized for their intellectual achievement.

That so many brilliant thinkers can be identified with faith is especially dramatic evidence of the "turning." However, for the most part their religious allegiances are not obvious in their work; generally they do not engage in religious advocacy. One may read many of the works of Ricoeur, for instance, without knowing certainly that he is a Christian. His work does not argue for Christianity, but he makes faith of one kind or another intellectually

music, voluble praise, bodily movement including clapping and swaying, personal testimonies, sometimes prayers 'in the Spirit' [a somewhat restrained form of "speaking in tongues," concerning which see below], a sermon full of stories and anecdotes, announcements, lots of humorous banter, a period of intense prayers for healing, and a parting song." From early pentecostalism, there are stories of levitations, that event associated with mystical practices in which the human body floats in air a few feet above the ground. There were also reports of healings, exorcisms, and miraculous signs such as a celestial light filling an auditorium and a glowing halo marking the divinely inspired.

If with pentecostalism in mind we now recall the writers of affirmation, in whom there has been an intellectual shift away from the Enlightenment, it may prove reasonable to imagine that we have in view two poles of a cultural continuum. It is obvious, of course, that we are dealing, on one hand, with people attracted to very primitive emotional excitement and in some cases the grossest kind of superstition. On the other hand, we are considering an intellectual elite.[32] Can there be a continuity between the kinds of change that have been described in the two very different psychic realms? What, if anything, is happening between the two apparently opposite poles of experience? Is anything relevant going on in what we may refer to as a cultural middle-class?

In the broad cultural middle-class, standard measurements do not reflect any increase during recent decades in overt religious activity or commitment. Relative to the total population, the proportion of membership and attendance in main line denominations has changed little over three decades.[33]

Yet it seems unquestionable that a spiritual change is under way. Some rather frail indices take on importance as they become cumulative. Between 1972 and 1980 bachelor's degrees in theology increased from 3.9 percent of the total degrees conferred to 6.2 percent. Doctoral degrees in theology increased from 1.4 percent to 4.2 percent. Between 1978 and 1981 the

number of people receiving religious instruction of some sort outside of worship services increased from 17 percent to 26 percent. By comparison, and a point of perhaps some importance, the number of people involved in Bible study groups did not change. There is a striking figure concerning Protestant-supported religious schools. These increased in number by 47 percent between 1971 and 1978. Obviously, this change may reflect, at least in part, an increase of crime and a loss of confidence in public schools.

A point of central interest concerns the publication and sales of religious books. Between 1970 and 1980 the number of religious books published remained virtually constant. The sale of religious books, however, increased in the same period. As a proportion of all books sold, religious books rose from 5.4 percent in 1970 to 7.8 in 1980. More recently not only the purchase of religious books, but the publication of religious books has expanded enormously. *Writer's Market* trumpets the interests of editors in books on "spirituality." A week rarely passes without notice of one or more religious books in *The New York Times Book Review*. Regularly religious books appear on best-seller lists. The number of religious titles published annually grew by 40 percent from 1990 to 1996 and sales reached $1.1 billion a year.[34]

The rising interest in religion has no better testimony than the fact that major television networks decided to exploit it in prime-time programming. In 1998 there were six regular programs catering to one or another aspect of religious interest: "Touched by an Angel" CBS; "Promised Land" CBS; "Soul Man" ABC; and, briefly, "Nothing Sacred" ABC; "Good News," UPN, and "Seventh Heaven," WB. NBC often schedules the "Billy Graham Crusade." On a more impressive level, the Oscar-winning actor Robert Duval produced, at a cost of 5 million dollars of his own money, the movie "The Apostle." In a radical departure from the usual alternative patterns of sentimentalism or satire in treating religion, Duval, in the leading role as a pentecostal preacher, gives the character dignity and unquestionable sin-

cerity of faith. Nothing of this sort has ever come out of Hollywood before.

Astonishingly, religion reached New York theater. The play "Home," by Samm-Art Williams, appeared on Broadway and at the Riverside Church theater. It is the story of a man who suffers as a veteran of the Vietnam war and as a victim of racial injustice but is a man of steadfast religious faith.[35] As part of a "Next Wave Festival, the Brooklyn Academy of Music produced the operatic drama "Missionaries," by Elizabeth Swados. The show, called "a dramatic requiem," honors three nuns and a lay missionary assassinated in El Salvador in 1980. Far more than a political statement, the performance is filled with stately solemnity of religious feeling.[36] In another theatrical presentation, the Tony-winning actress and television star Tyne Daly appeared in a one-woman play, "Mystery School," by Paul Selig. Daly plays a series of five very different women, each of whom is searching for religious faith.[37] One is also struck by a phenomenon almost unique in the twentieth century until its final year, a movie of stark religious integrity titled *The Confession*, starring Ben Kingsley and Alec Baldwin and based on the novel *Fertig*, by Sol Yurick.

A journalist commenting on religious programs on television, says, "Church attendance is down and people seem to be searching for religion anywhere but in the pew."[38] Searching—that is the nature of the religious activity of Tyne Daly's women. Searching is the form of the new religious phenomena of our time. Even within the framework of orthodoxy, perhaps especially within that framework, spirituality is a searching. In his five-year report to Rome Bishop Joseph A. Fiorenza, President of the American Council of Bishops, wrote as follows concerning his diocese:

> There is increasing hunger for the spiritual life while at the same time many reject the Church's moral teachings. The parish Churches are full but many do not participate in the sacrament of penance or have a Catholic understanding of the Eucharist. Divorce and re-marriage is also a problem for a significant number of

people. There is also a problem of Protestants proselytizing among Hispanic Catholics.

In spite of these serious concerns the Church continues to attract new members and there are signs that young adults who are estranged from the Church are returning.[39]

In an article in *The New York Times*, Michael Novak, a theologian at the American Enterprise Institute, cites statements by significant figures of our time. In an interview Normal Mailer said, "Religion to me is now the last frontier." Vaclav Havel comments on the crisis of moral responsibility in this "first atheistic civilization in the history of humankind." The crisis, Havel said, results from our loss of the feeling that "the Universe, nature, existence and our lives are the work of a creation guided by a definite intention." Novak comments that when such men, "ripe with years and not particularly known as pious men, join in emphasizing the new importance of religion, and evoke perspectives introduce into the literature of our time by Aleksandre Solzhenitsyn, you may be sure that the 21st century will be the most religious in 500 years."[40]

Harvey Cox speaks of "the religious renaissance" and of "the larger religious upsurge " of which pentecostalism is a part. Cox says something else that is of great importance. It is a suggestion of Heidegger's "Turning." Cox speaks of a "coming tidal change in world culture." He feels that the new religious movements during the last three decades "provide an invaluable set of clues about an even more comprehensive set of changes. The religious dimension may be the tip of the iceberg, but the underlying cultural shift is the sea in which the iceberg is floating"

It is especially notable that the historian Gertrude Himmelfarb speaks of "the current revival, which has been called the Fourth Great Awakening," this making reference to earlier periods of resurgence of religious fervor in the United States. The movement, beginning in the sixties, Himmelfarb points out, involves

The prophetic pose becomes grandiose: "I tell you this: you have just learned the secret of all life, and seen into infinity."

To the credulous reader, the argument is deeply flattering. The central theme of the book is: Life is about the discovery and realization of the Self. The isolated individual self is the source of truth. The first thing to learn about the self is its relationship to God. Quite simply, says the author, you are "His equal." Indeed, God says to the author, "You are already a God. You simply do not know it." Egomania is unabated.

The elevation of the Self is manifest in its total freedom. "God" says, "You call a life of complete freedom 'spiritual anarchy.' I call it God's great promise." The self is to enjoy total gratification. Its purpose is "infinite joy—which is What I Am."

Strange as it may seem, religious salvation is conceived in this book as the establishment of what Christopher Lasch calls "the narcissistic personality of our time" and which he sees as our basic cultural sickness. In the strangely corrupt book being described here, the self is granted limitless power: "There is nothing you cannot be, there is nothing you cannot do. There is nothing you cannot have." "For God's plan is for you to create anything—everything—whatever you want." "There is nothing you can't have if you choose it." This is the conviction of Narcissism—the infantile illusion of omnipotence. "God's" profile of this infantilism is complete. The individual possesses total knowledge. He is indestructible: "You never do die. Life is eternal, You are immortal. You never do die. You simply change form." The entire text, of course, is given such unity as it has by the central presumptuous and infantile irrationality: *There is only one reason to do anything: as a statement to the universe of who you are.*

The book's "theology" is supported by allying the "spiritual" message with the entire range of values and attitudes propagated by mass media. The past and everything that represents it are totally rejected. Every institution that is mentioned is discredited. It is centrally significant that in this document the conception of society does not really exist.

Such individualism must be considered a psychological symptom rather than a political or social concept. It is most conspicuous in the notions concerning morality. Having raised various basic moral questions, the author ("God") says, "There is no 'right' or 'wrong' in these matters." In moral questions, you must act entirely on feeling and on your own feeling. Acting simply on how you feel in each case "is called acting on your own authority." "Renunciation in the classic sense of self-denial is not required." Restraint is repudiated. "Never deny passion, for that is to deny Who You Are and Who You Truly Want to Be." The "God" here does not hesitate to exalt what general decency would consider obscene: "I do not love 'good' more than I love 'bad.' Hitler went to heaven. When you understand this, you will understand God."

The counsel of total gratification blossoms when "God" turns to the question of "relationship." Relationship is what you share with "your mate," or a sexual partner with whom one cohabits. "Relationships are sacred," and it really doesn't matter, so the message goes, whether relations are brief or enduring. They are sacred because "they provide life's grandest opportunity . . . to create and produce the experience of your highest conceptualization of Self." And we must not be sentimental about "relationship." *Let each person in relationship worry not about the other, but only, only, only about Self. . . .* The most loving person is the person who is Self-centered." And "Blessed are the Self-centered, for they shall know God."

Gross intellectual shabbiness pervades even the details of the text. We are treated to the gnomic fakery of esoteric knowledge: Matter is said to be created by "the slowing down of the unfathomable speed of all vibration (thought form)." We are given an "explanation" of miracles based on a distorted echo of freshman physics: "Jesus did this [created miracles] regularly. He understood how to manipulate energy and matter, how to rearrange it, how to redistribute it, how to utterly control it." There are outrageous non sequiturs such as the following: "God cre-

ated *relativity*, the greatest gift God ever gave to Itself. Thus *relationship* is the greatest gift God ever gave to you." There is a reference to the "psychic" in the sense of presumed paranormal experiences such as predicting events and communicating with the dead. "God" says, "Someday–perhaps in Book Two–I'll explain to you exactly how psychic energy and psychic ability works."

The publication gives rise to a poignant irony. As we have seen in the previous chapter, many distinguished writers of the twentieth century have seen a return to religion as the only possible curative for the steady deterioration of values and the growing tendency to social disintegration. In the publication described above, Walsch, a local radio talk-show host in Oregon, promulgates what he calls religion, not only to approve, but to celebrate and sanctify the most debased values of our time.

So while aware that the inward change, the contemporary spiritual resurgence of our time, is inevitable and needed, we must not ignore the spiritual pornography of such as Bakker, Swaggert, and Walsch. The danger of the turning is that it can become cultural deformity and moral monstrosity. It will do so unless, more and more, intellectuals who are the remnant core personnel of modernist civilization help to define it. That will require a new spiritual commitment of their own.

Chapter Five

SUBJECTIVE KNOWLEDGE AND TRUTH

Undisciplined subjectivism can give rise to enormities, as we have seen in the previous chapter. But both subjectivism and objectivism, if either is taken as an isolated and independent source of knowledge, will produce deformity and illusion. The crucial development, which has been noted above, is as follows: Quite recently, after many thousands of years of the existence of full fledged human beings on earth, and after some ten thousand years of civilization, something quite extraordinary took place. Elaborate processes were devised that for brief periods permitted a few privileged people to submit in total passivity to imprints of the external world; this, presumably, produced our knowledge of the truth. Surely that strikes us as surpassingly strange. It is an entirely fair statement of the conception in which science, or objective knowledge, as it is usually understood, is confused with metaphysics and taken for the source of truth. If this bizarre notion is to be avoided, the confusions clustered in it must be dispelled.

For the literate person of the modern world the technique of faith will depend strictly and from the beginning upon an adequate conception of subjective knowledge and the restraining conditions under which it can serve life. From Shakespeare we learned that beauty is in the eye of the beholder. The rose exists

objectively; it has an existence independent of the beholder. Presumably we are capable of knowing this objective existence—presumably with indifference. But being stirred by the rose as a thing of beauty is brought about by conditions or processes within the beholder. Beauty, we would say, has a subjective source. Since the last quarter of the Eighteenth Century we have understood that experience, not only of beauty, but of all things whatever has two sources. There is an outward source of the external world impinging upon perceptual faculties, and an internal source influencing how the external stimulus is experienced. The outward source we call objective. The inward source we call subjective. The challenge posed for present purposes is in realizing the range and diversity of kinds of factors, both external and internal, that shape experience and fill our lives.

Modern neurology makes it clear that outward forces and inward are at work in even the apparently most simple seeing and hearing. The objective-subjective duality prevails absolutely. Color has no external existence. We cannot see the light moving from the surface of the red carnation to your eye. But it moves in specific wave lengths, and because certain light-receptive cells in the cornea of your eye are sensitive to certain wave lengths of light, you experience the redness which you think of as existing in the carnation. Thus far we have considered only a physical object and the immediate response of the senses. Even here the basic objective-subjective duality is at work, but we know that immeasurably more is involved in one's response to a red carnation and in any other apparently simple perception.

The great achievement of Immanuel Kant in the last quarter of the eighteenth century was the first modern break-through. Kant *particularized* the fundamental subjective components of mental response to the external world. He assumed that the senses brought the imprint of outward objects to the mind. But, he argued with great force, that in order for us to experience these objects, concepts related to the objects had to be activated. In

other words, we see objects only when we also think them. This conception explains much that we must constantly keep in mind.

Fundamental to Kant's insight are a limited number of "categories," or concepts, which are inherent in the mind and which are the foundations for knowledge generally. They are such conceptions as "totality," "negation," "cause," "necessity" which are links holding together the world as we conceive it. Kant found also inherent in the mind the conception of and impulse to unity, which we may take as the basic impulse driving human thought. This impulse we will later relate to the origin of consciousness. The inherent, or "apriori," concepts of most importance historically were the concepts of time and space, which, according to Kant, do not exist except as they are observed. This conception, as Einstein testified, lies behind his thought on the relativity of time and space. Time and space are the structuring principles of the physical world as we understand it. For Kant, large elements of knowledge, indeed its very foundations, were subjective and all the rest of knowledge resulted from the combination of subjective and objective components.

From Kant it is not a very large step to another conception of the massive role of subjectivity in human experience. This is the idea, common today and held by many over a period of three centuries, that human beings are conscious because they have language. This, as we shall see, is one of the conceptions fundamental to modern authentication of faith. The virtuous atheist is not likely to find his way back to faith in oblivion of the contemporary understanding of language and human consciousness. Let us pause over that conception. The reasoning concerning the nature of language is essentially as follows. Consciousness is knowing, which is a continuous awareness of relationships. Relationships are summarized by concepts. Concepts are the meanings of words, but words are not simply sounds; the meaning is part of the word.[44]

Words in their turn are centers of complex networks of relationships. It might seem at first that the relationship between the

sound or letters and the actual object is the only relationship involved. Considering more closely, we realize that the word/concept "cup" is a center of complex networks of relationships. "Cup" in its most common identification is part of a category called "dishes." It has especially close relationships to other "dishes"— "saucers," "plates," "platters," "bowls," "pitchers," "glasses." It is also related, though less intimately, with "silver," or "knives," "forks," and "spoons." It is more closely related to the articles of the kitchen and dining room than to those of other parts of the house. In links of diminishing strength, however, "cup" is related to all the objects of the larger categories called "domestic furnishing" and "household equipment."

In a fundamental relationship, "cup" is linked with "drinking," which is related to the more general activity of "taking nourishment." "Cup" has especially close relationships with certain contents—"coffee," "tea," "milk," "soup." "Cup" also has links with decorum. Good manners require that it be drunk from in certain ways and not in others. In one context "cup" is a standard of measurement used constantly in "cooking." In a broader sense "cup" belongs among all "containers." In a still more abstract relationship "cup" is related to all concavities. In special cultural contexts "cup" may have romantic connotations, being, for instance, a synonym for wine. Linked symbolically with "sword," "cup" has a feminine connotation. In contexts of ritual and faith it is linked with the "Eucharist." It may be a synonym for "the Holy Grail."

The kinds of relationships described here are not just abstract inventions. They are the kinds of relationships in which words are stored in memory. This fact has been fully established by psychological testing, especially by different kinds of word association tests. For instance, such a test asks you to utter the first word you think of after you hear the word "cup." Evidence is that you are much more likely to say "saucer" than "household equipment" and overwhelmingly more likely that you will say "dishes" than that you will say "dinosaur."

The networks of words are linked in a single, total network, constituting the verbal and conceptual content of the human mind. Activation of the memory of any word has far-reaching reverberation in the activation of other word memories. The total word memories activated generate the implicit knowledge that is the constant knowing of consciousness. In the basic activation of language a visual image activates the memory of the sound of a word, with reverberations among all the networks of words with which it is connected. Conscious seeing is the foundation from which the rest of consciousness develops.

So deeply ingrained are our habits of mind that it is difficult for our imaginations to grasp that associations exist only in our minds. Only a special force of reason will make it clear to us that in the object *saucer* there is nothing whatever that relates it to an object *cup*. The relationship is there because we have used *saucers* with *cups* and the words "saucer" and "cup" are memories that include the memory of that use. External objects are brute foundations of our reality but they come into existence for us because of the kind of association that exists in our mind between "cup" and "saucer." In the world revealed by language objects seem to exist in objective simplicity but they are in large part constructed as is the relationship between "cup" and "saucer."

Language brings us into consciousness, into life as human beings. It is not only the primary subjective knowledge, but it is accountable for all knowledge whatever. Objective knowledge is possible because of subjective knowledge. But language is only one of the elements of subjectivity, and it is not usually recognized as such. More generally, subjectivity is any factor of inward origin influencing the way we see things, the way we think, or the way we behave. Subjectivity is massively generated from within the body as emotion. Unfortunately, emotion in Western culture is too often thought of as disruptive of reason, which is identified with objectivity.

Cultures massively shape and control subjectivity. In Western culture there is a tradition of Romanticism that, outside of

scientific contexts, values emotion and sees an unemotional disposition as lacking in humanity. In contrast, Javanese culture conceives emotion as dangerous; it requires management and control to preserve a calm equanimity of life.[45] Subjectivity has the form of the ethos of a people. The ethos is the "tone, character, and quality of their life, its moral and aesthetic style and mood; it is the underlying attitude toward themselves and their world that their life reflects."[46] The ethos of a people, anthropologists tell us, is shaped in consonance with the world view of that people. The Navaho ethos prizes "calm deliberateness, untiring persistence, and dignified caution." It is the corollary of a world view in which nature is seen as "tremendously powerful, mechanically regular, and highly dangerous."[47]

In one way or another subjective forces are influences upon consciousness, many of which are organized in the brain but generated by the larger organism. In this respect the mind is enormously responsive to the body. The relationship produces fantasies and dreams, which are present during much of our lives. Fantasies and dreams are considered by some as psychologically diagnostic, but even as such their actual content is considered trivial, even contemptible. The reason is that fantasy and dream function outside the boundaries of human control and responsibility. That is to say they are free of the control of objective knowledge and of objective, consciously directed processes. When the well-springs of fantasy and dream are cultivated and controlled, they are highly valued. Under conscious cultivation and control, they are the source of art.

A dimension of the development of the artist is what Michael Polanyi calls "personal knowledge." Its most elemental form is "how to" knowledge, consisting of those skills which you may perform perfectly and yet would be hard pressed to say in any detail "how" you do it. Notable examples are the ability to ride a bicycle and the ability to swim and the advanced ability to play a musical instrument.[48] These abilities begin in conscious prac-

tice. Practice is eventually assimilated by the organism, in which unconscious controls are muscular and neurological.

The study, the necessary initial imitation, the endless practice essential to the development of an artist—let us say a painter—has as its purpose that technique becomes personal knowledge. It is assimilated by the organism and becomes a largely intuitive and unconscious activity. In its assimilation by the organism, the technique takes on distinctive characteristics peculiar to the artist. It becomes a style, which in a fundamental way is the goal of artistic achievement. The style liberated by the personal knowledge is the largely unconscious expression of individuality, that is to say, a distinctive organism as shaped by the culture. The painter's work, if he succeeds, becomes a new way of seeing.

Personal knowledge, however, is by no means all that goes into the painting. The organism exerts unconscious controls, but the artist has assimilated the culture both intuitively and intellectually. The final artistic product results from an interplay of conscious and unconscious controls, in both of which the culture is a primary factor. The culture assimilated by the organism—as the scrim of being and the dance of presences—is the primary unconscious power generating artistic execution, but at virtually every step there are controls of conscious appraisal shaped now in some measure by the body and temperament, but far more by the artist's intellectual assimilation of the culture. The process here is one we must keep in mind in the context of religion.

The point of importance for our purposes is that, at least from the Renaissance onward, the individual artist makes a conscious judgment and appraisal of what unconscious processes have produced. He makes a judgment, for better or for worse, as to the fittingness of the work for the culture as it is embodied in the social environment. In such a judgment, of course, he may be wrong, and the work will fail. If the work succeeds, it is integrated into the culture, having effects usually of both conscious

and unconscious kinds. Eventually the culture will decide the fate of the artistic work, but the artist alone makes the judgments that bring it into being.

Let us not hesitate to recognize that the successful artistic work is a part of knowledge. It you are an artist, it may be knowledge that you can use. In any event, for human beings generally, it is knowledge that, we might say, uses them, shaping in some measure their future knowledge and ability for experience. It becomes a part of truth as we can know it. The processes of the artist and the culture, processes of creation and selection, are those we must expect in the origin of religion.

The next step of the argument is to consider the kinds, range, and intensity of influences upon the human organism, and to discriminate them from those found in the animal kingdom. An animal is affected by light and warmth, by cold and by changes in the weather. It flees or is aroused to combat by the aggression of other animals. It is sexually stimulated by body chemistry or activity of the opposite sex. It flourishes or languishes in response to variations in the availability of food. Everything that affects it is part of the immediate environment and the effect is instantaneous.

A basic effect of human consciousness was to extend in time and space the range of influences upon the human organism. Consciousness results from the activation of memory. Visual stimuli activate memories of word/concepts, and word/concepts activate the memory of other word/concepts. Continuities of the same kind of visual and auditory-vocal memories that generate consciousness constitute narrative memories. The recall of the past is the recall of a conscious past. The kinds of memory stimulus generating consciousness also elicit memory of the past and makes possible the projection of the future. This is the foundation of culture and history. A thought in millennia past can bind the lives of endless generations to come. Thought penetrating cosmic immensities can shape the content of human experience. It can inform it with the anguish of isolation. (Pascal can say, "Those

empty spaces frighten me.") It may bring also the consolation of beauty and promise!

There is also another kind of effect of time and distance. Transformations of the organism thousands of years before the emergence of consciousness shape the content and nature of human subjectivity. Some of these transformation may have effects emerging into consciousness in a distinctive kind of experience that is not implicit in, is totally irrelevant to, its origin. Let us consider a few examples.

Such results seem clearly to be reflected in the presence of the same conceptions, symbols, and practices in diverse and widely separated human cultures. Many phenomena of this sort are of the greatest antiquity, being present among Paleolithic populations. It will serve the purposes of imagination and argument simply to list at random some of the patterns and motifs constantly repeated in cultures of all times and places. The very incomplete list that now follows is drawn from the work of Mircea Eliade, the great student of comparative religions at the University of Chicago for many years. In reading the following list, it must be kept in mind that every item in it is either recurrent or universal in religious phenomena far more primitive than any of the major living religions. The items are numbered, simply as a way of visually distinguishing them in the text:

1)Cosmogonic myths, or myths of the origin of the cosmos, especially the version in which the Creator derives the world from primordial waters. 2) The origin of the earth in a hierogamy, or sacred sexual union, of a male god of the sky and Mother Earth. 3) The sky as sacred and related to spontaneous notions of transcendence. 4) The origin of the earth in a hero's separation of the sky and earth. 5) The origin of man as growing from the ground like plants, or as fashioned from clay by divine artisans, or as formed from the blood of immolated gods; divine creation by "the power of the Word." 6) The lives and conduct of humans as determined by divine powers. 7) The myth of an original paradise. 8) Trees or megaliths, or trees accompanied by mega-

liths, providing central imagery, and the sacredness of the universe represented in a World Tree or a Cosmic Tree considered to be at the center of the world (as prototype of the Christian symbolism of the Cross). 9) Myths uniting the images of a naked goddess, a miraculous tree, and its guardian, a serpent. 10) Human culture as the result of a theft from higher powers and punishment of the theft. 11) The deluge that destroys and cleanses humanity and permits its new beginning. 12) The cosmic order as continually troubled and periodically regenerated. 13) Sexuality conceived as having a religious character. 14) The notion of circular time and a cosmic cycle. 15) Fertility cults of Mother Goddesses. 16) The Mother Goddess in terrifying aspect. 17) The idea of the soul's survival after death. 18) Cults of the dead. 19) The assimilation of caves and mines to the womb of Mother Earth. 20) Furnaces conceived as wombs. 21) God as bisexual or androgynous. 22) The bull as symbol of male fertility. 23) Initiation rites which introduce the novitiate to sex, death, and the sacred. 24) Models of temples and cities conceived as preexisting in the sky. 25) The habitation or temple conceived as an image of the world. 26) Belief in the pre-existence of words and institutions, as in Platonism. 27) The goddess who descends to the underworld in a fatal effort to abolish death. 28) Ritual confrontations, jousts, combats conceived as stimulating the creative forces of life. 29) Techniques of divination, especially by examining the entrails of a victim. 30) Young gods who die and are resurrected annually. 31) The death and immolation of a divine being as essential to human welfare. 32) Cults of the dead. 33) The king considered a "son of God" and an intermediary between gods and men. 34) The monarch as an incarnate god. 35) The god who dies and returns to life. 36) Gods as triadic powers. 37) Imitation of a god as the key to a "royal destiny" in another world. 38) The replacement of an old creator god by a more dynamic young god, who rejuvenates the world. 39) Cults of a Mother Goddess.[49]

In this listing of recurrent patterns and motifs we recognize

basic building blocks of the living religions. Most religions are in some measure built of fragments of other religions, fragments that they adopt and transform. This fact must not lead us to miss the truly significant point of the list above. For the most part the recurrence of the religious configurations is not the result of communication, transmission, or inheritance between cultures. The fact of greatest significance is that the same religious motifs, conceptions, practices occur anew and independently in different cultures in different times and places, and they do so continuously.

Furthermore, what must now be recognized is a point to which Eliade gives the greatest emphasis. "The 'sacred," says Eliade, "is an element in the structure of consciousness and not a stage in the history of consciousness."[50] Special reasons for assuming that to be true will be suggested below (pages 99–100). The point to be emphasized is that evidence of recognition of the sacred is reflected in the earliest clear records of human consciousness, during the Upper Paleolithic period some 40,000 to 30,000 years ago, and all the elements in the list above are of the greatest antiquity. Eliade says, "Almost all the religious attitudes man has, he has had from the most primitive times."[51] He emphasizes that "the major religious attitudes came into existence once and for all" from the moment when man first became conscious of his distinction from the universe in which he found himself.[52] Our hope is to come to some understanding of the meaning of this.

From time immemorial gods have been associated with intimations of transcendence associated inevitably with the sky. That association remains even today in the notion of heaven as a realm "up above," providing we do not specify "a region beyond the sky." Within all civilizations there has developed the notion of the stars as controlling human destiny. Indeed the first modern blow to traditional religious faith consisted in the Copernican theory. Copernicus removed the earth from the center of a divinely ordered celestial universe and left it homeless in an endless

desert of stars. Astronomy became the primary instrument of the scientific assault on faith.

Advocates of the big-bang theory—and they include most astronomers—assure us that the theory leaves no function to be performed by a creator. That is certainly true if we conceive the Creator in a purely anthropomorphic way. For the moment, it is sufficient to observe that if only because astronomy has presented a major obstacle to faith, it must be a fundamental concern of a reorientation to faith. It is obvious, indeed, that we must attempt to incorporate what we really know about the physical universe in our conception of God. However, we must not assume that astronomical knowledge is complete or final or even that it is fully credible in every respect.

The big bang theory rests upon quantum theory and we must understand that the phenomena of quantum mechanics are discoverable only by mathematical processes which are not otherwise available to human consciousness. They may not be represented in the spatial and temporal dimensions which govern the content of the human imagination. The phenomena of quantum processes cannot be imagined. Indeed, what are called "quarks" are purely theoretical entities, but they are taken to be the building blocks of protons and neutrons. No one has ever seen a quark. Outside of mathematics quantum processes may be discussed in metaphors of very limited validity. It is true that quantum processes under carefully controlled conditions within the universe as it now exists have observable and very real results—atomic and nuclear explosions, for instance. It seems likely that the quantum processes of matter and energy as they are now described would have occurred at other cosmic times and in other conditions of the universe. However, we have no way of being certain of that.

There can be no doubt that many contemporary astronomical observations are consistent with the Big Bang theory. However, crucial gaps in the theory remain to be filled. And mathematical projections filling some of the gaps require the assumption of

consequences to which we need not necessarily consent. Granted the general inadequacy of common sense and of our imaginations when confronting Big Bang theory, there are points at which the protests of our imaginations must be respected.

Much of the Big Bang theory consists in the projection of mathematical descriptions of quantum processes into the unimaginably distant past. The most fundamental of these projections tells us that the present universe evolved entirely from a beginning in which it was a small volume of space "a billion billion billion billion times smaller than an atomic nucleus."[53] Except within this infinitely small space, we are told, absolutely nothing existed. We must not abuse ourselves by imagining physicists creating anything remotely resembling this original condition. The result would be another universe. We are confronted exclusively with mathematical projections. We need have no doubt that the mathematical projections are mathematically correct. But we are unquestionably justified in doubting that all these projections describe reality.

We should also be mindful of some of the specific limitations of Big Bang theory. The fact of the matter is that the mathematical projection that is taken to describe the beginning of the universe does not quite reach the beginning. The explanation is as follows. In quantum activity as we know it today, only three of the four basic forces controlling the structure of matter (the strong force, the weak force, the electromagnetic force, and gravity)are at work. Gravity has no influence. So the mathematical description of quantum phenomena that is projected for the beginning does not include the effect of gravity. But in the horrendous concentration of matter and energy proposed as the beginning, it is necessary to assume that gravity would be as strong as the other forces. Modern knowledge has no explanation of how matter would behave when gravity is so intense.

So the mathematical projection is assumed to carry us back to a point assumed to be an unimaginably brief time after the primordial explosion, a period so fantastically brief that it can be

described only mathematically, as 10\-43 of a second. At this point the universe would have expanded enormously to reach the size of a sphere one-thousandth of a centimeter in diameter, or about the size of the point of a needle. Beyond positing the expansion to this size, modern physics has no means whatever of explaining what happened prior to this and cannot exclude the possibility that the 10\-43 second was not actually billions upon billions of light years in duration.[54]

Modern knowledge is considered to be most reliable in telling us what happened during the 300,000 years following the primordial explosion. The picture of what happened between then and now—a period of between 10 and 20 billion years—is confused. The problem is, first of all, that we do not know the amount of matter in the universe. The only model that seems to fit requires the assumption that even in the range of the universe generally visible to us most of the matter present is cold and totally invisible. The model requires that from 90 to 98% of the universe consists of such invisible matter. We have no proof that such matter exists and no idea whatever of what its nature might be. But the model requiring this matter is the one most favored by cosmologists today.

Another problem concerns the stars. The earliest chemical constituents of the universe were hydrogen and helium. Stars are the "cosmic furnaces" that forge the heavier chemical elements essential to the development of life. We do not understand how the stars came into being. How they were formed is a fundamental problem of astrophysics.[55]

The questions raised thus far reflect truly crucial deficiencies of knowledge. There are other problems of a more "local" sort that are perhaps less significant. The Big Bang theory predicts that the galaxies are expanding as is the space between them. Sure enough, spectral analysis indicates that most of the galaxies are expanding. Here and there, however, there seem to be movements that are not accounted for by the original explosion. Our galaxy, the Milky Way, is part of a Super Cluster, which

is an assemblage of 10,000 galaxies. Our Super Cluster and the Hydra-Centaurus Super Cluster do not simply follow the expansion of the universe. Their movement includes another direction in which they are moving at several hundred kilometers per second. To account for this astronomers have posited a gravitational attraction of enormous power, which they have named the "Great Attractor." Astronomers are now attempting to prove the existence of the Great Attractor.[56]

Astronomical knowledge is far from complete, and some of its most fundamental perspectives may be changed in the future. Much of astronomical knowledge, however, is authentically attended by wonder. And this wonder is part of the unquestionably significant knowledge of our time. For the lay reader, astronomical figures quickly numb the mind and become totally meaningless. Let us consider only certain facts selected to reflect the awesome magnitudes of the universe.

Light, we will remember, travels at the speed of 186,000 miles per second (and according to Einstein, nothing can ever exceed this velocity). Light from the moon reaches us in 1.4 seconds, light from the sun takes eight minutes. Light from the nearest star takes four years to reach us. To move from one edge of our galaxy to the other, light takes 100,000 years. (A light-year is the distance light will travel in a year, which is 5,878,000,000,000 miles. So we multiply this figure by 100,000 to get the distance across the Milky Way.)

The Milky Way consists of several hundred billion stars. The closest galaxy to the Milky Way, the Andromeda galaxy, is 2.3 million light-years away; that is, light from Andromeda takes 2.3 million years to reach us. Science fiction of the star-wars variety confuses the popular mind about these matters, suggesting that we might be able to travel to any point in the universe. It is certain, for instance, that we could never travel to Andromeda, because even if we could travel at the speed of light it would take us 2.3 million years to get there.

Within the observable universe there are hundreds of bil-

lions of galaxies, and about ten new ones appear every year as the universe ages and light has more time to reach us. The Big Bang theory means that at certain extreme distances galaxies are receding from us at the speed of light, and for that reason the light from these galaxies will never reach us. Such galaxies exist beyond the limits of the observable universe. We inhabit an extremely minute niche in a universe of heart-quenching immensities. If we want exercise in the impossible effort to glimpse the enormities of God, here is opportunity in abundance.

The sheer magnitudes that the cosmologists report to us might lead those of us who are laymen to take their intellectual authority as absolute. That would be a great mistake, but we have no cause to doubt the general structure of the universe as it is described by modern astronomy. Indeed, we have every reason to assume that some version of the Big Bang Theory is true. The Big Bang Theory is based on quantum mechanics. This presents the possibility for a new perspective on the relationship of man to the universe. The alienation of man from the universe begins with his expulsion from its assumed physical center by the work of Copernicus published in 1543 and has been confirmed by astronomical observation ever since. Quantum Theory and the Big Bang Theory suggest that we may examine man's relationship to the universe in new dimensions. We will consider man, not in relation to a spatial center of the universe, but in relationship to the origin of the universe and to the structure of the matter that makes up the universe.

Cosmologists tell us that certain numbers are sufficient to describe the universe. These numbers designate physical relationships and these relationships seem not to vary. They are constants. There are some fifteen such numbers.[57] One such number is called the "gravitational constant." This is a quantitative statement of the proportionality involved in the law of gravity. The law states that the gravitational force attracting a ball toward the earth varies in proportion to the product of the masses of the ball earth and inversely in proportion to the square of their dis-

tance. Two other constants are the parameters controlling the strength of the weak and strong forces. Another constant is the speed of light, or 186,000 miles per second. There is a constant that describes the mass of the proton as 1,826 times that of the electron. What is called "Planck's constant" determines the size of an atom, which is about one hundred millionth of a centimeter.

The point that has been made about the basic constants of nature is that they have created a universe that is precisely attuned to the emergence of planets like our own and to the emergence of life and eventually "toward self-consciousness through the creation of intelligence."[58] The slightest change in the basic constants of matter and energy, and human life could not have emerged. So the constant might be looked upon as reflecting either an accident or a plan. The cosmologist Trinh Xuan Thuan, of the University of Virginia, says that stating without proof that there is not a plan "is no more scientific and is as dogmatic as maintaining that one does not exist."[59] The question here cannot be resolved, but the question itself has meaning. What it can do is to neutralize the materialistic and mechanistic arguments against spiritual reality in the universe.

The fact that the constants seem to be valid everywhere supports what is called "the cosmological principle," the idea that the universe is unified in the sense that it is everywhere the same. There is basic evidence of more organic aspects of unity, evidence that all the parts are related to each other and interact with each other. If this is so, then we too are part of the universe related to all of its parts. The unity of the universe is basic to Einstein's general theory of relativity (1916) and to his description of space as curved. The unity of the universe is assumed by the Big Bang Theory which is taken to explain that unity. The theory says that in the beginning all the parts of the universe were in effect so intimately related as to be one. With the primordial explosion the parts were increasingly separated from each other, but we are compelled to affirm that they "remember" their

original relationships.[60] (We are thus in some sense an incarnation of "the word," the basic principle of the structure of the universe.)

That "remembering" is required by the best theory we have, and two experiments may be taken to reflect the continued operation of original cosmic relationships.

In 1851 the French physicist Léon Foucault hung a pendulum at the end of a long cord from the vault of the Pantheon in Paris. His intent was to demonstrate that the Earth rotated. To reflect the earth's rotation, the plane of oscillation of the pendulum would have rotated a fraction of 360 degrees every 24 hours. A great deal more than this actually happened. The plane "pivoted around the vertical axis as the hours passed. If it began swinging in the north-south direction, it oscillated in the east-west after a few hours."[61]

This phenomenon is explained by Trinh Xuan Thuan as follows: The plane of oscillation moves in relation to the earth so the earth must not be controlling it. What is controlling it might be identified if we could discover something that does not move in relation to the plane of oscillation. The plane of oscillation may be aligned successively, with the Sun, with the closest stars, with the closest galaxy, the Andromeda Galaxy, with the Local Super Cluster of galaxies. In every case, though with decreasing rapidity, the celestial body moves away from the plane of oscillation. Finally, the plane of oscillation is aligned with a cluster of galaxies so distant as to be visible only in the largest telescopes. Finally, there is no drift away from the plane of oscillation.[62]

According to Thuan, the behavior of Foucault's pendulum "is influenced by the most distant galaxies or, since most of the visible mass in the universe is in galaxies, by the universe as a whole. In other words, what happens here is determined in the vast expanse of space, and what takes place in our minuscule planet is dictated by the whole hierarchy of structures in the universe. Every part contains the whole, and depends on everything else. The universe is interconnected." In any case," Thuan

continues,"the behavior of Foucault's pendulum forces us to conclude that there exists a sort of interaction totally different from
those described by recognized physics, a mysterious interaction
that does not involve any form, nor exchange of energy, but that
connects the whole universe together."[63]

Another principle provides basis for the assumption of the
interconnectedness of the universe. The phenomenon of non-
locality has its origin in one of the basic experiments in quantum
mechanics.[64] Photons are emitted from the same quantum state,
say calcium or mercury atoms. Provision is made for polarization
of one of the photons in flight under conditions in which there
could not possibly be communication of any kind with another
controlled photon. The extraordinary fact is that despite the elimi-
nation of the possibility of causal relations existing between the
two photons, the second changes to reflect the polarization of the
first.

The phenomenon is sometimes said to manifest "non-sepa-
rability," meaning that in some totally inexplicable way the two
photons cannot be separated; it is also referred to as "non-locality," meaning that an effect has occurred in the absence of
conditions for causation required in the terms of Newtonian physics that are easily understood by everyone. The relation between
the two photons is called "complementarity," and it is a relation
completely unknown to science prior to the development of quantum mechanics and, of course, completely unknown to the world
as interpreted by common-sense which is in accord with
Newtonian physics. In more recent experimentation, non-locality has been shown to be effective at a distance of seven miles,
and theoretically it would be effective at any distance in the universe.[65] Non-locality has been called the "most profound
discovery in all of science."[66]

The significance of all this is that it provides an explanation
that is crucial to our understanding of the human spirit. It provides a way of authenticating the most important facts that
naturalistic observation reveals about human spirituality. The

most elementary of those facts are that certain principles—the impulse to narrative, the perception of stillness, the impulse to unity—are inherent in consciousness. These principles are essential to the origin and development of religion. Furthermore, the sacred is inherent in consciousness. The structure of the sacred is identical to the structure in which consciousness originates. At another level of human nature, naturalistic observation reveals that all the building-blocks of the more advanced religions emerge in the most primitive conditions of consciousness and occur perennially. These facts are the particulars basic to the irrefutable proposition that religion has subjective sources, that the knowledge of spiritual reality is subjective knowledge.

The fact that all religious faith and all its contents have a subjective origin has often been taken in this century as the result of an accident and thus totally meaningless. Let us keep in mind that the assumption that an accident explains this is essential to preserving the world view that many scientists and many philosophers cultivate. To assume that subjective knowledge is not an accident is to acknowledge the authentic existence in the world of something that is inherently alien to positivistic observation and assumptions. It is to abolish the facile world view central to the notion of the autonomy of science and of man. What the specific facts of concrete scientific knowledge actually tell us is quite different.

Lets witness the expression of the meaning of scientific knowledge by the astronomer Trinh Xuan Thuan: "Science has taught us that we share a common history with all the matter in the universe, that we are children of the stars, brothers of wild beasts, and cousins of the red poppies in the fields. It also tells us that we carry the universe within us, and that we are indivisibly part of it."[67] This does not bring us to proof of the existence of God. But what it does is incalculably momentous. It defines and limits a single leap of faith necessary to belief in God and it makes the leap easy. That single necessary leap of faith is affirmation of the proposition: We have subjective knowledge of God because we

carry the universe within us and are indivisibly part of it. Our subjective knowledge of God is authentic knowledge because it is a register in the human psyche of the presence of the universe.

Chapter Six

REALITY ANEW

The preconceptions of the secular world are deeply ingrained in our psyches. These preconceptions are mistaken but they completely dominate the world-view of the secular person. They consolidate as a virtually immovable obstacle to spirituality. It is this obstacle that makes the effort for faith an intellectual quest. It yields only to the intelligence, imagination, and discipline required to follow the processes of thought developed in this chapter. It deals with linguistics and formal philosophy and undertakes a kind of close reasoning that does not occur elsewhere in the book. We will be dealing with theories, remembering that all significant knowledge is theoretical knowledge. Readers who persist will quickly realize that the conceptions here are equipment for saving our souls.

When we examine ourselves closely, we will find that our most important conceptions of reality are conflicting versions that alternate in our consciousness, without clear distinction or control. We assume much of the time that the world we see, hear, touch, feel is "the real world." This we assume is the realm of finality and certainty. At any moment, however, we may be talked out of this conviction. We are told over and over again that this sensory world we live in is illusionary. It is a dream world concealing the real world. The true world of reality is a skeletal world of unseen abstractions. We can know it only in the mathematical

descriptions of science. Without question, our mathematical knowledge of this world is useful, but with careful thought we understand that this shadow world has no meaning. So the popular thought of modernism tells us that the world we live in is a veil of illusion and that the other possibility of ultimate reality, the world of abstractions described by science, is a meaninglessness. The sting of this is especially sharp when it cancels our response to those works designed to bring meanings, the meanings of *our* world, into focused realization—the works of art and myth.

The path to spiritual transformation begins with the realization that objective reality does not exist. We will discover what we will call reality, but it does not have the solidity and permanence that we generally associate with the word "reality." We must resolve to train our imaginations in accord with this fact. This is a perilous undertaking, We know that there are deviant conceptions of reality that can produce disaster. So a disciplinary reservation must control our thought from the first. That reservation is as follows: Although there is no objective reality having the finality and certainty that we have usually associated with the word "reality," there are clear principles for choosing between other possible conceptions of reality. Our basic assumption does not commit us to chaos. And the basic argument here is that we can and must choose.

What we must achieve is the constant realization that the realm having, not finality and certainty, but priority claims to reality is the humanly perceptible world in which we live. This is not a world that of itself generates meaning, but it is the world in which we have deposited all meaning. To understand our world as the depository of meaning, we must first understand the sense in which it is a realm of qualified reality. This requires an understanding of how we, the race of human beings, got to be here in the first place. Although a course of biological evolution lies behind us, we were not present during this course of evolution. Never at any point in this course were there human beings on

the way to their modern condition. The totality of the past that lies behind us was a process of exclusively animal evolution. We came into being at what, in so far as we know it, is the end of this process. There was an evolution producing our biological inheritance. There was no evolution of man. We came into being when the first human eyes came into being, when the first eyes beheld the world. The human race came into being with the dawn of consciousness. There is only one theory that explains how this came about. This theory, whether right or wrong, is the best possible way of bringing us to the kind of understanding crucial for the modern intellect. The theory of consciousness to be presented will take some time, but this theory, or something very like it, is fundamental to modern thought about God, and at every step it will sustain our spiritual progress.

The Nature of Consciousness

The explanation of consciousness proposed here may be stated simply: We are conscious and therefore human because we have language. It may be helpful from the first to point out that while many educated readers may never have heard of this conception, it is almost three centuries old. From the eighteenth century onward there have always been thinkers of some prominence who accepted this explanation. During most of the twentieth century, language has been at the center of philosophical interest, and a number of participants in this "linguistic turn," have assumed the proposed conception of the cause of consciousness to be valid. As this is a conception that can never be finally established, there will be some point in acknowledging that a large number of distinguished people in the nineteenth and twentieth centuries who have been convinced of its validity.[68]

A radically simplified formulation of the theory of consciousness may begin with two assumptions. One is that what we call "concepts" are devocalized memories of words or of patterns of words. The other assumption is that animals do not experience

human seeing. The eyes of animals are light detectors. As such they are sufficient to explain that the animal reacts to various kinds of visual images.

The theory of consciousness is, first of all, a theory explaining human seeing, the kind of seeing that involves a great deal more than animal response to patterns of light. Human response to a visual image activates two kinds of memory, visual and linguistic (conceptual). The activation of visual memory is what we share with animals. The linguistic memory introduces something very different. Let us bring to mind, then, the enormity of language—the thousands of words in vocabularies of natural languages, every word related to all other words, words as part of fields of meaning (or grouping of words, called "semantic fields") and fields of meaning overlapping fields of meaning in a single continuous fabric constituting human knowledge and embodying the totality of human culture. All or part of this enormous system is fully or partially activated in a form pressing toward overt expression when we experience a visual image. To a large extent this form of activation is what is called "implicit memory." The discoverer of the concept of implicit memory, Daniel Schacter, describes it as follows: Implicit memory occurs "when people are influenced by a past experience without any awareness that they are remembering."[69]

The first response of the human organism to a visual image is a generalized activation that probably affects the entire brain.[70] This is also the animal response to a visual image. This generalized activation initiates a searching. But in the human brain, the searching finds, perhaps first of all, the representation of a semantic field and then searching within the semantic field finds the memory of the sound pattern of a word. This sound pattern, we may now call, following Saussure, a "sound-image."[71] Activation of this sound-image results in a spreading of intensified activation—in the primary semantic field, in the more closely related semantic fields, in narrative (biographical) memories related to the image. (Only a very small part, if any, of this activated

system, a few words, perhaps, is likely to emerge as actual vocalization.)

This activation of language is an activation of conceptuality and constitutes a subtle and partly unconscious knowing. Knowing is a response to relationships. This subtle knowing is what constitutes consciousness. This knowing is largely generalized and occurs on the verge of consciousness. The object exists in the realm of this knowing. It is brought into focus and illuminated: it is caused to be seen. It is both a visual object and a meaning. Some small part of the range of language thus mobilized will emerge in overt expression, speech or writing, only if one initiates some kind of action concerning the object of which he has become conscious.

Our theory requires that every thing you see evokes a visual memory which evokes the memory of the sound-pattern of a word. Every word you hear evokes the memory of the sound-pattern of the word which evokes an image from the visual memory system. (We are concerned here with substantive words—nouns, verbs, adjectives and adverbs.) Obviously, with the development of abstract thought (abstract language), there are developed words in which the visual element virtually disappears.

The interaction of the auditory-vocal memory and the imagery memory systems is the basic neuronal mechanism of consciousness. The two systems are always in interaction with each other, this interaction is present in all instances of recall, and it is this interaction with which the development of consciousness begins. Two assumptions are now necessary. First, neuronal movement within the animal brain is always toward action, and the activation of the foundation of semantic elements in the human brain is a tentative suspension of this movement toward action. Second, in basic consciousness the activation of linguistic memory is implicit and not consciously verbalized. Consciousness, then, is the experience of the verge of knowing and of a potentiality of action, all knowing and action attended

by affectivity. These conditions, powers, and tendencies are the product of language in the biological organism.

The World Created by Language and Consciousness

By virtue of language and consciousness we build vast structures of knowledge overlaying the meaningless body of physical existence. In these structures we build morality, values, politics, right, religion—all institutions, all meaning. A part of our environment is made up of unseen objects which science has described in mathematical terms. Mathematics is a specialized derivative of language. Our world is made up of language that generates meaning which gives objects existence in our consciousness.. Language that creates consciousness provides the substance of all human culture.

We come to realize that even at the most elementary level of experience we do not know a finite reality. We can see a physical object only because our memory brings a concept to bear upon it. We inevitably see the object in terms of that concept. That concept is colored by the totality of the culture which is stored in human memory along with it and of which the concept is a part. This means that no perception is an experience of "truth." Every perception is an interpretation, and thus built by human fallibility and subject to inevitable change. Science seems to imply, and many scientists assume, that behind the world we live in, the world shaped by our culture, there is a more stable and certain reality.

The world reported by science—or, or to be more exact, partially reported by science—can be described only in mathematical terms. We feel that these reports are valid, that they reflect some partial insights into our universe, because they permit us to make changes in the interpreted world of experience. But we have not the smallest notion of how mathematics relates to the totality of

this pre-world (the world that exists prior to our perception of it). Does mathematics grasp only some small sliver of this pre-world? Or does mathematics reflect the totality. If so, that totality eludes our comprehension because, mathematical discourse eventually contradicts itself. It is important that we are aware of these philosophical shortcomings of mathematics because the assumptions of science claim a total monopoly on our ability to know reality. They thus collaborate with that postmodern nihilism which denies any measure of reality to the world we experience.

The Life-World

To exorcize the bad dreams of postmodern nihilism, we must train our imaginations again in the realities of the everyday-world in which we live, the world that we can see, and hear, and touch. It is called the *life-world*. It is defined in part by its contrast with the *theory-world,* which designates the unseen world described in some part by the mathematical language of science. The term "life-world" comes from Edmund Husserl in the first third of this century. He describes the life-world as the world of "natural life," the product of "the natural attitude."[72] The life-world, says Husserl, is "the one that is actually given through perception, that is ever experienced and experienceable." It is "our everyday life-world." It is "the 'world of us all'—it is *identical with the world that can be commonly talked about.*"[73] Heidegger, who was Husserl's graduate assistant, distinguished the life-world and the theory-world in this way:

> Let us think of the sun. Every day it rises and sets for us. Only a very few astronomers, physicists, philosophers—and even they only on the basis of a specialized approach which may be more or less widespread—experience this state of affairs otherwise, namely as a motion of the earth around the sun. But the appearance in which sun and earth stand, e.g. the early morning landscape, the

sea in the evening, the night, is an appearing. This appearance is not nothing. Nor is it untrue. Nor is it a mere appearance of conditions in nature which are really otherwise. This appearance is historical and it is history, discovered and grounded in poetry and myth and thus an essential area of our world.

Only the tired latecomers with their supercilious wit imagine that they can dispose of the historical power of appearance by declaring it to be "subjective," hence very dubious.[74]

For Husserl the life-world was not a fiction; it was the real world. The theory world of the symbols of mathematical science is merely "a garb of ideas" covering the reality of the life-world and in this "garb of ideas" we mistake "for *true being* what is actually a *method.*" He maintains that reaffirmation of the life-world "is the only possible way to overcome the philosophical naivete that lies in the 'scientific' character of traditional objectivistic philosophy."[75] This is the first necessity for fulfilling "the spiritual need of our time,"which, Husserl said, "has in fact, become unbearable."[76]

Husserl's distinctive contribution was his insistence that the theory-world is a derivative of the life-world and it is the life-world from which philosophical thought must begin. He is thus the father of the school of thought called "phenomenology." In the hands of Husserl's graduate assistant, Martin Heidegger, and Heidegger's graduate assistant, Hans-Georg Gadamer, his thought was transformed by the idea of the centrality of language but he has had enormous influence as the beginning of developments that would reject "analytic philosophy," or the philosophy that sees itself as part of science.

Heidegger and Gadamer are two of the most important influences on contemporary thought. Husserl came first, however. It must be acknowledged that in his emphasis on the fact that the life-world is to be explicated linguistically, there is an approach to the idea of the centrality of language, and in his later writing there is the unmistakable seed of another idea of tremendous importance: "we, each [of us] and all of us together belong to the

world as living with one another in the world; and the world is our world, valid for our consciousness as existing precisely through this 'living together'."[77] In other words the authenticity of the life-world has a social origin.

The problem solved by the embrace of the life-world is very ancient. Long before Plato, Heraclitus, inspired by a scientistic vision, declared that all things change except change itself. Thus at the beginning of philosophy, he attempted to bring it to an end. If we are to be able to say anything of significance, there must be something enduring for us to talk about. The eventual responses to Heraclitus were two world-famous affirmations, declaring the existence of the unchanging and the eternal: the atoms of Democritus (the unsplitable atoms with which atomic theory began) and the Ideas (or Ideals, or Forms) of Plato. For Plato the life-world was the "everyday" world, and the realm of Ideas, existing in heaven and in the memory of man, was made up of the perfect forms of which objects in the everyday world were copies. According to Stanley Rosen, the real purpose of the Ideas was not to establish a transcendent beyond but to restore authority and reality to the everyday world. Rosen says that the Ideas by preserving our everyday knowledge also preserve "the context of scientific and technical thinking, including the technical thinking of philosophy."[78]

From the invigorated scientific thought of the Enlightenment, the great poet William Blake sought refuge in the life-world. One's salvation was to be found by living in a world defined by one

> Standing on his own roof, or in his garden on a mount
> Of twenty-five cubits in height, such space is his Universe;
> And on its verge [contrary to Newton] the Sun rises & sets, the clouds bow
> To meet the flat Earth & the Sea in such an ordered Space.

Blake goes on to speak of "that false appearance which appears to the reasoner / As of a Globe rolling thro Voidness." It is, he says "a delusion" of Hell.[79]

Influenced by American pragmatism rather than phenomenology, George Santayana wrote a beautiful book entitled *Skepticism and Animal Faith* (1923) arguing that civilized men must embrace the life-world as reality. Animal faith he defines as "practical intellect" that deals with the world as it finds it.[80] The philosopher P. F. Strawson distinguished what is in effect the life-world by the attitudes of those involved in it. Theirs is the "participant attitude," which he contrasts with the "scientific attitude." [81] Heidegger said, "The closer we come to the danger, the more brightly do the ways into the saving power begin to shine."[82] Stanley Rosen says simply, "In order to turn away from reductivism, we must turn back to the everyday intelligibility of the beings because there is nowhere else to turn."[83]

If we are to make such a turn, we must not expect much help from intellectual sources. Nor must we look for a philosophical analysis, for an "explanation," of the life-world. Husserl, who identified and named the life-world, characterized it as the product of consciousness. When he went on to conclude that consciousness is an absolute, identical with the ideal of "transcendental idealism," he was, for one thing, acknowledging that there is something mysterious about the life world. Rosen points out that to return to the life-world is to abandon the hope of certainty that has inspired most thought since Descartes. He says, "There is no philosophical doctrine or definition of what constitutes everyday life."[84] It is sufficient to say, as Husserl does, that the life world is "the world that can be commonly talked about." It is clear that the intellect founded on the life-world must work with a great deal of what Michael Polanyi calls "personal knowledge," which is tacit, intuitive, and non-objective.[85]

Like all affirmations whatsoever, affirmation of the life-world is a "leap of faith." Restoring the life-world is to be achieved, not by analysis, but by a practice. What is required is changing ourselves. We must, first of all, cease to pretend that the conditions of our minds are inevitable. That they simply reflect the way the world is. We must understand that our modernist way of seeing

the world is the result of a an obsessive paradigm controlling our minds. Our educations have drilled us incessantly in obedience to this paradigm. A great deal of modernist egomania has sanctified this obsession, complacently confirming it as truth. The paradigm is in two parts. One part says that where knowledge is concerned we are totally passive recipients, completely impotent, essentially victims. The other part says that the only real knowledge is scientific, or positivistic, analysis. (The logic of the paradigm is outlined in Appendix B.)

The paradigm is a profound falsification of our nature and the nature of the world. Training ourselves in that realization is the primary means of restoring the life-world. Our need for this is a corollary of the impulse to conservation and environmentalism. The project of restoring the life-world is a moral and aesthetic corollary of these technological correctives. A regimen to transform our minds and restore our souls is essential. Scheduled moments of concentration, of stillness, of self-unifying reflection on ourselves and the nature of the world can achieve much. There is needed the practice of a kind of prayer. The resolve upon such a solitary practice is itself a recognition that we as individuals and our world are real. Such moments are given special importance in the rush and clutter of the modern world. We need the practice and discipline of a litany declaring that we do indeed exist because the life-world that fills our consciousness is reality. The tree is the reality, not the chlorophyll.

As "humanists" we must accustom ourselves to living in two worlds, the life-world and the theory-world. Desire tells us that we must beware the metaphysical allure implicit in the theory-world, or in some aspects of it. Desire is desire for unity, and materialism is the most radical fulfillment of that desire imaginable. Here in the realm of mind is a totalization that makes us the primary actors of the universe. Here is a fulfillment of desire that cannot be imagined in any alternative metaphysics. In that sense, materialism is a radically religious notion, driven by religious impulses.

We must remind ourselves simply to look at things again. Experience of the arts can be of great help, for their subject matter is the life-world. Painting during most of its history stills and concentrates the life-world, and Impressionism may be of special value. The truth of the life-world is that we are all impressionists. It must be recognized, of course, that much of the painting of the twentieth century has been a gesture of allegiance to the abstraction of science, an exorcism of the life-world.

We understand that consciousness is in large part an unconscious creative process. In conscious practice of this process, in consciously shaping it, we become artists. However, we are not artists free to create the world again from scratch. We understand that creativity is part of a condition and a process larger than we are. In creating the world, we collaborate with the community, which is the surety of reality. A great deal has been given to us. We are indebted on all sides, indebted to the human collectivity and to the totality of things that brought us into being and made us creators. We must recapture the piety that is loyalty to our origins. But our reflection must be neither passive nor mindless. It must include discrimination of different aspects of the environment.

A part of the life-world is the product of technology, creating elements of comfort and beauty. But in part technology has been a desecration of the life-world, eliminating humanity and poisoning the debased survivors. For instance, technology intensifies communication between people while making them anonymous as persons. We cannot make the needed discrimination concrete without resolving to change things. This means that ours must be an art in which morality is inextricable. Our art—both our art of living and our art as artifacts—must be a new art, but it will be very old in being an art of adoration. All art, said John Ruskin, is praise.

-SOUT

Reason and the Goodness of the World

With the advent of the life-world, we will have recovered discourse and human rationality, and "no theme," says Santayana, "lies closer to the heart of man."[86] There will again be "things" to think about and the word/concepts that bring them into being will become again part of reality. In our embrace of rationality, however, we must guard against incontinence. If we look closely at postmodernism, we find that when it is not totally discrediting reason, it is bestowing upon reason, in its most extreme, scientific form, the power of final truth. The rationality we recover with the life-world is of another sort.

We discover that we are in possession of two rationalities, one verbal, the other mathematical, and we must sustain both. We guard the reality of the life-world against the invasion of the theory world, but value science and mathematics within the realm of physical phenomena. We are committed to a dualism, for we affirm both worlds. We understand, furthermore, that they can never be reconciled. We must live with the frustration of our hope of human achievement of ultimate unity, a hope active whenever we require an explanation. We must understand that the meeting of the two realms is a mystery, an insoluble dualism. Rationality meets its limitations in "a contradiction at the heart of things."

To make the distinction between the life-world and the theory-world is in a very real sense to make Kant's distinction between phenomena (life-world) and noumena (an unknowable reality behind phenomena). Like Kant we affirm rationality at the expense of limiting its claims. It no longer nurtures that jealousy of God that aims at total explanation. Reason is no longer the substance of the universe. It is no longer autonomous but, like the life-world, it depends on something else, that original choice and affirmation of the goodness of the world. This is essentially the choice that has been made by all those modern thinkers who have abandoned analytic philosophy. Rationality, says Hilary Putnam, "is at bottom, just one part of our conception of human

flourishing, our idea of the good." In these terms Putnam authenticates rationality, "for reference and truth are notions we cannot consistently give up."[87] Stanley Rosen says, "What we need to learn from the ancients . . . is the intimate connection between reason and the good."[88]

Iris Murdoch says, "The contemplation of experience must be connected to, enlightened by, seen in the light of, something good (pure, just)." She says also, "Love is truth, truth is love."[89] Charles Taylor takes the same stand: "We cannot understand the order [of the world] and our place in it without loving it, without seeing its goodness, which is what I want to call being in attunement with it." He continues: "Those who see the world-order purely in terms of accident and chance are not thereby led to love it more or to be happier with themselves; and this means they must be wrong, if knowledge and wisdom are closely linked."[90]

Rationality, then, is never a free and independent power. It works always within a context of which it is a part. Every act of analysis, says Rosen, presupposes "unity."[91] And unity is not a product of reason but of intuition. Kenneth Burke says, "We differ from those who would eradicate 'word magic': we hold that it is not eradicable, and that there is no need for eradicating it. One must simply eradicate the wrong kinds and coach the right kinds."[92] Taylor agrees: "Our emotion language is indispensable precisely because it is irreducible."[93] The neurologist Antonio Damasio, who has written an entire book on the subject, says, "I suggest only that certain aspects of the process of emotion and feeling are indispensable for rationality."[94]

It is through the emotions that all other influences participate in reason. The environment of which rationality is a part is first the body but also the larger environment. Wittgenstein spoke of language (thought) as part of "forms of life." And rationality, to begin with, results from, a social context, as the theory of consciousness makes clear. Alasdair MacIntyre says, "It is only by participation in rational practice-based community that one becomes rational."[95]

Unfortunately, coming to understand the dependency of rationality has spawned a virulent kind of anti-intellectualism. Commenting on the postmodern world, Alain Finkielkraut says that we reject reason and thus abandon all distinctions: "We are living in a time of *feelings*, where there is no truth or lie, no stereotype or invention, nothing beautiful or ugly, but an infinite palette of different and equal pleasures."[96] The postmodern sophistry discrediting rationality has been encouraged by a famous statement of Heidegger: "There is a thinking more rigorous than the conceptual."[97] This and the example of his later writing suggests that philosophy should become a sort of prose-poetry, a suggestion that Murdoch calls "a terrible wish."[98] In absence of a clear focus in this matter, Taylor points out, "scientism remains smugly satisfied with its half-baked explanations, and the subjectivist conception of experience veers towards formless sentimentalism."[99] Understanding the limitations of reason, says Damasio, is not warrant for abandoning reason: "Knowing about the relevance of feelings in the processes of reason does *not* suggest that reason is less important than feelings, that it should take a backseat to them or that it should be less cultivated."[100] What the limitation of reason requires is not abandonment to emotion but recognition of human finitude, something that is extremely difficult for the modern temperament and imagination, because it has religious implications. Humanity comes into being with consciousness, which is generated by a concept. Reason is a frail craft in a troubled sea, but it is all we have that is peculiarly our own. We come to understand that reason is the gift of life. Because consciousness is always conceptual, reason is that from which all else follows. Without this small craft there would be no sea—of emotion, of imagination, of faith—threatening to overwhelm it. When reason would turn back to destroy the foundations of faith, we recall that it too is based upon faith and is part of a reality that we create. Its possibility is based on the meanings that it may be employed to destroy. Its claim to reality is limited, but firm. Reason is necessary for life.

Linguistic reason and the life-world, made up of objects and their human meanings, are our qualified but foundational reality. Bringing ourselves to understand that science is a fantasy, though one of tremendous value, and that the life-world is the realm in which we must live and think go far toward restoring our cultural health.

Understanding that all realities are realities that we create will open our minds again to the myths that we create. And we will come eventually to comprehend that we do not create alone.

Chapter Seven

HISTORY AND THE ADORNMENTS OF SPIRIT

We can have come this far because we wish to believe in God—or at least because we continue to entertain that possibility. We can make an effort to believe only if we can first conceive of God, and we realize quickly that attempting to do that is not only a perilous intellectual effort. It is more essentially an effort of prayer. To wish to believe in God is to wish to be able to pray. To wish to believe in God is to give up the effort to be his intellectual equal. That sacrifice brings us close to the possible experience of God. The great scholar Etienne Gilson confirms the insight of Kierkegaard, saying "that to seek God is to have found him already."[101] We must add: "providing that we remember that our finding is a seeking."

The first chapter outlined a special faith taken from G. W. F. Hegel, Pierre Teilhard de Chardin, and, especially, Karl Rhaner and assumed to be a body of belief which in its general tendency is inherent in all mature religions. This creed is coherent, not with the metaphysical assumptions of modern science, but with its purely scientific assumptions. For this reason and because of its abstractness, this creed may be received with relative ease by modern minds. Such an acceptance would be rich in potentialities. If this creed is inherent in all mature religions, then it is a framework, largely unconscious, on which these religions have

been built. It is a schema on which mature religions have bestowed spiritual adornments. And if this is so, this abstract creed–a creed for the mind, easy to accept but also easy to forget—may serve as the framework on which the modern minds may build again a more substantial faith–a faith, not only for the mind, but for the whole of life. The following paragraphs adumbrate the construction in part of such a faith. Fundamental articles of belief are outlined. They lie beyond our power of belief at this point in the argument. We only gather ideas about them that may become auxiliary to belief.

We cannot emphasize sufficiently that the human mind is irremediably inadequate to God and that although any characterization of God is a truth, it is a limited truth. This has always been Catholic teaching. For St. John Chrysostom, in the fourth century, God is "the inexpressible, the incomprehensible, the invisible, the ungraspable." In the sixth century the Pope who was called Gregory the Great and who was truly great, said, "Then only is there truth in what we know concerning God, when we are made sensible that we cannot fully know anything about him."[102] In the thirteenth century Saint Thomas Aquinas says that "concerning God, we cannot grasp what he is, but only what he is not, and how other things stand in relation to him." (SCGI,30.) This is the essential meaning of the "negative theology" of Nicholas of Cusa (1401–1464). Without embracing this insight, we founder in the most abject and chaotic form of fundamentalism.

We must recognize two other inevitable limitations on our prospects. A basic assumption of this book is that it is virtually impossible in the modern world to arrive at a faith that is not continuously shaken by doubt. Furthermore, such faith as we may achieve will be partial, incomplete, riddled with rejections, in some ways a fragmented faith conforming entirely to no orthodoxy. So we must be on guard against exaggerated claims to explain spiritual phenomena. Such exaggeration is characteristic of simplistic literalism and of misguided claims of intimacy with God. Such naiveté fabricates wooly reasons for God's provi-

dence in the world and pretends to explain evil. Such intellect is incapable of resting in mystery. A comparable kind of exaggeration is the abiding presumption of theologians.

In this we may take as our guide the great Erasmus of Rotterdam (1466–1536) who managed to be, both at the same time, a very devout Christian and perhaps the most complete embodiment of Renaissance humanism and who was a vigorous a proponent of reform within the Church and an opponent of the solutions of Martin Luther. He inveighed against the excesses of theology, the effort to explain what cannot be explained. He cites for instance a question as to whether Jesus, being both man and God, could feel pain. He deplores the tendency of those "who raise so many meddlesome, not to say irreverent questions concerning matters very far removed from our nature, and who formulate so many definitions about matters which could have been either ignored without loss of salvation or left in doubt."[103]

We do not so much conceive of God as to make a very small number of limited but crucial assumptions. We assume that God's being is radically different from our own. If civilized people are to conceive of God at all they must assume an infinite being of infinite knowledge and infinite power. We recognize that any effort to imagine God tends to diminish and contradict the nature of God. For instance, if we imagine God as thinking, we make him less than God. Thinking is a means of overcoming a lack of knowledge, of meeting a need which could not exist for infinite knowledge. When we encounter stories about God in anthropomorphic images, we know that although they may express truths, they are partial truths accommodated to the limitations of human minds.

The possibility that anthropomorphic stories about God express profound truths derives from another result of our limited number of basic assumptions about God. While we will not participate in truly primitive notions of a limited God, we will discover grounds for assuming their authenticity. We acknowledge that if there exists one drop of divinity, it saturates the universe. That is

implicit, for civilized minds, in the idea of God. We thus acknowledge that anything can happen. To believe in God is to believe in an unqualified way in the possibility of miracles. One of the miracles in which we can believe is that God reveals himself in ways compatible with the finite understanding of human beings. We accept an anthropomorphism qualified in this way.(The theological term for this is the doctrine of "accommodation.")

We do not thus believe that miracles often happen–not in our time and our world. To exclude their possibility, however, would be a gross presumption. It is, indeed, difficult to credit the occurrence of miracles in our time, but it is difficult not to credit miracles in some periods of history. One of the things that historians can tell us is that during the early centuries of Christianity, the reports of miracles and belief in miracles were abundantly commonplace. Miracles occurred regularly among Christians and just as frequently among others—among Jews, among those of the traditional Graeco-Roman faith that continued to be dominant during most of the first three centuries, and within the many oriental cults proliferating within the Roman empire.[104] Historians can depend ably report this fact to us. They cannot provide a definitive interpretation. We need, however, to say this: To credit miracle is to acknowledge that here and there the otherwise separate realms reflected in objective and subjective knowledge have come together. This we cannot presume to understand.

Indeed, to assume that we can understand miracle is to assume that it does not exist. Speculative questions can do no more than delineate the margins of the mystery. It is sufficient to recognize some very special characteristics of the age of miracle. The early Christian centuries were filled with intense activity and movement within the far-flung Roman empire, a period of the intermixture of people, of cultures, and faiths. A period of disorientation and of new and intensified psychic needs, a period of ferment.[105] Were these conditions that could bring together the separate realms that must unite if there are to be miracles?

We have reason to believe that new faiths arise from the confrontations between cultures and we know that new faiths tend to be held with great intensity.[106] Some historians maintain that it was always among believers that miracles occurred. If miracles were common during the first centuries, we cannot be satisfied with purely sociological explanations.

Here and there and in various ways there has arisen a compelling idea as to one of the aspects of change in the regime of miracle. With the passing of time, and especially with the rise of the secular mind in the West, faith has become more difficult. At the same time it seems to have taken on possibilities of greater complexity and a new kind of intensity. A reality that requires no care and attention slips into the nebulosity of the commonplace. It is not only the modern world that contrasts with the flourishing of miracle in the first centuries. Even in the sixth century such a contrast was evident. Pope Gregory the Great recognized it in a way that is of interest for modern faith. He addressed the clergy as follows: "Now my brethren, seeing that you work no such signs, is it that you believe not?. . . . Not so. For holy Church works daily now in the spirit, whatsoever the Apostles then wrought in body. . . . And, indeed, these miracles are greater for being spiritual: all the greater, as uplifting not the bodies but the souls of men."[107] With Gregory we affirm the validity of objective knowledge without denying spiritual reality. We surely believe in the objective *causes* by which we attempt to *explain* positively everything, but with Saint Thomas Aquinas we must believe that these are secondary causes (See page 251 below) and that, in some sense we cannot understand, they are sustained like everything in existence by God, the primary cause.

One may imagine that within the historical process spirituality evolves in increasing purity and strength. Robert Browning's great Pope in *The Ring and the Book* suggested that at earlier levels of civilization, miracles were necessary for the creation and sustaining of faith and that with strengthening intellectual and spiritual resources miracles were no longer needed. Fur-

thermore they were a crutch the absence of which fostered spiritual growth. (See pages 136.) The story of "doubting Thomas" has been taken as a paradigm of the principle involved. Thomas required direct physical evidence of the identity of the resurrected Christ. For this reason Jesus rebuked him with the words: "Oh ye of little faith!"

The modern person confronting an elaboration of articles of faith, will inevitably attempt to discriminate. One may say, "Why, yes, I believe in God, but not in that kind of God. Of course, I can't believe in miracles." This reflects intellectual chaos, or hardly any intellect at all. It must be understood that in the modern world faith, as it has always been, is faith in an absurdity. Faith exists only when it is faith in the absurd. So far as one's dignity is concerned, the realization definitive of the contemporary intellect is that if one has any dignity at all it is bestowed by God. The effort to achieve and maintain faith in the modern world is a struggle that must be repeated over and over again, but it is a struggle that succeeds only in so far as, over and over again, it ceases to be a struggle and becomes submission. Faith is *submission*.

It is not intellectually or psychologically possible to submit to God in the abstract. One submits to God as He is represented in the particularities of doctrine. Doctrine is an articulation of miracles. Faith first and last is faith in miracles. So turning to faith, we submit to a record of miracles. From some of them, perhaps most of them, we may simply turn away our attention. However, we do not presume to the impudence of denial. And we know that turning away our attention can become scorn. We pray for deliverance from pride. We pray for the grace of submission.

It is not only that the idea of God implies the idea of miracles. We must have miracles in order to believe in God. We cannot believe in an abstract God; miracles are necessary if God is to be particularized. We get some idea of the problems involved here by considering the language we use about God. We can hardly say anything about God without speaking of God as "He," or, if

you prefer a feminist alternative, as "She." In either case we are anthropomorphizing: we are attributing to God the traits of inferior beings—human beings. But language makes us aware that we have no choice. We cannot refer to God as "It."

We realize that although we may posit intellectually a God infinitely superior to human beings, we cannot imagine such a being. We can construct a God manque, combining human with animal traits–the human traits of language and consciousness with, let us say, an ability to fly. Such a being would not be spiritually superior. It would be human with an added alternative mode of movement. If we imagine a being superior to humans, it turns out that this being simply has one or more superior human traits. A being superior to humans is possible as a conception, as a vague notion, but it is not available to the human imagination.(That we are made in the image of God is, nevertheless, an article of faith, which remains to be considered.) When our imaginations entertain a being without human traits, it turns out to be inferior to humans, something like a chemical element, or a gas, a fog, a miasma. This is the truth understood almost uniquely by William Blake.

Therefore it must be a mystery, a kind of miracle, that gives God a human form. God as the fulfillment of an intellectual need, God as an abstraction, is not enough. Faith requires a tangible and living object, a sacred image of life. For Judaism Israel was that object. Israel was the visible presence of a community. Israel's fate was the correlative of God, a concrete reflection and assurance of God. Judaism survives so long as Jews are part of Jewish communities, which are remnants of Israel.

Community is inseparable from the elementary form of religious life, as Emil Durkheim made clear. When most local communities were dissolved, dispersed in the military and political whirlwind of the Roman empire, souls stood alone, profoundly lost. The crucially human image of Christ as the Incarnation of God made God real again, affirmed the existence of God in the only form in which we–the Gentiles of the West—can

conceive of God, in human form, not collective but individual. Christ was made necessary by Rome. As denizens of increasingly one world we are the heirs of Rome. Christ as God incarnate redeems us from the ambiguity of an abstract conception of God and presents us with an image capable of being loved. The God, not of a particular people, or of a community, but of all mankind.

No historian doubts that Jesus of Nazareth existed or that he suffered and was crucified under Pontius Pilate. It is equally certain that from his life there grew the faith for which the Roman empire was waiting: it spread with astonishing speed and within three centuries was the official religion of the Empire. No one doubts that from Jesus' teaching there grew the faith that was fundamental to Western civilization. These facts alone seem almost sufficient in themselves to make us in the twenty-first century believe what was believed in the first century, that Christ was the Incarnation of God. But Christianity proposes a belief more difficult than that: Jesus Christ was both human and divine. This is the central mystery of Christianity. Every effort to escape from the oppressive burden of this mystery is a denial of Christianity.

With this central and divine absurdity in mind, we may now survey more particularly what is to be believed.

The conception of God as the Father is deeply ingrained in the tradition which it is our purpose to authenticate and embrace. The conception, like all significant conceptions, is metaphorical, but it is also completely coherent with any rational conception of God. God has in some way generated us. We result from his being. We have his likeness. God has the fatherly character of being the source of both love and discipline: love in giving us life, discipline in giving us death, which marks our limitation and illuminates all meaning.

Implicit in the idea of God is the idea of heaven. In constructing our meaning of heaven, we may start with Plato. His heaven was like our world, but it was a realm of perfection, badly mirrored in our imperfections. In another sense his world was a realm of abstract forms, conceptions that gave meanings to our

world. If by virtue of being "star stuff" we are endowed with spiritual knowledge, then the abstractions, the mathematically formulated principles governing in perfection the movement of the galaxies, are part of heaven and the mind of God. God is the maker and sustainer of the setting of our existence, of both the material and the spiritual worlds, the physical universe and the *noosphere*, as it was called by Teilhard de Chardin, or the "thinking sphere" of evolutionary development, or the sphere of the human soul.[108] The noosphere may be equated with the realm of human reality which was described in Chapter 6 and called the "life-world."

We have first an authorizing belief, which is as follows: We are connatural with the stars, which are intermingled with our beginnings. We believe that our star nature is involved in the human organism and human consciousness as they are shaped by human society. The totality of our beings thus formed is expressed in the cooperative efforts of human imaginations in service to human flourishing. These elements tempered in the arduous processes of history arrive at truth. So we believe that, in ways that we do not understand, the story of Christ is true.

We believe—as our first defining belief—that Christ is the Incarnation of God and that he is fully God and fully human. We receive this as a mystery but a condition at one with the enveloping mystery of the being of all that is. Though we do not understand this, it is made in some measure intellectually tractable for us because we believe that we too, in a distinct way, are also an incarnation of God.

The act of God is not distinct from what it accomplishes and does not occur in the medium of time and so is not to be lost in a past. It is sustained in all eternity. Christ, begotten by the father, is begotten by the father through all eternity. We believe that the articles of our faith are a coherent whole but we do not believe that its unity depends on or can be represented by articulations of human rationality. In a way that we do not understand, we believe that the divine begetting of Christ was one with the total

creative act of God which sustains the universe.. We believe that the creation and the incarnation are one.

We remind ourselves that, although we are given small hand-holds of knowledge, the nature of God is beyond human comprehension.

Ours is a triune faith. We believe first that there is a God. Then we believe three things: that he created the world, that he has made himself intelligible to human comprehension, and that he continues as a force in the life of men. (We believe that wherever God has been believed, these are believed to be acts of God.) If we attempt to conceive God as a rationally comprehensible principle in these functions, we conceive of God as less than human. We believe that God has revealed himself in the highest form which we are capable of comprehending, the form of persons. We believe necessarily in the Father, and the Son, and the Holy Spirit.

After attempting to understand everything possible to be understood, we submit to belief in what we cannot understand. That is the fundamental religious act. We gasp, near suffocation, to *say something* about it. The Council of Florence (1442) put it this way: "The father is wholly in the Son and wholly in the Holy Spirit; the Son is wholly in the Father and wholly in the Holy Spirit; the Holy Spirit is wholly in the Father and wholly in the Son." The words do not clarify, nor are they meant to; they are a way of possessing the mystery.

The theologians, always attempting to explain, to make understandable, characterized the Trinity as three *persons* in one *substance*. We may say that the *substance* is God; the *persons* are God the Father, God the Son, and God the Holy Spirit. (For the conception of *substance*, see Chapter 13, pages 262–263.) God then exists in each of the three persons and in order that this not come to consist of three gods, the idea of persons must become something other than the individual *substances* that we intuitively conceive them to be. Persons must be conceived as capacities for relationships and a capacity to come into being through those

relationships. This is erudite and satisfactorily modern, but it is essential that we acknowledge both the necessity and the eventual failure of rational effort in this matter.

Saint Basil said, "It is by his energies that we know God; we do not assert that we come near to the essence itself, for his energies descend to us but his essence remains unapproachable."[109] So we will not *know* (conceive of) what the Persons of the Trinity *are*. What we can conceive, if sometimes only metaphorically, is what they do. In the conception of God the Father and Creator our basic need for a unified conception of the totality of things is realized. God is the fulfillment of our intellectual need. The conception of God is essential for our conception of the other Persons of the Trinity.

Christ in this world is God become also man. This is the central miracle, and we do not propose to understand it. All miracles exist on the fringes of our mind because they are out of reach of the analytic processes at the center of our minds. We turn from this center, not to reason but to adore, not only with our minds, but with the fullness of our being.

In the most horrible, most painful, most murderous form of death Christ's humanity was made dramatically evident. He dies for us. Forever after, his mangled body hangs in an image of death that is cathartic, ridding life of death. In the image of death as the crucifixion and in the love of this image the Catholic daily realizes Heidegger's "freedom toward death" which is a "resolute" acceptance and affirmation of death in which consciousness (*Dasein*) finds its authenticity and wholeness and an attendant "unspeakable joy"[110]. This comes as subtle subliminal knowledge before one goes on to rationalize it consciously in the paradox of immortality. (Puritanism can be defined as the rejection of this cathartic image. For the Puritan the image is offensive, intolerable. With this image we come to the heart of Catholicism.)

Although Jesus as a man "suffered, died, and was buried," he was also divine and could not be permanently lost to mortality. We are assured of this by the New Testament. As man Jesus

died. He arose as divine person and son of God. The divine principle focused here as person in history returns to the incomprehensible realm of the divinity sustaining the universe. We know that all the processes we know about on this earth come to an end. Are we to say that some obstruct the process of history and fall into the oblivion in its wake, and others contribute to the process of history and participate in its consummation in the eternity of Christ? Are we to say. . . ? Are we to say. . . ? We are attracted, placated by abstractions, suggesting that God is within reach of our intellects. But as soon as we embark on abstractions we know that we face a sea of the incomprehensible. Every abstraction is in part a betrayal. We can only hope that abstractions give us some small intellectual purchase on the larger meaning living in what seems the simpler but is the more comprehensive expression. We must turn back to the concrete story: "He will come again in glory to judge . . . and his kingdom will have no end."

With the Father barely comprehensible by reason and the Son communicated to us only through history, the form in which we know God as an unseen power working within the world is the Third Person of the Trinity, the Holy Spirit: The Holy Spirit is seen as working in the world: By the power of the Holy Spirit Jesus was born of the Virgin Mary. Now the Holy Spirit is seen again as working within the world.

There is a fourth embodiment of God. The Church is "catholic," meaning "universal," because Christ exists within it and because its call is to all human beings. "The Church," says the *Catholic Catechism* (Article 845), "is the place where humanity must discover its unity and salvation." The Church is "apostolic" because its Bishops are the successors to the Apostles. The Catholic Church is called the "one" Church having this nature. This was taken throughout the past to mean: "Outside the Church there is no salvation." Vatican II dispelled that idea. Those who know neither Christ nor the Church "but who nevertheless seek God with a sincere heart, and moved by grace, try

in their actions to do his will as they know it through the dictates of their conscience–those too may achieve eternal salvation."[111]

The fact that salvation can occur outside the Church and outside Christendom is not taken to deny the special powers invested in the Church by its inheritance of the Keys of the Kingdom from Christ. Fundamental among these is the power of the Church to forgive sin. The first step in the exercise of this power is Baptism by which one is delivered from original sin and by which one is received into the Church. The power of forgiveness of sins continues in the sacrament of Penance.

The last sentence of the Nicene Creed, in whatever sense we may take it, is distinctive of and fundamental to Christianity: "We look for the resurrection of the dead and the life of the world to come." We may not hesitate to take "the resurrection of the dead" as a figurative reference to the immortality of the soul. That leaves us with hardly less a problem. A historical perspective can be of help. For instance, Etienne Gilson says, "It would probably surprise a good many modern Christians to learn that in certain of the earliest Fathers the belief in the immortality of the soul is vague almost to non-existence."[112] The brilliant Gilbert Keith Chesterton said, in essentially these words, "As a Catholic I must affirm the immortality of the soul, but it is not a article of faith that I must think much about." In effect, Chesterton gave to the idea of the immortality of the soul an "assent of religion" without quite an "assent of faith." (See also Chapter 14, page 272, for this distinction.) We may best focus on what this means in light of the modern stage of spiritual development. To do this we may imagine four historical conditions of human consciousness:

1) Among primitive people death is always considered an accident.

2) At an early stage of development within civilization, the inevitability of death is dimly understood, but it is submerged in the hurly-burly of human activity. In this stage

we are encircled by the kinds of danger to which animals respond instinctively without any consciousness of death. Struggling instinctively to stay alive, we have no time to contemplate death. Death, an unstable concept exists only on the fringes of the mind, while instinct is unremittingly alert against it.

3) At a stage of civilization propitious for contemplation, every person becomes in some degree a philosopher. Life as a beginning and a duration comes into view and communal experience implants an inductive conclusion: Life which has a beginning and a duration also has an end. All humans die. I will die. An anguished instinct for survival rushes against this concept in consciousness and makes it unforgettable. Life flourishes but is regularly visited by a recurrent chill.

4) For a while in civilization an implicit faith sustains an animal optimism and fires the energies exploring the possibilities of explanation in the physical world. This ends with the reduction of all meaning to physical explanation. Life is then seen as an illusion, Nihilism triumphs. Death pervades all consciousness and becomes the only reality. Death as knowledge sickens the human organism.

Because we are human and uniquely have the knowledge of death, we must acknowledge death. The secular alternative of forgetfulness is a mindlessness, which is more inconsistent with our sense of integrity than is a deliberate embrace of faith. But thinking death poisons life. To be faithful to life we must somehow think, not death, but life, to the very end. Even toward the end we must not let life, for so long as we have it, be sickened by the thought of death. And yet, although faith is rich in beliefs that help to sustain life, this belief in the immortality of the soul seems to lie beyond our reach. But our belief is in a religion that proclaims that as truth. So belief in the immortality of the soul is

not denied; it is just consigned to the fringes of the mind, There on the fringes, deposited there by words to be summonsed again by words, the belief in life after death sustains belief in life during life. Whatever else may be the truth, this is a way of saying life is good.[113]

Unquestionably our power of faith falters before all this. For our desert-crippled souls our abstract special creed, which cannot sustain itself, is needed to sustain all this—and can be sustained by it.—We are part of divinity in the world. As spiritual beings we participate in the creation and the sustaining of the reality of the world. Always, and in response to the doubts raised by every advance of material knowledge, it is within ourselves that we find God. As the result of the dialectic of material and spiritual knowledge in history, we have increasingly intense, complex, and comprehensive knowledge of God. Spirit arises from matter and ultimate spiritual realization is the goal toward which the universe evolves.

Even all this, which is still only an intellectual exercise, will end in sterility unless it becomes part of an action. One must somehow find the spiritual hardihood to undertake a specific religious practice, strengthened by the thought "that to seek God is to have found him already." We will turn next to the embodiment of the greatest of all forms of religious practice.

Chapter Eight

WHORE OF BABYLON
OR BRIDE OF CHRIST

The Challenge

The culture of the West is ripe for transformation, The fact
remains, however, that the institution capable of bringing it health
and unity is undergoing uncertain fermentation. There are con-
troversial proposals, for instance, concerning contraception,
abortion, clerical celibacy, female ordination, annulments, and
homosexuality, not to mention the hotly contested question of
Papal Infallibility, which will be considered later in this
chapter.[114](In all that follows I identify Christianity and Roman
Catholicism, unless otherwise indicated.)

We must turn to the Catholic Church because either we accept the decay of everything we value or we engage ourselves in
an epic reconstruction of history—an abatement and displacement of movements dominating Western culture that were both
profoundly creative and ultimately destructive. From the Renaissance onward, the major tendency in Western culture has been
the displacement of traditional knowledge, the reduction to atomic
components of cultural, social, and political institutions, and the
generation of individualism in every phase of life. With
Promethean energy we have taken all things apart, and now that
they have disappeared, we confront with empty hands the pur-

poses that they served. We must put things back together. What we achieve now will be new, but to build it we have only the past to draw upon.

A Faith and a Culture

The great fructifying institution at the center of the pre-Renaissance Western culture was the Roman Catholic Church. The disruption of that culture came in the Renaissance and the Reformation. The Catholic Church and the world of Protestantism occupy opposite poles in the dialectic of history. The powerful individualistic impulse of the Renaissance had its most radical effect in the Protestant Reformation. The individualistic character of Protestantism is witnessed by the great commentators Max Weber and Emil Durkheim. Weber saw individualism and the "Protestant ethic" as the driving forces in the growth of capitalism. Durkheim saw individualism as explaining a higher suicide rate among Protestants. The same general contrast between the faiths has been developed most recently by the distinguished sociologist, Father Andrew M. Greeley.[115]

Catholics, according to Greeley, see the community as sacramental, a medium for the revelation of God. The Protestant sees the community as sin-filled and God forsaken.

The individual stands alone, essentially independent of all worldly relationships as he confronts God. The Catholic in his relation to God is supported by the intermediary of the community as the Church and by the psychological and artistic paraphernalia of the world embodied in the Church. The difference shapes the innermost beings of Protestants and Catholics.

The difference is explored by David Tracy in a book entitled *The Analogical Imagination* (1981). The Protestant imagination is analytic. The Catholic is analogical; it sees similarities and unities, conceives the individual always as part of a universe. Within Christendom, the Catholic Church is the institution that turns toward community. Against the centrifugal force of Protes-

tantism, Catholicism represents the force of communal cohesion. The special need for God in our time is the defining communal value of the Catholic Church. The Church is the original, primary, and comprehensive embodiment of the religious faith that is needed in our time.

The project envisioned by everything in this book is a transformation of our culture that does not sacrifice the political gains and the genuine intellectual and spiritual gains that have been produced by history. We must achieve now a new cultural conservatism that does not compromise what has been gained in the legitimate freedom and political equality of the individual. It is this that can be accomplished through the growing influence of the Church.

Historical Deformities and Purification

All that will be said hereafter about the function of the Church in society has one of its basic grounds of justification in a single awesome fact. This is the historical transformation of the Church. Most of the essential sins within the Church arose from its taking the role of a nation among competing nations and as a military power among competing military powers. (See Chapters 11 and 12.) The effect of the processes of history, which we must consider divine processes, has been to purify the Church by removing it from the arena of competition with nation states. Its material power is sufficient to sustain it, not as a material competitor with the states, but as a spiritual counter-agent to the materialistic dynamisms of the secular state. We cannot escape the conclusion that the growth of democracy—not in the Church but in nations of Europe—and the purification of spirituality within the Church are part of the same divine process.

The purification of the spirituality within the Church by the growth of democracy in secular states is part of the same historical movement in which the growth of knowledge disciplined and refined religious faith. In this development, democratic factors

first emerge in the development of local monarchies which, although autocratic, depended upon public opinion in their resistance to the aristocracy.[116]

With the growth of scientific knowledge and rationalistic assumptions, faith ceased to be an easy and primitive literalism. a simplified assumption of anthropomorphic powers directly superintending the world. In *The Ring and the Book,* Browning's Pope considered the role of the Enlightenment, that seventeenth and eighteenth-century upsurge of modern knowledge.(X, 1844–1860) Was its role in history to shake

> This torpor of assurance from our creed,
> Reintroduce the doubt discarded, bring
> That formidable danger back. we drove
> Long ago to the distance and the dark?

That "formidable danger" to be reintroduced is the reality of death, which "the torpor of assurance" has hidden under the doctrine of immortality of the soul. Thus would "man stand forth again, pale, resolute/ Prepared to die, which means alive at last?" The eventual gist of the Pope's proposal is to reject faith as based on objective observation ("faith in the report"), which is "Man's God," and accept "God's God in the mind of man," which is God known in human subjectivity.[117] The truth that the Pope glimpses is the historical truth of the paradox of faith in the modern world. This paradox is that faith inherently sustains life, but a literalist faith, a faith mistaken for objective knowledge, falsifies and deadens life. Faith posed against the objective power of denial requires robust intellectual effort for its support and calls upon spiritual energies of a kind unknown in less complex historical periods. At least a part of this truth is represented in the office within the Church popularly known as that of "the devil's advocate."[118] Science must not be denied or forgotten. In its absence faith reverts to a primitive childishness. Objective knowledge is the essential antithesis of modern faith, as death is the vitalizing

antithesis of life, and democracy is the vitalizing antithesis of Christendom.

While its degeneration undermines the morale of the culture, democracy is originally and essentially an instrument for ennobling the human spirit. The integrity of humans as spiritual beings can be maintained under the rule of a benign monarch, but only democracy is designed to permanently safeguard the freedom necessary to this conception of human beings. The Church is in a sense antithetical to democracy, but it cannot flourish in the modern world if political democracy of the state does not survive. The Church, which achieved its maturity in the Medieval lineaments of Empire, has been deprived of its material power by states shaped by democratic influences. The Church can continue to exist now as a spiritual power only within an international community dominated by democratic states. We must understand, nevertheless, that the relationship of Church to democracy is and must remain extremely complex

If by "democracy" one means the general conditions prevailing in contemporary European democracies, then it is a grave error to think of the Church as a democratic institution.[119] We will return to this point later. A spiritual obligation of the Church is to support genuinely democratic elements in all states, but an essential spiritual function of the Church is to counteract tendencies to cultural and spiritual degeneration inherent in democracy. Our argument cannot move one step further forward without recognizing that, as Winston Churchill said, among all possible forms of government, democracy is to be preferred because it is the least of many evils.

Modernity: Public Morality vs. Private Morality

The role of faith in Western cultures may be viewed in light of an awesome transformation of secular society accomplished by history. Until the earliest dawn of the modern world, the con-

ditions of the world affecting the lives of human beings were taken to result simply and directly from the will of God and entirely immune to human power. Coeval with the growth of democratic aspirations in connection with the French and American revolutions was the growth of another possibility.

People came to realize that to a very large extent conditions of the world affecting human lives could be controlled by human beings, who were responsible for those conditions. This created a new kind of moral obligation. Ones political allegiance became a morally compulsive allegiance. In addition to the older "private morality," there came to the front now what we can call a "public morality," the morality of how you vote and the kind of political policies that you support, which has been discussed in Chapter 3. In the course of time public morality took on increasing importance. This occurred in step with the growth of the "human" sciences. Every human science is based upon a determinism of its own making.

There are, of course different determinisms. For the psychologist, human actions are controlled, not by the will, but by psychological forces. For the economists, economic forces determine human actions, for the sociologist, social forces, etc. Eventually determinism captured the minds of most intellectuals and the demi-intellectuals who produce the media. With this development there emerged the idea that human behavior and the conditions in which humans lived their lives were totally determined by factors so large, abstract, and impersonal that they could be controlled only by the collectivity, in other words, by the state.

An enormous transformation occurred. An index of the change can be seen in the renaming of disciplinary institutions. Penal departments were now named Departments of Public Corrections. This was a giant hypocrisy, but none the less significant. In the minds of the educated, the perpetrators of anti-social acts were no longer criminals; they were victims. They were not to be punished but reformed. The guilty were the larger body of citi-

zens who had not acted collectively to correct the social conditions making criminal behavior unavoidable. In fact the citizen's neglect of social responsibility was the only kind of guilt.

The ethical change was embodied in a wide-spread collectivist movement in politics, the most conspicuous case of which was Marxism. This development represented an epochal advance in the potentialities of the human spirit. And yet something had gone wrong. Public morality now conflicted with and overwhelmed private morality. Private morality is primarily concerned with regard and care for other individuals and is based on the notion that individuals are responsible for their action. To persist in private morality was to obscure and resist public measures for the correction of the abstract forces that actually controlled how people behaved.

There had occurred one of those disastrous exaggerations that create massive human tragedies. Real social responsibilities had at last come to be understood. What had not been grasped was fundamental. Human society cannot be totally engineered. While the responsibilities of individuals for social reform are authentic and morally urgent, the amelioration of social conditions cannot be made stable unless individuals come to take responsibility for their personal behavior. Individuals can do this only when the standards of personal morality are an integral part of ones identification of oneself as a psychological, that is, spiritual, whole. Ones identification as a whole being involves a grasp of ones relationship to a totality of things. That is a preposterous requirement except as religion consists in a summary and symbolic conception of the whole.

If we ask what remains of private morality in contemporary society, we must conclude that the effect on it of a distorted and misapprehended public morality has been devastating. The effect of public morality has been to make democracy the exclusive moral principle. This means that ones relationship to the state is the relationship overriding all others. Only democratic relationships can be recognized. The primary democratic right is equality

before the law which means equality before the power of the state; from this flow all other legal and political rights. In so far as public morality retains its exclusive authority, there is no other measure of status or individual value.

An essential weakness of democracy develops as the notion of public morality penetrates all cultural levels of society. Large numbers of people conceive of themselves, not as the bearers and practitioners of public morality, but as its beneficiaries. For these people the only criteria for identification of the self are public criteria–political and legal. One is defined simply and only by equality. One takes his being–inevitably a quite amorphous being–from his equality. As there are no criteria other than legal and political, everyone is equal to everyone else and there are no grounds justifying distinctions of any kind. It follows that the only restraints upon freedom are the laws of the state. This means that freedom is what you can get away with. The prevailing logic leads to social dissolution. Democracy becomes a moral shambles.

The survival of democracy is totally dependent upon a number of values other than equality, conspicuous among which is the value of reason. Democratic principles are the product of the eighteenth-century Age of Reason. (The so-called democracy of ancient Greece was built upon the backs of an enormous population of slaves.) Both democracy and reason, in somewhat different ways, depend upon the integrity of the influence upon society of certain eternal sacred postulates. These postulates– these spiritual principles–have their origins in religion and are dependent upon it for their survival.

The tendency to permit public morality to usurp all moral function and principle is strong, both in Protestantism and in the Church, but has not prevailed and will not prevail within the Church.[120] On the other hand, the Church was the first to recognize the sacred status of public morality. This concern was present in Saint Thomas Aquinas (See Chapter 13)but occurred most notably in the nineteenth century. This concern was a primary

emphasis in the Second Vatican Council. The Church preserves the claims of public morality as one of the various sacred claims of morality. In this fundamental instance among many, the Church poses a counter-balance to the drift of secular society.

Vatican II, the Modern Transformation of the Church

The Church is a reagent for modernism, a test for sifting the dross from the gold.

In the nineteenth century all the institutions of the West were under attack and most were making concessions in the form of liberal transformation. A single institution turned against the current. The Catholic Church enunciated a number of doctrines to retrench its internal liberal currents and fortify its resistance to external influences. In 1854 Pius IX enunciated the dogma of the Immaculate Conception of Mary. In 1864 he issued the "Syllabus of Errors," which condemned most of the tenets of nineteenth century liberalism. The First Vatican Council meeting in 1869–1870, declared the dogma of Papal Infallibility. This stiffening of orthodoxy caused tremendous controversy both within and outside the Church throughout Europe, but there would seem to be no doubt that in the long-run it strengthened the Church. For instance, Marian devotion spread quickly throughout the Catholic world.

To many people the Church had come to seem a bastion of permanence amid the seemingly catastrophic changes that were sweeping the world. This accounts for the large number of conversions to Catholicism in the nineteenth century among European intellectuals who felt overwhelmed by the chaos that was eliminating the world of the past. The crisis they then recognized now verges on catastrophe. The Church changes in history, and it must change now, but it changes slowly and sometimes must react against external currents which would destroy it in demands for change for which it is not ready. This is a fundamental strength of the Church.

No one living in the modern world can doubt that change has moved too rapidly, that it threatens to overwhelm us. A part of the stabilizing power of the Church is in its power to slow history to a rate that makes possible the fruitful assimilation of change.

Vatican I braced the Church against the whirlwind of Modernism. After the passing of time for the sedimentation of the real values of the new, Vatican II, the second most important event in the history of the Church after the Council of Trent in the 16th century, embraced those aspects of Modernism that could serve the human spirit. This great Council, of the years 1962 to 1965, opened all the noblest prospects for reform and change in the future of the Church. Vatican II created great enthusiasm and a renewal of confidence. Its purpose, said its originator John XXIII, was an *aggiornamento*, an updating of the Church, an opening of the Church to the modern world. Its purpose, in the words of John XXIII, was "the recomposition of the whole mystical flock of Christ."

The achievement of Vatican II was enormous. It recognized that previously the "Church" had seemed to mean the hierarchy. The Council declared that the Church is identical with the community of human beings. It extended the role of the laity in the Church, describing all baptized persons as participating in what is called "the common priesthood." This provided the opening for the work of a wise, informed, and dedicated laity in the transformation of the Church. This is a task that cries out for the enforcement of the role of noblest Catholics of this priesthood by increasing recruitment of the secular spirits.

Vatican II also transformed the liturgy, abandoning for the first time since the Council of Trent the use of Latin and providing that the entire Mass be conducted in the vernacular. It called also for the full and active participation of the laity in the liturgy. Yet another document clarified and adjusted the relationship between Scripture and tradition, declaring that both "flow from the same divine wellspring" but that Scripture is the word of God

and the function of tradition is fidelity to Scripture in handing it on. The contribution of tradition is not denied, but Scripture is given a new and clear primacy. The document calls for a major role of Scripture in the liturgy. It also places a new emphasis on modern methods of study of the Bible and on liberal schools of interpretation. This addresses a Catholic wound inflicted by the Reformation. The new Biblical emphasis is in part a deliberate opening of ecumenism toward Protestantism. Ecumenism is emphasized repeatedly by Vatican II and one result is that contemporary translations of the Bible are the work of Catholic, Jewish, and Protestant scholars.

Another document provided a new, firmer foundation for the Church's social teaching, its engagement of the problems of society. The "Pastoral Constitution on the Church in the Modern World" had as its major concern what I have called above "public morality." This liberalization of the political perspective of the Church had begun much earlier, in the encyclical *Rerum Novarum* in 1891(by one of the great Popes, Leo XIII), and its accelerating expansion has continued in the social encyclical of John XXIII and those of John Paul II who has emphasized the need for social justice in the effect of the international economy upon the developing countries.

The Council also broached faintly another social area, that of the family which is at the heart of Catholic teaching. While the past teachings of the Church had recognized only the procreative element in sexuality, the Council also recognized another element that was "unitive" in its effect. Sexuality served, not only procreation, but the bonding of sexual partners. In this formulation the way has been opened for resolving the crucial source of turmoil within the Church, the much disputed prohibition of artificial contraception. This possibility, however, was averted for the immediately foreseeable future when Pope Paul VI withdrew the subjects of celibacy and contraception from the consideration of the Council, an act for which he has been much criticized. The kind of conservative restraints upon the effect of

the Council by Paul VI have been continued by John Paul II. We must understand why.

Vatican II was a magnificent moment in the history of the Church. In this Council the Church assimilated contemporary conceptions and knowledge consistent with faith and created ways of more complete administration to the spiritual needs of a society that had been transformed by modern history. In this sense it was a liberal movement. To accomplish this it inevitably opened itself to a current of liberalism in modern society which becomes a totalizing ideology. It thus ceases to be liberal and becomes a fanaticism. We will shortly examine, in the case of Gary Wills, an instance of liberalism thus deformed.

John Paul II: A Liberal Conservator

Liberals must not rush to judgement of John Paul II. Amidst the chaos of the cultural revolution of the sixties, the exulting response to Vatican II, especially in some radical experiments with the liturgy, must have seemed a reckless abandonment and an assault on the past that would eventually leave nothing standing to believe in. It is also true that in some respects, John Paul II has been a liberal Pope. He has labored ceaselessly for the expansion of the social teaching which was a basic objective of Vatican II.

John Paul has been even handed in his criticism of Marxism and irresponsible capitalism. He has become a powerful voice in defense of the poor and of social justice for developing nations within the international economy. There is no doubt that he has taken significant steps toward ecumenicalism. Many who dissent on other issues cannot feel less than sympathy for John Paul's eleventh encyclical *Evangelium Vitae* (The Gospel of Life) 1995, opposing the contemporary practice of abortion as what he called a "culture of death." Nor can we fail to admire the intellectual distinction of his *Fides et Ratio* stressing the importance of rationality for faith and of the study of philosophy for Catholic minds.

For a century the Church was immunized against modernism behind the sanctions of Vatican I. Then in renewed health and a perspective matured by time the Church opened itself again to the world. Sustained by the fundamental allegiance of John Paul II, Vatican II fitted the Church again for cultural leadership of the Western world.

A Faith for the Intellectual

The character of the faith that can stem the dissolution of society is patterned to fit the soul of the spiritual aristocrat. Such a person is by definition an intellectual, though he may not be employed in intellectual occupations. Like all of the best in society he is also in some measure an heir of the old military aristocracy. The strong values of discipline are chiefly inherited through middle-class lineages, but they reflect their origins. Furthermore, if intellectuals are to embrace a faith, it must be something very definite. The religious intellectual requires clarity and completeness in his intellectual world. It is required because a responsible religion must be nicely articulated with its secular environment. The intellectual finds ambiguity and conceptual mushiness offensive. There must be no doubt about the nature of the step the intellectual is to take.

Only if a faith is precisely elaborated can it be engaged by an acute and comprehensive intellect. If there are to be areas of obscurity, their margins must be defined. The intellectual will not be offended necessarily by the radial character of an article of faith, but he must have a clear conception of its foundation and its relationship to the totality of doctrine. For modern minds in the modern world, faith must have a large intellectual dimension. The intellectual also understands that if he is to embrace a faith, it must present him with the possibility of a total experience.

All this means that the faith to which an intellectual may be attracted must be a difficult faith. It cannot require simply a mild

change of opinion. It must have a radical structure of doctrine that challenges the individual's power of belief. It must, furthermore, require a clear and definite discipline. Such a belief can be achieved only in a commitment that goes beyond intellectual affirmation. There must be not only conceptions but a practice, and this means that body, attitude, and feeling must be engaged. Among all the varieties and interpretations of Christianity, only Catholicism meets these criteria.

The Disappearance of History

If we are to maintain in Western society any element of continuity with the past, then the nature of postmodernism will tell us that the Church is not only an embodiment of what we need. It has become a necessity. A radically different proposition is maintained in a brilliant book entitled *The Disenchantment of the World: a Political History of Religion*, by the French scholar Marcel Gauchet. He undertakes to explain and confirm the permanent demise of religion. We will see that the change in Christianity, which Gauchet thinks the sign of its inevitable disappearance, is the opportunity for a reawakening of Christianity that is already underway. However dubious Gauchet's argument concerning the future of Christianity may be, he provides the only coherent explanation of postmodernism that exists.[121]

Distinctive characteristics of postmodernism are the loss of the sense of temporal continuity and, integrally related to this, the end of ideologies, among which we may join Gauchet for the moment in including Christianity. These basic structural conditions of postmodernism, though Gauchet does not use this term, are, according to Gauchet the result of the bureaucratization of the democratic state. The function of massive bureaucracy is to so manipulate society as to control the future, but in its obsessive effort to do this it saturates society with partial controls that make any prediction or direction utterly impossible. Ideology, religious or secular, is defined by a prescription for the future.

Democracy, which freed us from the religious orientation of the past, now eliminated the possibility of an ideology.

There is general recognition of the disappearance of the future in the pervasive contemporary mind set. Serious anticipation and long-term planning have become unthinkable. The postmodern world may be horrified by the nameless rush of time, but it has no conception that can make the future comprehensible or controllable. The amorphous condition called Postmodernism, which is the result of democracy being permitted to go to seed, will be significant when we consider the necessary development of the relationship of the Church to the state. There can be no doubt that the current cultural catastrophe will continue and democracy itself will die unless powerful religious influence can serve as a counter-poise to the influence of democratic bureaucracy.

The Church as Counterbalance to the State

The Church is socially and culturally necessary precisely because of its conservatism and its power of continuity. Other institutions are relatively free of internal conflict because they have conformed easily and quickly, bending to accommodate social change. By immediately accommodating social change, they relinquish their power to influence social change. A part of the key to the Church's strength is that it does not simply change its own character in response to social change. It is not simply a part of a larger social organism interacting in a condition of equality with other smaller parts. While supporting the legitimate democratic powers of secular society, it must remain a spiritual counterpart to secular society.

The Church's response to social change must be a change that occurs within the Church and in conformity with the spiritual reality that is embodied in the Church. A strength of the Church is that it responds to social change very slowly. That means resistance to social change. Resistance creates the inner

ferment from which change shaped by spirituality can emerge. The result will be a Church which retains its power to influence the lives of human beings. The Church may undergo some important changes, but the Church must not abandon its always guarded response to new departures. For religion to remain religion, certain principles and conceptions cannot be sacrificed.

Implicit in the permanence of the Church is an element of permanence in the intellectual architecture of the human race. Traditionally and in the Church that element of permanence is called "the order of nature." It is an element which can be expanded but it must not be abandoned. In the words of a contemporary writer, Wilfred M. McClay, we must "be prepared to endorse some set of normative standards inherent in nature." McClay warns that "we are rapidly approaching the point where . . . liberty is taken to include the sovereign right to do whatever one wants with the human body and mind, including the comprehensive genetic or pharmacological refashioning of both." Thus, he says, we "risk making ourselves into the first posthuman creatures." As McClay points out, the only reason for not doing that is "the Judeo-Christian understanding of the human person as a *created* being whose dignity and fundamental characteristics are a divine *endowment* from that Creator."[122]

The validity of the importance of social and intellectual elements of permanence was historically manifest in the second half of the nineteenth century, when, as we have seen, the Church constructed barriers to the influence of modernism. By contrast the democratic state is attuned to rapid assimilation of social and cultural change.

The history of the Church has been in a fundamental way the history of its relation to the state. It is clearer now than it has ever been that the Church, to be true to itself, must live in permanent tension with every state. The Church's commitment to the democratic elements in all states is fundamental, but its loyalty to any one state is necessarily qualified. When its spiritual commitments are in conflict with such loyalty, its spiritual commitments must

rule. I believe we will come to understand that if the Church is to stem the rising tide of chaos in the West, we must envision anew the relation of church and state.

What is now to be urged depends rigorously upon the existence of two conditions. The first is that the Church does today in fact exist outside the realm of the competition of nations; except for meager areas necessary for administrative integrity, the Church is not and cannot become a territorial power; the Church, despite the requirement of great material resources to achieve its purposes, has been purified by history and is a power concerned exclusively with spiritual objectives. The second necessary condition is absolute. It is that the principle of the division of Church and State be preserved and it must be strengthened in a way that will rigorously prevent the direct intervention of either institution in the affairs of the other. Only thus can the inherent functions of each institution be maintained with integrity.

Church and state are antithetical to each other but also essential to each other. Balanced against the massive power of the state there must eventually be an institution capable of effectively counteracting the materialism inherent in the secularism of the state. Balanced against the giant secular bureaucracy of the state there must be a giant spiritual bureaucracy. The role of the Church must be that of spiritual adversary of, and counter-influence to, the state in so far as the state cultivates and does not attempt to restrain the culturally degenerative tendencies that need not arise from democracy but regularly do so. If religion is to withstand the onslaught of contemporary secularism, there must be an element of social unanimity which only the Church can provide. If democracy is to be capable of nourishing humanity, it must depend on certain values which can be sustained only by religious faith. In democracy the state is a secular state and as such it must be prevented from secularizing the spirits of individuals.

The Church has not remained immune to the toxic influence of the circumambient culture, but more than any other institu-

tion the Church has shown itself capable of resisting the degeneracy of cultural democratization. The Catholic Church is the largest religious organization on earth. It is the only organization of such magnitude as may be imagined to constitute a binary opposition with the state. A religious world made up of innumerable divisions cannot confront the secular power of the state. The Church identifies itself with society as a whole, and then with the whole of the human race, and in this it represents a magnitude imaginably great enough to counter the spiritual influence of the state.

What is being proposed is a radical social dualism. Vital to its feasibility would be a legal separation of the Church and the State more rigorous and circumspect than it is now. The influence of the Church in the affairs of the State would, indeed, be immense, but this would occur only by the Church's influence on the souls of the population. The spiritual values of the Church—the spiritual foundations of reality, reason, and morality—are, in fact, essential to sustaining democratic processes in the secular realm. On the other hand, great evil has arisen from the influence on their souls of the secular order. The Church will innoculate against the self-destructive elements inherent in democracy. Yet, the Church for its own good must assiduously defend and protect democratic institutions in the political arena.

The Church itself must explicitly and overtly assure that religious influence on the state does not convert it into a theocracy. In what the Church cannot achieve spiritually, it cannot ask for, and it must reject, the help of the state. The Church must insist that the state treat it as it does all other institutions, spiritual and secular. It must also identify and define clearly the areas of life that are essentially spiritual and hence areas from which the state must be excluded. On the side of the state, only by the vitality of democratic institutions can the province of the Church be maintained as exclusively spiritual and its authority thereby justified. We must learn to live in two radically different orders.

For a century the Church was immunized against modernism behind the sanctions of Vatican I. Then in renewed health and a perspective matured by time the Church opened itself again to the world. Sustained by the fundamental allegiance of John Paul II, Vatican II fitted the Church again for cultural leadership of the Western world.

A Faith for the Intellectual

The character of the faith that can stem the dissolution of society is patterned to fit the soul of the spiritual aristocrat. Such a person is by definition an intellectual, though he may not be employed in intellectual occupations. Like all of the best in society he is also in some measure an heir of the old military aristocracy. The strong values of discipline are chiefly inherited through middle-class lineages, but they reflect their origins. Furthermore, if intellectuals are to embrace a faith, it must be something very definite. The religious intellectual requires clarity and completeness in his intellectual world. It is required because a responsible religion must be nicely articulated with its secular environment. The intellectual finds ambiguity and conceptual mushiness offensive. There must be no doubt about the nature of the step the intellectual is to take.

Only if a faith is precisely elaborated can it be engaged by an acute and comprehensive intellect. If there are to be areas of obscurity, their margins must be defined. The intellectual will not be offended necessarily by the radial character of an article of faith, but he must have a clear conception of its foundation and its relationship to the totality of doctrine. For modern minds in the modern world, faith must have a large intellectual dimension. The intellectual also understands that if he is to embrace a faith, it must present him with the possibility of a total experience.

All this means that the faith to which an intellectual may be attracted must be a difficult faith. It cannot require simply a mild

tion the Church has shown itself capable of resisting the degeneracy of cultural democratization. The Catholic Church is the largest religious organization on earth. It is the only organization of such magnitude as may be imagined to constitute a binary opposition with the state. A religious world made up of innumerable divisions cannot confront the secular power of the state. The Church identifies itself with society as a whole, and then with the whole of the human race, and in this it represents a magnitude imaginably great enough to counter the spiritual influence of the state.

What is being proposed is a radical social dualism. Vital to its feasibility would be a legal separation of the Church and the State more rigorous and circumspect than it is now. The influence of the Church in the affairs of the State would, indeed, be immense, but this would occur only by the Church's influence on the souls of the population. The spiritual values of the Church—the spiritual foundations of reality, reason, and morality—are, in fact, essential to sustaining democratic processes in the secular realm. On the other hand, great evil has arisen from the influence on their souls of the secular order. The Church will innoculate against the self-destructive elements inherent in democracy. Yet, the Church for its own good must assiduously defend and protect democratic institutions in the political arena.

The Church itself must explicitly and overtly assure that religious influence on the state does not convert it into a theocracy. In what the Church cannot achieve spiritually, it cannot ask for, and it must reject, the help of the state. The Church must insist that the state treat it as it does all other institutions, spiritual and secular. It must also identify and define clearly the areas of life that are essentially spiritual and hence areas from which the state must be excluded. On the side of the state, only by the vitality of democratic institutions can the province of the Church be maintained as exclusively spiritual and its authority thereby justified. We must learn to live in two radically different orders.

We must not permit them by intermingling to corrupt and destroy each other.

What is at issue may be seen in a single measure of the deterioration of contemporary society and a point on which many presumably sophisticated people would take great pride. This measure of decay is the disappearance and holding in contempt of the principle of hierarchy. The only hierarchic principle in our society is in monetary compensation. Here the vast rewards granted to sports figures, entertainers, and the top administrative officers of corporations form the apex of a radically differentiated hierarchy. Despite this real hierarchy, all collaborate in the pretense that everyone is equal. This is another horrendous mass hypocrisy, and it is an insuperable obstacle to the development of those implicit principles and unconscious habits of restraint and control that sustain the structure of society.

We can sustain democracy only by reinterpreting it. It must be understood that equality is not absolute. It must be understood that we participate in two orders of being. We are participants in an order in which the civil law applies to all of us equally and fully. Hence in the world of law and politics we are each of us equal to all the others. Because in the contemporary world this seems to be the only order that exists, equality is conceived as an absolute and universally applicable principle. It is assumed that before all human beings and all institutions each individual must assert his equality, his autonomy, his absolute justification.

Values and the Need for Hierarchy

To have any values is to have a hierarchy of values and that means a culture sustaining distinctions of value and merit in a way that will not undermine but will nourish democracy. We must maintain political and legal equality, while insisting on the recognition of moral, intellectual, and spiritual inequalities.

It is uniquely the Church that in the course of history has

In isolated primary communities, change in subjective knowledge does not jeopardize cultural unity and spiritual vitality. This fact must be realized in the light of the central thesis of this book: Religion is the product of subjective knowledge shaped by consensus responding to communal need. Because a primitive community is small and occupies a limited geographical region, its members all respond to the same environment, and constant direct interaction between them assures solidarity of consensus. Change within civilization is a very different matter. The condition of civilization is a multiplicity of communities. Within civilization the equivalent of primary communities are diversified. There also develops a vertical diversification creating what are in effect new kinds of communities. By interaction with each other, their internal principles of coherence are weakened.

Among the communities internal to civilization are what have been called the multiplicity of "languages" constituting civilization. These are the special vocabularies and usages of human activities differing as cultural and scientific pursuits differ.[123] The communities also correspond to the different languages of different trades, professions, intellectual specializations, social classes, and geographical areas. In these different languages, or communities, or worlds, the effects of the integrative processes are diversified and come into conflict with each other. The unifying of subjective knowledge that occurs in the isolate primary community and that gives rise to religion and culture to begin with, is no longer possible. Remnants of primary communities are totally dissipated. Conflicts of gods and of values spawn chaos. Spiritual resources are desiccated. Subjective knowledge becomes the isolated function of individuals. As such it spawns new religions which compete with each other to dominate society. Eventually, they vitiate each other totally.

The effect of a diversity of doctrines is that under the force of individualism that brought them into being, they multiply. During the Protestant Interregnum in England, the period 1649 to

1660 during which the Protestant dictatorship ruled England, an effort was made by the government to record all the religious sects but there were so many of them and they multiplied so rapidly that it was found to be impossible to keep up with them. Appallingly, at the end of the twentieth century there are in the world almost twenty-five thousand Protestant sects. The smallest and most numerous of such sects survive in pockets of ignorance and in enclaves of fantasy fashions in developed countries and in the isolation common in undeveloped countries.

Conflict generates dogmas in which subjective truth degenerates into the illusion of objective factuality. In the end there occurs something more fundamental than the loss of credibility of individual systems of belief. Having lost its moorings in community, subjective knowledge itself is completely discredited and repudiated. All subjective knowledge is now understood as dream and fantasy. The spiritual resources of humanity cease to exist. The final remnant of subjective knowledge is despair.

In civilization, spirituality dies unless institutions are devised that can fulfill the unifying functions that occur naturally in primary communities. In civilization there must be made effective, in one form or another, a doctrine of infallibility that recognizes the historicity of faith, even a doctrine of infallibility that knows it is required by the historicity of faith. Otherwise religion is diluted beyond existence or it survives only by virtue of brutish ignorance sustaining literalistic sects. In the major currents of society, religion becomes irrelevant.

The infallibility of the Church with the Pope at its head is simply a corollary of the necessity of stable and unified religious doctrine and ritual and both are corollaries of the necessity of instrumentation and convention in art. The individual cannot be left to contemplate and endure alone the infinity of spiritual possibilities. The essential and inevitable mediation of discipline, form, and convention in doctrine, ritual, and art is a manifestation of the radical limitation of the human capacity to conceive of God. Subjective knowledge is always only a particular limited

form in which we can comprehend God. The agon of faith is defined by the obligation to believe what we can conceive of God while knowing the limitations of our conceptual grasp. The unifying function of a primary community or of a civilized institution integrated with our particular culture must determine the form of faith.

It is unquestionably true that action is needed to avert the ills that have resulted from the doctrine of Infallibility. This is one of the many projects of reform in which the influence of new modern spirits will be greatly needed to support the noblest and best of Catholic intellects. The required action must come in the improvement of the deliberative procedures of the magisterium and in the process for the election of the pope. It must not involve an abrogation of the principle of Infallibility. Long centuries before the Church enunciated the doctrine of Papal Infallibility, Saint Augustine said, "The whole body of the faithful . . . cannot err in matters of belief."[124] When we look closely, we discover that our horror at Papal infallibility is a factor of our lack of belief in God.

We may note here an attack on Papal Infallibility which seems to prove the need for that doctrine. This is to be found in the most virulent attack on the Roman Catholic Church in recent decades. It is a book by Garry Wills entitled *Papal Sin: Structures of Deceit*[125]. A defense of Infallibility may be based on the condition of the faith of Wills, who professes to be a loyal Catholic. Wills rejects all the fundamental doctrines peculiar to the Church. He rejects the authenticity of tradition which the Church, with the contemporary support of Vatican II, has always considered one of the agencies of revelation. Correspondingly Wills rejects the Apostolic Succession, the doctrine that the Pope is the heir of Saint Peter and the hierarchy and the body of priests the heir of the apostles. Hence for Wills the Church ceases to be a divine institution. His position is in no basic way different from that of the Protestant Reformation. His practice is the futile Prot-

estant effort to return to a purely scriptural Christianity and restore the condition of the earliest Christian communities. It is, furthermore, impossible to distinguish Wills' conception of truth from that of nineteenth-century positivism.

It is only when we reach the final chapter of the book that we fully realize the appalling depth of Wills' assault on the Church. The final chapter is an attack on the doctrine of the mass, the central doctrine of Catholicism. In effect, the doctrine of the Church associating sacrifice with the Eucharist is "unclean" and a "structure of deceit." Generally Wills tiptoes, avoiding the word "transubstantiation," which defines the central doctrine. His eventual position emerges only in an outburst of anger when he characterizes priests as "magicians of the eucharistic transformation." The doctrine of the Eucharist for Wills is part of a deception that "returns one to the lying system of the Prince of This World, where one prevails by darkness." It need hardly be said that the book is in extremely bad taste. Without the doctrine of Infallibility secular intellectuals of the stripe of Wills will play Luther and Calvin within the Church and chaos will have come again.

Papal Infallibility becomes no longer an outrageous conception when it is realized that Catholics believe that the Church, though constituted by fallible individual human beings, is literally a divine institution. We believe that along with Christ and the Prophets and all of Scripture, the Church is one of the sources of divine revelation.

The principle of infallibility maintains the unity of the Church. That unity will come to have a new and unexpected value to Westerners if our apparent political future is fulfilled. There is abundant evidence that modern nations and the democracies they nurture will give way to new borders, spatial and ideological, of entities defined by religion and ethnicity.[126] With this the West will return to the condition of the Middle Ages, and once again the Church will be the single international institution uniting the Western world and sustaining its civilization.

Chapter Nine

THE GARDEN OF HERESIES

Because we are intellectual human beings, we cannot possibly approach the question of religious faith except through an intellectual process. We must become philosophers before we can become religious. We must rely upon secular resources of thought. This means that we may of our own happen upon any of the historical vagaries of the past. Before achieving a true faith, we may achieve any of the heresies. For this reason, we should be aware of the historical heresies beforehand. And not only to avoid them. Along with the Church we participate in a process of history that is creative, that is to say, divine.

The creative powers of history draw inevitably upon the past. In what was error we may discover elements that will augment and revivify the truth. While we cannot master the entire record of heretical achievements, we can get an idea of its nature. Here the prospective Christian may exercise his unused religious imagination. In addition, we will come to understand better than in any other way that religion is a historical product. A part of the historical process was explained in the fourth century by Saint Augustine: "Heretics are given to us," he said, "so that we might not remain in infancy. They question, there is discussion, and definitions are arrived at to make an organized faith."[127]

The Mediterranean world was a garden of religious fermentation, of innumerable growths of faith, most of which Christianity

came to consider heresies. It was, nevertheless, from this garden of heresies that Christianity grew and from which in the future it may draw unsuspected elements of strength. For instance, an anticipation of our conception of the revelatory power of history, we will find in "Gnosticism," of which more momentarily. Again, if we put aside the magical trappings from Egyptian Hermeticism in the thought of Giordano Bruno, and ignore his rash and subversive methods and attitudes, we find that in his universalism and his sense of God's agency in nature he shares something with the special formulation of basic faith that we have derived chiefly from Father Karl Rahner. That Bruno was burned at the stake in Rome at the soul-chillingly late date of 1600 affects us with remorse and a sense of loss.

We do not say that Christianity was the one divine element among all the multifarious growths of the spirit. We say that they were all divine and that Christianity was the one that could serve historical humanity and that the divine processes of history selected it for survival. We thank God in the faith that history has given us an enlarging share in the perspective of God on these heresies, some of which we will now describe briefly.

First of all, we will look at the heresy that almost overran the world in which Christianity eventually became dominant. In its various forms, it was called "Gnosticism." Gnosticism was long considered a heretical development of Christianity, but it is now recognized that its origins are obscure and that various sources may have contributed to its development—Jewish, Iranian, Babylonian, Egyptian, and other Oriental sources and ideas. It embodies, however, an inner unity of thought distinct from all the contributing sources. It is an intellectually complex system and represents an extremely high degree of philosophical sophistication. It has been called Christianity Hellenized. What follows is a profile common to nearly all bodies of Gnostic doctrine.[128]

The supreme deity is radically transcendent. He is almost totally removed from the realm of human life and from the physi-

sustains the entire universe which the archons have created. So they must resist by every possible means the escape of the spirit from their cosmic imprisonment. (We may be reminded of the jealous thrust for total autonomy in scientistic minds.) In opposition to the archons, the upper powers seek this liberation as a means of regaining the wholeness of their divinity. The means of liberating the imprisoned spirit of man is knowledge—hence the term "gnosis." which is from Greek.

The achievement of saving knowledge is a process continuing through the entire experience of man on earth. It begins with the Paradise story of Genesis, which the Gnostics render with all its values reversed. The divinity that denies knowledge to Adam is the evil Demiurge, the Creator of the universe. The serpent is the first bringer of knowledge, and thus becomes in Gnosticism a general symbol of the extra-cosmic spiritual principle and gives rise to cults of the serpent among some Gnostic sects.

In the same logic other rejected figures of the Old Testament, such as Cain and Esau, become bearers of the pneumatic heritage. Gnosticism conceives of a revelatory lineage running through history and culminating in Jesus, and, in varied versions of Gnosticism, in such figures as Buddha and Zoroaster. As in contemporary Catholicism, spirituality of other faiths is recognized.

Obviously Gnosticism is a system loaded with explosively revolutionary possibilities, which are realized in various forms in different sects and versions of Gnostic doctrine. An unfortunate major expression of this revolutionary impulse is an anti-Judaism that runs throughout Gnosticism. The pride, ignorance, and malevolence, and the evil domination, of the Demiurge are taken as a caricature of the Old Testament God. The essential hostility to the universe and in general to the accepted nature of things is expressed in different way. It is often expressed as asceticism, a rejection of the pleasure of the body and of material existence. On the other hand, it becomes a deliberate rejection of the morality presumably based on the nature of the universe. This is

expressed by a few sects in studied libertinism with sexual orgy as liberating ritual and an opening to the spirit. In a less spectacular, though no less fundamental way, Gnosticism easily gives rise to the heresy called "Antinomianism," the doctrine that the moral law has no relevance to salvation because faith alone is necessary to salvation.

If the modern intellectual turns to consider historic religious possibilities, he must inevitably be attracted, even excited, by Gnosticism. He is, above all, an Antinomian. Moral values are entirely relative and they are insignificant in comparison with larger spiritual concerns such as political values and these are certainly more nearly in harmony with the remote Gnostic God than with the God of morality. He is inherently elitist, his interests very remote from the simplicities of the minds of people in general. He prides himself on the kind of intellectual complexity essential to Gnosticism, and is aware that they are not within the reach of the majority of people. If he is to have a spiritual life at all, it is certainly one that will flourish under his own intellectual authorization.

He will submit to no one on such questions. He is instinctively contemptuous of orthodoxy. The very word is offensive. He is compelled to embrace that which is new, creative, varied, ever changing. Within Gnosticism there are almost unlimited variations of possibility. Furthermore, the tendency of the modernist intellect is incorrigibly nihilistic. Gnosticism's concept of a world of deception designed by a totally ignorant and fallacious God and totally devoid of value is profoundly nihilistic, as is its eventual discounting of the discursive intellect. Gnosticism's exaltation of subjective knowledge gratifies his egotism and his sense of total autonomy.

Indeed, if we are to pause for a moment over religious possibilities, we cannot fail to be compelled toward Gnosticism, but while sharing in its philosophical orientation, we cannot but be abhorrent of the dangers it poses. Gnosticism, which is acosmic, is also asocial. What distinguishes orthodoxy from Gnosticism

most important of all the competitors of Christianity.[130] It flourished among soldiers and especially on the frontiers of the Empire.

Christianity and the mystery religions had some very significant characteristics in common. They were entered by the free choice of the individual. Membership was not limited by race, cultural background, or sex (except in the case of Mithraism). These religions were not an inherent part of a particular community in a way that made membership hereditary or obligatory. They filled a need created for many populations by the absence of such hereditary and socially integrated faiths in the social flux and cultural anonymity in much of the Empire. In the absence of the stabilizing power of cultural roots, they substituted the appeal of strong emotional experience. There were usually similarities in the conception of the deity, his earthly experience, and his salvational power. They may be seen as preparing the soil in which they were generally supplanted by Christianity.[131]

The religious ferment of the Mediterranean world cannot be imagined without at least some sense of the vividness and diversity of the Christian heresies. The spectrum may be suggested here only by noting the most important of the heresies not yet mentioned. We may begin, however, not with a Christian heresy, but a Jewish heresy that had some similarities to Christianity—the Essenes.

The Essenes were a Jewish sect who regarded the ruling priestly groups as hopelessly corrupt. They left the Temple to set up a purified place of worship in the city of Qumran in the desert near the Dead Sea. They had existed for some 150 years before the birth of Christ. We are warned against equating the Essenes and the Christians, but there are some striking similarities between the two forms of faith. The founder of the community was known as "Teacher of Righteousness." He was venerated as God's messenger. There are similarities in religious practice. Like the Christians, the Essene sect was apocalyptic and messianic. As in Christianity, the Messiah would appear at the end of time to reign over an eternal kingdom.[132]

The organization and ritual systems of the two sects present some similarities that Mircea Eliade considers "astonishing."[133] For instance, they developed the practice of a sacral meal of bread and wine. They practiced initiatory baptism. The highest office in their priesthood was that of a supreme leader, referred to as a "shepherd" which parallels the Christian bishop, a term coming from the Greek *episkopos*, which is also translated as "shepherd." A similarity of very special interest is that both employ a hermeneutic, or interpretational method which is not found in rabbinic Judaism: in the prophecies of the Old testament they read precise references to the history of their own time. In addition, both in the writings of the Essenes and in passages of Saint Paul, secret gnosis and esotericism are comprehended within the interpretative method. It is also true that some of the fundamental theological language of Essene writing is to be found in the Gospel of John.

This does not preclude the possibility of a direct influence of the earlier upon the later sect. It is considered almost certain that John the Baptist had been an Essene. He thus links Christianity with the reformist movement within Judaism. Furthermore, the idea of the Paraclete in John 14:17;15:26; 16:13 and elsewhere seems to be drawn from a theology like that of Qumran. A recitation of parallels is misleading because it simply ignores the great differences between the sects, but the similarities are of vital importance for our understanding of religion. In them we can see the same culture acting at different times and in different people to give the same shapes to different efforts to know God and to practice that knowledge. We understand more fully that history is a process of revelation.

While Jewish heresies may cast light on the background and origin of Christianity, we must entertain the thought that its own heresies pose recognizable possibilities for its growth in our time. At the same time we must speculate only with great caution.

All significant heresies are concerned with basic mysteries that constitute the heart of a faith. Heresies are of two kinds. One

One of the earliest and most vigorous heresies confronting a fairly well established Christian orthodoxy was Arianism. Arius(A.D. 256–336), a presbyter of Alexandria, was concerned to make Christianity more reasonable, more intellectually respectable. He was impressed by two points. On one hand, the idea of the Trinity, three equal persons in one, seemed to him unreasonable, and unnecessarily so. He found it incompatible with a philosophically sophisticated conception of God. An anthropomorphic God the Father was simply a childish notion. God necessarily transcended the range of human comprehension. God in his essential being was accessible to human knowledge only through his creation. His first creation was the Logos which was the medium for all the rest of his creation. The Logos, we may say, is the principle of reason governing the structure of the universe.

The Logos, Arianism maintained, was incarnated in Christ. For Arius, though not for others and not necessarily, this meant that Christ is not equal to, not "consubstantial" with, God the Father, but was made by Him. The orthodox doctrine of the Trinity is denied. Arianism brought intellectual turmoil all over the Empire. To refute it, the Emperor Constantine (see Chapter 10) called the Council of Nicaea in 325. Under his personal supervision and mediation the Council condemned Arianism and produced the Anti-Arian Nicene Creed which remains the statement of doctrine in the Catholic mass and is part of the ritual of a number of other Christian churches. (See Appendix C.) Among the most notorious of Christian heresies was Pelagianism.

Pelagius was a learned Briton who came to Rome in about the year A.D. 400. While insisting on his own orthodoxy, he promulgated the proposition crucially in conflict with traditional Christianity that there is no such thing as original sin and man could save himself by his moral effort without the special efficacy of the grace of God. Pelagianism was the *bete noire* of Saint Augustine during much of his career and it was repeatedly condemned in the Councils of the Church. In maintaining the

essential innocence of man, Pelagius proposed an idea that would come to dominate Western culture, though only in the Enlightenment of the seventeenth and eighteenth century. The issue is alive in nearly all the contemporary proposals for change in Christianity.

Heresies of less duration and import were innumerable. The doctrinal turmoil of the early centuries cannot be adequately suggested without having in view the great enemies of the heretics. In some cases it is only in their writings that we know the heresies.

First among the writers against heresy was Irenaeus, Bishop of Lyon, whose most important book, *Against the Heresies* (c. 130 A.D.) was directed primarily against Gnosticism. Until recently, with crucial discoveries in Israel and North Africa, we knew Gnosticism chiefly from this work. He was martyred under Septimus Severus.

Tertullian (c. 160-c. 220), of North Africa, was both learned and eloquent. He was the first Christian theologian to write in Latin. For him the Church was "a precious elite of believers, to be defended against contamination of from whatever quarter." "To him," says Paul Johnson, "Christians were supermen because the spirit moved them."[136] This conception he shared with Paul and with Gnosticism, though, like Paul, he was an enemy of Gnosticism. Although direct communication with the deity was fundamentally important to Tertullian, he realized fully the danger of schism in this. He was deeply puritanical and has been called "the first Protestant."[137] He broke with the Church because he rejected the power of the clergy to remit sin. Though he had attacked the Montanist heresy, which admitted women to ecclesiastical office, he became the leader of a Montanist church in Carthage.

To this day the idea of the Trinity remains the central tension of Christianity, at once threatening its unity and sustaining its vitality. The affront of the mystery to rationality means a permanent engagement of Christianity with the secular world which opposes it. Hence Christianity can never become a mysticism that turns away from the world. The engagement of the world in

its modern form appears when Christianity spawns the Western tradition of instrumental reason in the form of science. Christianity is a faith that remains permanently in tension with the rational processes which it justifies.

Councils in the years following that of Nicaea continued to condemn heresies and thus to give increasing definition to Christianity. The heresies are always eminently *reasonable.* They are more reasonable than the orthodoxy they reject, or at least they present a doctrine that is more rationally comprehensible. They represented the permanent tension in Christianity, the inevitable impulse to make a mystery more rational and thus, as an eventual and unintentional result, to do away with it. To eliminate mystery entirely is, of course, to bring religion to an end. Obviously the heresies initiate a process of which modern science is a continuation. The processes fulfilled by the councils are of central importance for basic arguments of this book.

The question of the roles of grace and nature has been cataclysmic for the Church. The Protestant schism of the Reformation turned primarily on this question, Luther returning essentially to the position of Saint Augustine, maintained that the effect of original sin is total corruption of man and that he is totally dependent on grace for salvation. The Church responded in the focal act of the Counter-Reformation, the Council of Trent (1545–1563), by affirming what was essentially the position of Aquinas and Scholastic philosophy, which affirmed that both grace and human nature are needed. Just as the fundamental tension of the secular and the sacred in Christianity cannot be finally eradicated, neither can the tension between the conceptions of nature and grace, which, as we will see, is vividly alive in modern religious thought.

The heresies and the Councils dealing with them are integral with the evolution of faith. They provide a model of part of the processes—sometimes spontaneous, sometimes deliberate—by which religions come into being. They are part of the means by which history participates in revelation.

Chapter Ten

AGENTS OF FAITH

SAINT PAUL, MARTYRS, AND THE GREAT EMPEROR

In the condition called Postmodernism we are stranded outside of time. In Modernism the past was repudiated. In Postmodernism it is totally forgotten. Or it is conceived as dead, the detritus of the past that may be collected and rearranged in interesting artistic assemblages. The future exists only as the next moment. Serious anticipation and long-term planning have become unthinkable. In the Postmodern world history is unthinkable. It does not exist. The transformation of ourselves that we are attempting to conceive is one in which we are reunited with, are integrated in, the continuity that is history. Where our time sees largely failure and error, our faith tells us there is a struggle and a fruitful ordeal.

So we come to the crux of the difficulty of contemplating a retrieval of Christianity. We cannot even imagine Christianity except in the perspective of history, and to write a "proper"history of Christianity–one that is respectably empirical and scientistic— is to do away with Christianity. The instrument of "scientific" history is instrumental reason. Instrumental reason treats everything as though it were a machine or a product of machine-like processes. Everything becomes a product or a process of cause

and effect. Everything has to be. Everything is completely comprehensible by instrumental reason. There is a further difficulty.

The purpose and responsibility of much contemporary scholarship has been, in the ecstacy of a warped liberalism, to denigrate much that we may come to value. It is especially important, then, that we be prepared to repossess major aspects of history in the faith that it is—despite much ignorance, tragedy, and error—a sacred process.

A conception of many academicians is that religion is "an irrational palliative for the growing mass of the world's outsiders."[138] Such a conception assumes that we, the presumably enlightened of our time, have astonishingly privileged knowledge. It also requires a remarkable perspective on the rest of the human race. It requires, among other things, our contempt for humanity during two thousand years of the history of the Western civilization. If, on the contrary, Christianity is to emerge into some kind of light from the miasma of modernist negation, we must have at least some general notion of how, beginning as a small outlaw cult in an underprivileged province, it came to dominate the Roman empire—and all that succeeded it until the advent of modernity.

Second only to Christ in the importance of his contribution to the foundation of Christian faith was Saint Paul. It has been said simply that he "created the religion that we now know as Christianity."[139] He was born in Tarsus, in what is now Turkey. He was a Jew and a Roman citizen. Receiving both a Hellenic and a Jewish education, he became a devout Pharisee, one of the relatively aristocratic Judaic sect having a few things in common with Christianity but differing especially in its rigid emphasis upon religious law and punctilious observance of external practices. In his deep piety he became an especially zealous and brutal persecutor of Christians. He was an official in the trial of Saint Steven, the first Christian martyr. He entered both synagogues and private homes to capture Christians and deliver them to Judaic courts. He persecuted them, he said, "unto death."[140]

His conversion to Christianity is one of the most famous of narratives of the New Testament. Saul, as Paul was called before his conversion, sought and received a commission from the High Priest in Jerusalem to go to Damascus, imprison Christians there, and return them to Jerusalem for trial. What afterward occurred is recounted as follows: "On his journey, as he was nearing Damascus, a light from the sky suddenly flashed on him. He fell to the ground and heard a voice saying to him, 'Saul, Saul, why are you persecuting me?' When Saul asked who had spoken, "The reply came, "I am Jesus, whom you are persecuting. Now get up and go into the city and you will be told what you must do." Blinded by what had occurred, Saul was taken into Damascus where, after three days, a Christian disciple named Ananias interpreted the experience as an entering into Saul of the Holy Spirit. His sight was immediately restored. He was then baptized by Ananias. Shortly thereafter, he began the missionary activity that would take him to most parts of the Mediterranean world.[141]

Paul's letters make up a large part of the New Testament and are the earliest written Christian documents. Paul had established or made missionary visits to Christian communities far flung in the Mediterranean world. The letters, some written in prison, are addressed to those communities. Of all Biblical documents none are more likely to attract the skeptical reader than these passionate, eloquent, and intensely human letters. For the moment, we need to get a glimpse of Paul as a player in the political processes involved in the propagation of Christianity.

In about 49 A.D., some sixteen years after the sojourn of Christ on earth, Paul attended the Council of Jerusalem to confront the apostle Peter, who was then the leader of the Jewish Christians. Paul raised a question that deeply affected his "mission to the Gentiles." He argued that converts to Christianity did not have to be circumcised or to commit themselves to obedience to the Jewish law. In this he was opposed especially by a wing of the Jewish Christians, which tended to revert to Judaism. At issue was the future of Paul's mission; many Gentiles resisted

(260–268), Christians experienced peace. But the last and most thorough of all persecutions was to come.

Diocletian (284–305) initiated the "Great Persecution" in 303. His fixed purpose was to exterminate Christianity. His first general Edict against the Christians required that all scriptures be surrendered and burned, all churches closed, and all meetings of Christians banned. A second Edict ordered the arrest of all the clergy. At his abdication in 305, persecution virtually ceased in the West although it continued with virulence in Egypt and other parts of the East until Constantine's Edict of Milan (313).

And now we must stop. Rome's gift to Christianity was an enormity. Looking for reasonable recourse in an unreasonable world, theorizing about faith, stumbling through the detritus of history, suddenly we come upon a startling improbability. We are shaken briefly with the truth about it all. But what we come upon passes without purchase through our minds. We have come to the essence of faith. Our problem to begin with is that we cannot believe in faith. Confronting ultimate faith, we instantly deny what we have glimpsed. It cannot be. There are no martyrs. They are simply the mentally ill, the quite insane. Our minds demand this treatment of the subject. We have no other intellectual possibility. And yet we must. And yet. . . .

A posted edict of Diocletian was torn down by a citizen expressing bitterness and contempt for the Emperor:

> He was burnt, or rather toasted, by a slow fire; and his executioners, zealous to revenge the personal insult which had been offered to the emperor, exhausted every refinement of cruelty, without being able to subdue his patience, or to alter the steady and insulting smile which, in his dying agonies, he still preserved in his countenance.[143]

> From the persecution of Lucius Septimus Severus, in north Africa there is the story of Perpetua, a young married woman who was still nursing a child; Felicitas, who was then pregnant, and

Revocatus of Carthage, a slave who was being taught the principles of Christianity. . . . ,

After an appearance before the proconsul Minutius in which she was offered freedom if she sacrificed to the idols, Perpetua had her still-nursing baby taken from her and was thrown into prison. Describing her faith and life in prison, she told her father, "The dungeon is to me a palace. [Later she was again given the opportunity to sacrifice to the pagan gods and thus to escape punishment.] She replied, "I will not sacrifice."

"Are you a Christian?" asked Hilarianus [the judge].

"I am a Christian," Perpetua replied.

. . . On the day of their execution, Perpetua and Felicitas were first stripped naked and hung in nets, but were removed and clothed when the crowd objected. Upon returning to the arena, Perpetua was tossed about by a mad bull and was stunned but not seriously hurt; Felicitas, however, was badly gored. Perpetua hurried to her side and held her while they waited for the bull to charge them again, but he refused to do so, and they were dragged from the arena, much to the crowds disappointment.

After a short time, they were brought back to be killed by gladiators. Felicitas was killed quickly, but the young inexperienced gladiator assigned to kill Perpetua trembled violently and could only stab her weakly several times. Seeing how he trembled, Perpetua held this sword blade and guided it to a vital area of her body.[144]

The Emperor Constantine (312–337) not only ended Christian persecution. He embraced Christianity and this was a crucial turning point in history. Henceforth the foundation of Western civilization on Christianity was assured. Constantine was an extraordinary figure to whose character and his role in history we must give some attention. Except for Saint Paul no other simply human person has done so much for the establishment of Christianity. He provides an essential focus around which to organize consideration of important dimensions in the history, and the meaning, of Christianity.

Constantine looms large in history and yet he remains a para-doxical figure and in some respects an enigmatic figure. There is no doubt that in some respects he was supremely gifted. Gibbon, the great chronicler of the decline of Rome, describes him as follows: "His stature was lofty, his countenance majestic, his deportment graceful; his strength and activity were displayed in every manly exercise, and, from his earliest youth to a very advanced season of life, he preserved the vigor of his constitution by a strict adherence to the domestic virtues of chastity and temperance." His leisure was dedicated to reading, writing, or serious meditation. He was con-centrated intently upon the affairs of state. Gibbon says that he "infused his own intrepid spirit into his troops, whom he conducted with the talents of a consummate general."[145] Both in military com-mand and in political administration he manifested genius.

Yet, Constantine's ethical nature is questioned. Maxentius, a brother-in-law who was a usurper bent on destroying Constantine, was killed after the battle in which Constantine defeated his army. Crispus, one of his sons by his first wife, was accused of conspir-ing to overthrow Constantine and of attempting an incestuous seduction of Constantine's second wife, Fausta. Constantine had him quietly executed, possibly by poisoning. It is generally re-ported that Fausta, one of the possibly false accusers of Crispus, was also executed, but that has been questioned.[146] One may modify or suspend ones judgment of these acts, considering the exigencies of holding power in a chaotic age and the scarcity of our knowledge of the circumstances. There seems to be no ques-tion that in his advanced years Constantine was guilty of a certain frivolity and of some irresponsibility in administration. During the last fourteen years of his life, when his power and the peace of Rome were secure, Constantine affected clothes of exorbitant style, flamboyantly emblematic of imperial majesty. His policies, according to Gibbon, combined "the opposite yet reconcilable vices of rapaciousness and prodigality."[147] To judge Constantine one must also comprehend the magnitude and character of his achievement and his meaning for history.

Constantine's public career begins in an outpost of the empire, in Britain. Following the death of his father in York, in 306, Constantine entered into conflict with other contenders for the empire, becoming co-Emperor with Licinius in 312 but overthrowing Licinius in 323 to become sole Emperor until his death in 337.

The crucial story begins on the eve of a battle nine miles north of Rome in which Constantine confronted the army of his brother-in-law Maxentius. On the day before what is called the battle of Milvian bridge (312), Constantine reported seeing the sign of a cross in the sky. On the following morning he said that in a dream a voice had told him to conquer under this sign. Subsequently Constantine attributed his victory to divine guidance. Thus begins the process by which he was converted to become a totally committed defender and proponent of Christianity, and, as Emperor, a sedulous propagator of the faith.

Constantine's role is to be interpreted in part by the condition of Christianity as he found it—or, we may want to say, as it found him. Historians and commentators of the past have unanimously commented on the rapidity of the spread of Christianity. More recently, however, dissent from this opinion by professional historians has been popular. So even the writing of history becomes a confrontation between the secular culture and religion. As sociologist Rodney Stark remarks, social scientists treating phenomenon of Christianity have been "far more concerned with discrediting religion than with understanding it."[148] This means that all the crucial points that will be made concerning the rapidity of the spread of Christianity and the conditions favoring it have been denied by one or more recent writers. They deny especially a number of points that would seem to reflect favorably on Christianity.

For instance, these writers deny, at least by implication, that Christianity spread rapidly, that it had become a clearly potential political force when Constantine came to power, that paganism was declining, and that there was a prevailing need which it

All the religions of the past had been indigenous; they were intimately related to a community, a human collectivity located in a specific and knowable space and small enough for all its members to fully comprehend it as a unified condition of life of which they were a part. The divinity or divinities of such a religion are associated especially with the fortunes of the community. In such a faith, religious observation is a community exercise. The individual exists for the divine agency primarily as a member of the society. Such a faith we may say is an "outward" religion. We are to find such religions giving way to "inward" religions. In inward religions the primary relationship is between the divinity and the isolated individual,

The effect of the existence of the Roman Empire was to dislocate elements of communities in which local religions were implicated. The community was no longer the entity in which and by which the fates of its members were decided. The structure of sovereignty with which the god had been intuitively associated disappeared. The god was thus deprived of the collective function for which it was constituted. For the individual, the narrow horizon of the community, which had been the world, disappeared and in its place there existed another of enormous horizon, both ambiguous and unfriendly, its borders incalculably distant and essentially unknowable. The margins of the world slipped away, leaving the individual naked and alone in an obscure and unfriendly universe. The individual was no longer part of a place; the place was the individual, who became the locus of need. The need was for a religion in which the primary relation was between God and the individual. The religious instinct, the need for God, turned inward.

It is true, as Hegel has told us, that significant developments within a culture tend to transfuse the entire culture. This is true even if the culture is as diverse as the Mediterranean world. Greek philosophy had turned inward, had turned to ethics and the individual, in the thought of the Stoics and the Epicureans. New faiths and newly immigrated faiths competed to fill the in-

ward need. There was a strong tendency to monotheism.[158] Because the new faiths served to replace a sovereignty that had disappeared there was an emergence of ruler-cults, the cults of a divinity that was both a personal savior and a Lord—the Lord of all the limitless world that had replaced local communities.[159] Judaism was an inward religion; in the early first century it was an evangelizing faith and had won many converts.[160] Although a vibrant and compelling faith, Judaism was handicapped in a sense. It carried vigorous ethnic associations and practices often disagreeable to the gentile world.

On the other hand Christianity benefitted from a legitimacy drawn from Jewish antiquity while being free of the ethnic handicaps of Judaism. As we know, a major element in the general religious ferment was Gnosticism, a pre-eminently inward religion. More than fifty Gnostic sects have been noted.[161] Nothing could make clearer the organic origins of religion from social and historical matrices than the case of Gnosticism. The fifty Gnostic sects are not progeny of a single source. Gnosticism arose not once, but at different times in different places, from different antecedents.[162]

The weakness of Gnosticism, however, was not only its intellectual elitism, but also its intense subjectivism, precisely its "gnosis" (knowledge, so called). Wherever such subjectivism has existed, free of unifying and restraining elements, it has spawned limitless group fragmentation. (As is witnessed in Protestantism, of which there are almost twenty-five thousand sects.) Gnosticism was doomed to be dispersed, with components of its power assimilated in random religious growths.

The first and indispensable condition for the success of Christianity was that arising among faiths tied to particular ethnic and geographical backgrounds but weakened by loss of their communal orientation, Christianity brought a faith in which the central relationship was between the individual and God, an individual anywhere, at any time , coming voluntarily together with other individuals in total freedom from social, racial, and national bar-

was authentically engaged by questions of doctrine. Eusebius was right, as we now know from evidence established fairly recently.[187] We now know that two months before the Council of Nicaea there had been a Council of Antioch, also concerned with the Arian heresy. On a Good Friday near the end of this council Constantine delivered a sermon some two hours long entitled "Oration to the Saints." This sermon fully justifies Eusebius's characterization of Constantine as a serious theological thinker, according to the opinion of Robin Lane Fox, one of the most skeptical of contemporary historians and one especially quick to question and discredit Christians and things Christian.[188] Fox's general appraisal of Constantine is essentially beyond question:

Constantine's actions may still upset Christian consciences, but they have to be accepted as those of a sincere and convinced adherent of the faith, the man whose massive gifts and legislation first promoted it against all expectations, whose reluctance to coerce pagans was only too seldom shared and whose simple fears of God's anger at heresy made him the most tireless worker for Christian unity since St. Paul.[189]

We will want to recall at this point that in the year 330, five years after the Council of Nicaea, Constantine, having consolidated his empire and having determined permanently, he thought, the nature of Christianity, began building the city of Constantinople on the site of the Greek city of Byzantium in modern northwest Turkey. He transferred the capital of the Roman Empire from Rome to this new city. We can say that when Constantine died in 337 all the "secondary causes" that would insure the success of Christianity were in place. Some fifty years after Constantine's death, Under the Emperor Theodosius the Great (379–395), who forbade practice of the pagan faiths, Christianity became the official religion of the Roman Empire.

Chapter Eleven

POWER IN THE WORLD AND THE SPIRIT

Invaders, conquerors, and kings come and go. What stays in European history are the Monasteries and Christianity. Essentially they create the cultural matrix in which all else occurs. But we cannot understand the shape of religious phenomena in the past unless we also have some understanding of the world of practical affairs in which it occurred.

As we approach the history of Christianity in the Middle Ages and earlier, there are three things that must be kept in mind. The first is that the faith of the past was something very different from what we mean by faith. Men of the Middle Ages believed with an intensity we cannot imagine. The barrier between that time and ours is difficult to realize and difficult to cross. The "non-judgmentalism" of our time is based on the fact that our faith—in whatever: in morality, in principles, in truth, in God—is ineradicably provisional. We can be constantly non-judgmental because we do not believe in anything with truly firm conviction.

The "true believer" is proverbially a villain in our time. If you are capable of being "a true believer" in this absolutist sense, you are to be considered an ignorant person. And it may well be that you have not assimilated modern knowledge. However religious we may become, we will be capable only of a faith that is in some sense provisional. That is simply to say that we live in a

culture in which faith is constantly under attack. There can be no easy faith. It is extremely important to acknowledge this fact in any consideration we may entertain about religion. Our incapacity for an absolute faith would have been unintelligible to most people of the past. This fact is fundamental in attempting to respond justly to religious history.

The second thing that must be kept in mind is that motives are always mixed. We labor for virtuous causes because we love virtue, but always and inevitably because we hope to be rewarded—with recognition, or praise, or money—for our virtuous labors. If the virtue for which we labor is in fact absolute, we will not be troubled by its admixture with other motives. Rather it will justify, will consecrate, our other motives. We will act with decisiveness and resolution.

The third thing we must keep in mind in our approach to religion in the history of the past is the general nature of society as a whole that prevailed during most of Western history. From the time of Constantine's death to the nineteenth century, what we know as Italy today was a political and military cockpit. Internally, diverse kinds of political interests—sacred and secular—were in tensions that repeatedly erupted into armed conflict. Italy was made up of autonomous or semi-autonomous principalities, who either were in war with each other, or they were agents in shifting alliances defending against external powers that constituted a permanent external menace. Foreign participants in the menace and the aggression were diverse. With the division of the Empire into two after Constantine, there was the Eastern Empire centered in Constantinople. Over the centuries the Empire was repeatedly re-united and divided again. Its different areas were continually overrun by various nomadic tribes—Germanic, Oriental, Arabic.

What follows below is a list that will help us to comprehend the extraordinary environment in which the Papacy, the central institution of Christianity during most of these centuries, struggled to serve Christianity and its own power. The notes following the

dates are brief and thus very crude. They serve only to distinguish the powers at work and to indicate their diversity. The notes indicate only raw military actions and say nothing of the historical circumstances. The list is certainly not complete. It is presented only for its impressionistic value.

The Italian Cockpit

380   B.C. Rome fought Etruscan cities to the north.

390   B.C. Gauls overran Etruscan cities and sacked Rome.

400   A.D. Alaric leader of the Visigoths invaded Italy. Sueves and Vandals also invaded Italy.

452   Atilla the Hun reached the gates of Rome. He was dissuaded from sacking the city by Pope Leo I.

455   Vandals from North Africa despoiled Rome.

535   Armies of the Eastern Emperor Justinian occupied Rome and Ravenna.

546   Ostrogoths occupied Rome.

554   Justinian's armies returned and expelled the Ostrogoths from Italy, occupying Rome and parts of the South.

568   The Lombards moved into northern Italy and within a century and a half occupied most of Italy.

754   Pepin, the first Carolinian Frank, invaded Italy, defeated the Lombards.

756   Pepin returned to defeat the Lombards again. He turned over to the Pope their area called the Exarchate of Ravenna, which became the Papal States making the Pope a secular ruler.

773   Charlemagne invaded Italy to end the reign of the Lombards who had remained in power in the north.

846   Muslims raided and looted Rome.

916   Byzantine armies (or those of the Eastern Empire) drove the Muslims out of Italy.

951   Otto I, of the East Franks, invaded Northern Italy to become King of the Lombards.

961   Otto I invaded again and was crowned Emperor of the Roman Empire.

1018   Byzantine armies defeated Lombards in southern Italy.

1071   Norman armies in southern Italy end Byzantine and Lombard power there.

1084   Normans drove the Emperor Henry IV out of Rome and sacked the city.

1176   Invading forces of Frederic I Barbarossa were defeated by Milanese forces.

1250+ The city states having come into being in the twelfth century, Venice and Genoa engaged in continuing warfare.

1400+ The city states, especially in the north. fought each other continuously.

1494   Charles VIII of France invaded to claim the throne of Naples. The French also took over Milan and imprisoned its Duke. There thus began fighting in Italy between French, German, and Spaniard armies which continued for half a century.

1527   Charles, Duke of Bourbon, lead into Rome an army composed of German and Spanish soldiers, who, after his death, sacked the city.

1701   Eugene of Savoy led an Austrian army into Italy.

1798   Bonaparte, who had invaded the Papal States occupied Rome, though Austria subsequently captured again most of Italy.

1800   Bonaparte again crossed the Alps to invade Italy.

1808   Napoleon's troops again occupied Rome.

1820   Austrian troops entered Naples to quell a revolt against Ferdinand I.

1840   By this time Austrian forces controlled all Italy.

1859   The French, under Napoleon III, invaded Lombardy to assist the Sardinians in an effiort to thrown off Austrian oppression. Thus the War of Italian Unification began.

1861   Giuseppe Garibaldi began the leadership of military action that, after alliance with Prussia against France, would

result in realization of the Kingdom of Italy that was proclaimed at this time.

1870   Rome became the capital of the Kingdom of Italy.

Major omissions from this list are the actions of Papal armies, especially of armies supporting the Papacy, against the German Emperor Frederick II in the incessant wars, called the wars of the Guelphs (supporting the Pope) and the Ghibillines (supporting the Emperor). This prolonged conflict will be noted as we turn in a later chapter to other major phases and personalities in the history of the Papacy.

Among other things, we will be aware of three strands in the history of the Papacy. The *first* is the development of the supremacy of the Roman see, the process by which the Bishop of Rome became the Pope and the ruling head of the Church worldwide. The *second* strand is the development of the wealth and power of the Church considered in itself, and thus, the development of the "Imperial Papacy." The *third* is the constantly shifting relationships of the Church to the secular power reigning at any particular time.

By the time of Constantine, the supremacy of the Roman see had been fairly well established. This was dramatically strengthened by Constantine's constant insistence upon his personally exercising Papal functions. Constantine thus also established the pattern in which the Church functioned as an imperial power and the expectation that it would continue to do so. It should also be noted that by his personal donations, chiefly in the form of the construction of church buildings, Constantine increased the wealth of the Church. Its wealth was eventually enormous. Even In the earliest centuries the Church benefitted from the dying bequests of wealthy Christians. But the generosity of living Christians was probably unparalleled. A people who valued martyrdom for Christ did not hesitate to lavish their worldly goods upon the living embodiment of their faith.

Wealth was needed because from the first the Church sustained large projects of charity. Wealth and the power that went with it was also essential if the Church was to withstand the constant effort of secular rulers to control it. Church wealth, of course, incited the envy of secular powers. They understood also that the Church was civilization, which meant the power of public opinion and the conditions of morale necessary to support hegemony in the long run. Only if secular rulers controlled the Church could their inveterate impulse to greater and greater power, and eventually to absolute power, be realized. Conflict between the Church and secular power can be avoided, if that is really possible, only where there is firm legal separation of Church and State. That, of course, is a kind of final triumph of the State although in another sense it is of enormous benefit to the Church..

At issue for the Church historically was much more than wealth and power for its own sake. If secular powers control the operation of the Church, especially if they control its wealth and its appointments, they can and will control doctrine, if only for political purposes. It is reasonable to assume that clergymen should expect to control the content of doctrine. The quality of faith found in past centuries thoroughly justifies that expectation, and it justifies extreme measures to achieve that end. That conception is inherent in all the arguments of this book. It by no means justifies all the many crimes that have been committed in the name of Christianity and the Church, concerning which see Chapters 12. We may understand, nevertheless, why active, and often violent, competition for power between the Church and secular rulers was virtually constant up to and through the nineteenth century. This will be a continual interest in the historical sequences and historical personalities that we will now adumbrate.

The most important clergyman of the fourth century was not a Pope but the Bishop of Milan, Saint Ambrose (d. 393). A powerful personality and heir of an illustrious aristocratic family, he had been elected governor of Milan at a very early age and made Bishop through popular demand. He was transformed from an

unbaptized layman into a Bishop within eight days. He brought to the bishopric the attitudes and habits of aristocratic command. Oblivious of the notion of the supremacy of the Bishop of Rome, he prized the power of all Bishops. His own power was demonstrated when he excommunicated the Emperor Theodosius for carrying out a massacre of Thesalonian citizens for the murder of an army commander. He required the Emperor to make public penance before being permitted to receive communion again. Ambrose brought to completion the great new basilica of Milan which became a model for medieval churches.

Ambrose was especially important in establishing particulars of Catholic worship. He began the use of splendid vestments and introduced antiphonal singing. He wrote hymns, four of which are used today. Assuming that clergymen would be drawn from the upper classes, he pressed the clergy to make large charitable donations. A leader in the fight against Arianism, he began what became an extremely important aspect of Catholicism, the cult of relics. He condemned commerce as a necessarily dishonest enterprise, considering agriculture the only innocent way of making money, thus establishing a medieval attitude toward wealth.

He was in part responsible for the attitude of the medieval Church toward sex. Virginity was the condition most highly prized. Married life would be a hindrance to a career in the church. Ambrose promoted celibacy. He encouraged the development of the cult of the Virgin Mary.[190] Of importance among his writings, are allegorical interpretations of the Bible, especially the Old Testament. In almost everyway he was important in establishing the character of the medieval Church. Ambrose played an essential role in bringing Augustine into the Church.

A very different figure was St. Jerome. (ca 340-ca420)) Let us note briefly in passing his major accomplishments A papal secretary famed as a peculiarly dour and acerbic exemplar of asceticism, he was a very great scholar. He translated the Bible from Hebrew and Greek into Latin, producing the first version of

entirety. 2) Revelation does not have its source only in the Bible. The Church and the Bible interact reciprocally and share in the process of revelation.

For all practical purposes it was Saint Augustine who created one of the two major poles around which the history of Western culture has turned. After a youthful apostasy from his mother's Christian faith, he was for some ten years a Manichean, a gnostic. This may account for a disposition of his thought which is painfully distressing for modern liberals and which was fundamental to early orthodoxy: his deep consciousness of pervasive and profound evil in the world. This led to a deep pessimism about life and human beings that colored much of early medieval culture. Saint Augustine is the author of the radical conception in the Christian tradition of Original Sin. Original sin does not result from sexuality, but because the defective human soul is trammeled in material interests, it is especially prone to subversion by the sexual appetite. Illicit sex is seen as unquestionably a dangerous and basic sin. Augustine's emphasis upon the sacredness of the Virgin Birth is seen to presuppose that even in marriage the sexual act is not free of guilt, although there are passages in which delight in the "conjugal embrace" seems to be authorized. There is no doubt about Augustine's position on Original Sin, and, though his position on sex may be somewhat ambiguous, Original Sin and a hostility to sex come to be the most conspicuous notes in Augustine's reputation.

Eventually Augustine's attitude toward sex, and that of the Church, must be judged against a broader perspective. Max Weber, one of the greatest social thinkers and one with a thoroughly secular conception of religion, has this to say: "Despite the widespread belief that hostility toward sexuality is an idiosyncrasy of Christianity, it must be emphasized that no authentic religion of salvation had in principle any other point of view."[193] The tensions between civilization and sexuality are, of course, inevitable, and essential to civilization. Reasons for this will be considered in a later chapter.

Augustine seems to have come to his position on Original Sin in his attempting, like many heretics, to rationalize Christianity. It was necessary to reconcile logically the panoply of pain and evil in the world with the existence of a loving God. The fault was man's, his inheritance of the Original Sin of Adam. All the evil in the world stems from this. So radical is the basic flaw in human nature that men are powerless to save themselves. Redemption is totally dependent on the grace of God. For redemption some are chosen. We have no way of knowing who are among the elect. Those who are not have no reason to object; the fault is totally theirs. Both the lost and the elect owe love to God for their existence.

For Augustine the mind is important, but subordinate to faith, which comes from grace, in the scheme of salvation. For Augustine, who was vividly aware of the unconscious, religious truth is an inner illumination granted by God. The knowledge of truth is an indescribable experience. The movement to God is not by thought but by love.[194]

Because of his eloquence and the richness of his mind and because his view of man and the world somehow fit the times, Augustine was the most influential of theologians in the middle ages. There was a deep pessimism in his idea of the original evil and the weakness of man. Augustine considered man powerless to achieve his salvation; man was dependent on an obscure working of grace in a not highly probable divine election. These conceptions conditioned the character of medieval culture.

We may be grateful that, increasingly from the thirteenth century onward, Augustine's pre-eminence gave way to that of Saint Thomas Aquinas. The fact that the two men agreed on so many things and that the shift of reputation and influence occurred slowly obscures the fact that the change was profound. The difference would be represented in the Reformation, perhaps the most significant historical event since the birth of Christ. Chapter 13 will be devoted entirely to Saint Thomas Aquinas.

Augustine and Thomas Aquinas represent poles around which major shifts of Western culture have turned. The Protestant Ref-

ormation in the sixteenth century returned to Saint Augustine for its authority, Calvinism and other sects actually deepening the tragic ruin in their conception of Original Sin. In the eighteenth century both Enlightenment and Romanticism had as their most fundamental assumption the innocence of man, the absence of Original Sin. That position has been also central to liberal thought in our time. However, in the darkness cast by the horrors of the twentieth century, many thinkers are looking again at the idea of Original Sin. A major historical writer says that Augustine was and is influential: he "came close to the inner reality of human life."[195]

As we will soon look at the Papacy in some of its disgraceful phases, it is well to keep in mind some of its most illustrious occupants. Perhaps the most remarkable figures ever to occupy the Papacy was Pope Gregory I (540–604), also called Gregory the Great. He is a figure over whom we can afford to dwell for a time. He was a Roman aristocrat. There were two Popes among his ancestors. His father was a senator. Gregory himself, at the age of thirty-three was appointed Prefect of the City of Rome, or city administrator. Upon the death of his father and the retirement of his mother into religious life, he disbursed a large part of his fortune to the poor and converted the family home into a monastery and for some time resided there as a monk.

He was recruited for a papal diplomatic mission to Constantinople, and shortly after returning to Rome was made Pope—at a time when he held only the ecclesiastical rank of deacon.[196] One of the few Popes who have been elected unanimously, he came to the throne of Peter in a time of disastrous conditions in Italy. Plague infested the city and the Lombards occupied most of Italy. The Roman Emperor of the West in Ravenna was totally helpless, and in Rome civil government had totally collapsed. Gregory's initiatives made him virtually the civil ruler of Italy. To provide food for the populace he reorganized "the patrimony of Saint Peter," which consisted of enormous tracts of land held by the Papacy in Sicily, Dalmatia, Gaul, and north

Africa. To the astonishment of the civil government, he personally negotiated with the Lombards and when they moved on Rome, he organized the army which succeeded in defending Rome against invasion. His ambition was to convert the Lombards, who were Arians, to Catholicism.

Though frail of health, he was a man of enormous will and energy. He organized financial processes for the administration of ecclesiastical affairs in Italy. He developed and expanded the Church's program of charity. Aware of the debility of contemporary secular government, he assumed administrative responsibilities of the state, concerning himself even with the regulation of slaughter houses and the level of rents. He arranged for the repair of aqueducts.

Within the Church his organizational innovations essentially completed the establishment of the medieval papacy.[197] His administration practiced strict oversight of the Churches of Western Christendom and achieved effective reform. He removed irresponsible and immoral prelates. He established a code to govern the election and the conduct of bishops. He brought essentially to completion the administrative structure that would govern the medieval Church. He enforced clerical celibacy. He accepted the position of Rome as part of the Eastern empire, but stanchly maintained the primacy of Rome among all episcopal sees. All churches, including those in Constantinople, he considered subordinate to Rome.

He made a number of changes in the liturgy, promoting liturgical music. He completed development of the Catholic scheme of penance that prevails to this day.

The conception of penance counteracted the pessimism of Augustine's conception of Original Sin, and contributed to making medieval Christianity an optimistic religion.[198]

He was largely responsible for the expansion of monasticism in sixth century.[199] As observed above, prior to election to the Papacy he had turned his family home into a monastery where he lived as a monk. On six family estates in Sicily he also estab-

lished monasteries. On diplomatic missions for the Papacy he had always lived as a monk in monastic residencies. One of his achievements was the promotion of the "Rule of St. Benedict," giving order to form and discipline in monasteries, and establishing supervisory practices to render monastic development uniform and assure that monasteries were a part of the Church.

He was very aware of the passing of the Empire, which he did not lament. "The eagle," he wrote, "has gone bald and lost his feathers. . . . Where is the senate, where are the old people of Rome? Gone."[200] The vitality of the future, he felt, lay with the nations north of the Alps. In 596 Gregory dispatched the monk Augustine accompanied by forty other monks, all from his own monastery, for the conversion of England. Five years later he sent another body of monks to reinforce the first missionary efforts, and he made Augustine archbishop of Canterbury. He personally prescribed regulations for the house to be established at Canterbury.[201] In his instructions to Augustine Gregory stressed that his teaching should be flexible, adapted for the assimilation of local custom by Christianity, thus establishing a brilliant and humane tradition for Catholic missionaries.[202]

The body of his writing is very large. His scriptural commentary is notable for its allegorical interpretations. His *Pastoral Care* became the basic guide book for the Episcopate in the Middle Ages. He was made one of the four original Doctors of the Western church, along with Ambrose, Augustine of Hippo, and Jerome. (A Doctor of the Church is a saint recognized as an eminent teacher of the faith.)[203] Among the many accomplishments of his extraordinary career, Gregory the Great, as we have seen in Chapter 7, provided a formulation concerning miracles that is of value for modern faith.[204]

We must turn now to a transformation of European spirituality and of the Church so momentous that it has been called "a world revolution," meaning a radical change in ideological outlook calling for a new order of the way the world is run.[205] All the circumstances involved were in one sense or another a result of

the success of Christianity. Europe had been exhaustively Christianized. The religiosity of the laity was achieving greater depth
and refinement. An essentially spontaneous religious revival was
underway. The texture of religious consciousness was changing.
Perhaps as a result of urbanization, a Christianity touched with
Old Testament harshness was giving way to a softer and gentler
image of Christ and the Virgin Mother and to a more intensely
personal spirituality.[206]

The spiritual transformation was preceded by a transformation of discipline within the Church. The success of Christianity
had meant that while the laity was becoming more religious, the
clergy was becoming increasingly rich and comfortable and increasingly worldly. In the great monasteries such as Cluny, the
rigors of the Benedictine rule were falling into disuse as aristocratic monks enjoyed isolated luxury. Among bishops and priests
the older emphasis of the Church on celibacy was ignored. Bishops commonly took mistresses and produced children, usually
designated as "nephews," whose interest they protected as would
any responsible parent. Parish priests were usually married and
the heads of families. As they tended to the welfare and the careers of their children, they became involved in the lay institution
of feudalism. In addition clerical offices were regularly bought
and sold, the crime which is called "simony."

The decline of clerical discipline and morality was associated in the minds of many with the political subordination and
consequent debasement of the Church. For two hundred years
the Church had submitted to lay princes, accepting their claim
to the power and right of making key appointments to clerical
offices, the practice called "lay investiture." At every point the
Church was being vitiated by contamination of the secular world.

The response to these conditions is called the "Gregorian
Reform," though it began before the Papacy of Gregory VII (1073–
1085) and there were other reformers in addition to Hildebrand,
as he was called before he named himself after Gregory the Great
upon becoming Pope. The reformers were inspired by the great

Cistercian reform of monasticism in the tenth century (concerning which, see below), and most of them, including Hildebrand, had been monks. Gregory's predecessor Leo IX (1049–1054) reformed election procedures, defined the role of cardinals, appointed reformers, like Hildebrand, to key positions in the church, and summoned councils to enforce the reforms. Among other things, the reformers exposed and attacked sexual scandals among the clergy.

Hildebrand was one of the truly radical reformers. As Gregory VII, he was one of the great Popes. He made reform of the Church the basic concern of his Papacy. He reaffirmed previous rulings against clerical marriages and against simony, or the selling of clerical offices, and sent legates throughout Europe to make sure these rulings were obeyed. Reform and purification had as a major interest the exclusion of lay control and exploitation of the Church. Of central importance was the question of lay investiture, the practice, as pointed out above, for kings and other lay rulers to appoint bishops and thus to achieve essential control of the Church. In this connection two of Gregory's deepest convictions must be kept in mind. He was convinced that states were created by criminals using criminal processes. On the other hand, he was deeply devoted to the poor and the weak, and inveterately hostile to their oppressors, the wealthy and the strong. He was convinced that social welfare could be served only on the basis of Christian principles, which only a reformed Church could make effective. These convictions must be kept in mind as we appraise his most spectacular actions.

Gregory promoted the development of canon law. On the legal basis provided by this work, Gregory issued an extraordinary paper, *Dictatus Papae*. In effect this claimed for the Pope the greatest power on earth. His personal sanctity was inherited from Saint Peter. He was supreme over all worldly princes and had the right to depose them. He had supreme legislative and judicial power. No one could judge him. We will see that in the condition of faith in the eleventh century such claims could be taken very seriously.

Subsequently Gregory issued a general ban of lay investiture. This brought him into conflict with the German Emperor, Henry IV, which led to one of the most famous altercations in history, one in which we see vividly the power of the Papacy in the middle ages. Following Gregory's ban on lay investiture, Henry proceeded to name his own people to bishoprics in Germany and in Italy. Gregory rebuked him. Henry called a synod of German bishops who solemnly declared the Pope to be deposed. Henry personally called on him to abdicate. Gregory promptly excommunicated Henry IV, suspended him from exercising royal powers, and freed his subjects from allegiance to him.

Henry, who had been weakened politically by rebellion in Germany, could not stand up under this virtual anathema. It was necessary to seek the Pope's forgiveness. At this time, in the winter of 1077, Gregory was a guest of the countess Matilda of Tuscany at her castle of Canossa in northern Italy. For political reasons Gregory did not want a confrontation with Henry at this time. When Henry arrived at the castle, he was refused audience. Henry, the most powerful ruler in the West though momentarily weakened, now dressed in penitential clothing and stood for three days in the snow outside the gates. Finally Gregory was prevailed upon by the countess, who was a relative of Henry and by another guest, the powerful Abbot Hugh of Cluny, to hear Henry's confession and grant him absolution.

Henry was eventually powerful enough to attack Rome and force Gregory to seek refuge among the Normans ruling southern Italy, but at Canossa Henry's qualified submission had strengthened the claim of the Papacy to supreme worldly power, and Gregory had initiated more than a century and half of struggle between Pope and Emperor, during which Christianity grew into its richest flowering in the thirteenth century.

The strengths of the Church were not drawn only from political and intellectual achievements. They were drawn also from a distinct development that is perhaps inherent in human nature.

Human consciousness results from an evolutionary success, a condition of relative animal luxury that permits a detachment from the world. The impulse to detachment is inherent in consciousness and it becomes a conscious and definitive characteristic of all the religions of the civilized world. Most of us must live in two worlds—the secular world on one hand and, on the other, a realm of detachment, of spiritual awareness. The Church too must live in these two realms, but within the Church spiritual detachment gave rise very early to a unique institution. This was monasticism. And as most of us, in weekday secularity, draw strength from the spiritual detachment of Sunday worship, so the Church has regularly drawn strength from monasticism. Monasticism was an organic growth from the experience of the Church. With the passing of time Christianity, even in the first centuries, was attended by an inevitable disappointment. The earliest Christian communities were united by excitement, passionate religious intensity, and nobility of incentive. The communities were welded together by the urgent dangers in the surrounding world. The communities seemed worth the danger. As Christianity was increasingly successful, however, there occurred a waning of religious intensity. With the peace of Constantine, persecution and the call of martyrdom came to an end. Conditions of dynamic tensions and the severity of challenge disappeared. There was a tendency to diffusion, to dilution, as Christians interacted more comfortably with the larger secular world and more and more took part in and were integrated into that world. There can be no doubt also that with the success of the Church in the proliferation of hierarchy and the complex elaboration of faith, the new serenity and order were attended by a certain rationalistic chill. The result was a wide-spread feeling of a need for renewal. This gave rise to a new strategy for the intensification of religious life: a recoil from the environs of civilization and establishing small communities sharing in simplified, often primitive, conditions of life.

The monastic movement developed in the third century, not

only in Egypt which was long thought to be the unique place of origin of monasticism, but independently in Palestine, Syria, and Mesopotamia.[207] It has been called a "counter-culture" movement: the culture of solitude, poverty, simplicity, asceticism, and concentrated religious devotion *contra* the worldliness of the city and the sophistication of the regular clergy. The movement seems to have begun with the practice of religious hermits, the communal groups coming later.[208] Once again common cultural conditions gives rise to identical social and cultural phenomena in different places.

The East is the original source of Western monasticism. Yet, nothing in the East could have led one to anticipate the vigorous, rich, and noble flowering of monasticism in the West. One may argue that, after the first century, it was in Western monasticism that Christianity came to its finest realization in Western culture. St. Benedict of Nursia (ca.480-ca.547) was founder of monasticism in the West and author of the "Rule of Saint Benedict" which was the foundation of the great monastic reform of the eleventh and twelfth centuries and is the basis of organization of monasticism today.

Perhaps most important for European monasticism was the monasticism that grew up in Ireland. In contrast with the East, Irish monasticism, as nearly always in the West, was first of all a product of the upper classes or the controlling powers of society. Most Irish Abbotts (the heads, or "supreme moderators," of monasteries) were members of a ruling clan or tribal family. Some monasteries controlled thousands of acres of land.

Yet Christian humility was highly valued. It was considered wrong, or actually a sin, for a Bishop or an Abbott to ride a horse, thus suggesting his superiority to the common people. Spiritual discipline and integrity gave rise to intense scholarly and artistic activity. The Irish monks were learned in scriptures and achieved superior Latin scholarship. Their influence was immense. It has been said that Irish monasticism was the Church in Ireland.[209] The Irish monks, impelled to missionary activity, evangelized

parts of Scotland and Northern England. In 575 Columbanus, an Irish tribal leader and head of a family monastery, took a shipload of monks into Europe. By the death of Columbanus in 615 they had founded forty monasteries, in France, Italy, and the Alps. Some of these were renowned as centers of scholarship and were among the jewels of medieval culture.

We have seen the importance of monasticism for Pope Gregory the Great. He was so impressed with the Rule of Saint Benedict that he wrote a biography of Benedict. He promoted the use of the Rule as a means of assuring balance, sanity, and integrity in Western monasticism. Under this influence and that of the Irish example monasticism flourished. The Benedictine monks were literate and thus capable of complex and intense spiritual exercise and of intellectual development which permitted them to contribute to the preservation and development of philosophical, literary, and artistic culture. They were also committed to hard labor, and their combination of talents and commitments made them the master agriculturists of the time. They improved crops and planting methods. To a large extent they were responsible for the clearing of forests and the draining of swamps, which has been called the basic economic fact of the Dark Ages.[210]

The abbots were, like Pope Gregory I, from the ruling classes, and their prestige and power were often greater than that of the Bishops and the land-owning secular Lords. Under their leadership the monasteries developed the additional social function sustaining and promoting culture. From the very earliest beginning the monks had been engaged in the copying of manuscripts. The monasteries became the major agency in the preservation of the learning and arts of Greece and Rome and bringing them into continuing fruitful interaction with Christianity and native cultures. It has been said that "the leading abbeys were the universities of the Dark Ages."[211] They played a central role in the shaping of Christianity and making it the culture of the West.

The estates of the Church were expanding until about the

middle of the ninth century. They tended to contract under the impact of Scandinavian invasions. The power of the abbots and bishops gave way to that of lords whose power and possession of land was based solely on military power. While military rule of feudalism remained the social order until the nineteenth century, there was a great regeneration of monasticism from the end of the eleventh century. A conspicuous part of this development was the founding of the magnificent Cistercian order, so named for the city of Citeaux in Burgundy where it was first organized in 1098.

The Cistercians began with twenty-one members. In twenty years they established seven houses. By the middle of the century there were 328 houses and by the end of the century there were 525. The strength of the Cistercians was drawn from the hereditary energy and talents of its members, who were of aristocratic origin, and from the renewed energy with which they imposed the Benedictine discipline upon themselves. Their energies were liberated by the favor of the Papacy, which gave them complete freedom from the control of local lay and ecclesiastical authority. They achieved huge expansions of the resources of the Church in Spain, Portugal, Hungary, Poland, Sweden, Norway, Denmark, Bohemia, Austria, Wales, northern England, and the Scottish borders. The land of one monastery in Bohemia included 1,000 square miles and its development involved the creation of seventy villages.[212]

Part of the Cistercian success was due to Bernard of Clairvaux (1090–1153), a member of the order who became the dominant figure of the Church in the early twelfth century. The order benefitted as well from the fact that a number of their members became Popes. There are today two Cistercian orders, the order of the Strict Observance, called "Trappist," and the order of the Common Observance. Today the Trappists have throughout the world one hundred houses for monks and sixty-nine for nuns. The Common Observance has sixty-one houses for monks and ninety-one for nuns, a total of 321 houses. The Cistercians were

and profound faith and that he was a favorite Saint of the middle ages. Almost everyone knows that he was murdered by four knights who had misunderstood a remark of King Henry II. Everyone knows that Abelard was castrated by his lover's relatives. Few know that he was a major theological thinker. Everyone knows that six million Jews were murdered in the Holocaust. Very few understand that they failed to protect themselves because until the very last hours of their lives their very religious and deeply civilized imaginations could not conceive of the monstrosity of the Nazi imagination.

Where the Church is concerned, history is chiefly interested in those moments when it was least a Church. The Church at times became a military power, acted at times with brutal violence. The Church was embattled by the most powerful monarchs in Europe. Sometimes it withstood those secular military and political powers. Sometimes it was momentarily defeated. At times Priests, Monks, Archbishops, and Popes became wolves in sheep's clothing, or in the most extreme cases, let us say lower forms of animal life battening on innocence. People acting in the name of the Church became bloody marauders ravaging for power. These are the things history most easily records, the news that history most popularly disseminates.

History must relegate to brief paragraphs and cursory acknowledgment the meaning of the Church. Through most of twenty centuries the Church was present in all the large and all the very small places throughout the vast extent of the Western world. It sustained awareness of a permanence and splendor behind the moving shadows of actuality. Fear, pain, regret, grief, and sorrow are a constant of human experience in an uncertain world. The Church brought a stilling of fear and a softening of sorrow. The Church made possible the only sure surcease of anxiety and regret that human beings can experience—the balm of faith. To the infinite pliability and consequent anguish of human potentiality, the Church gave direction and peace. It alleviated much physical hunger and assuaged much pain.

The Church made possible civil order. It garnered and preserved both classical and oriental as well as its own learning. It
bestowed visions of incomparable beauty on impoverished lives.
It gave rise to the disposition of mind that makes reason possible. It cultivated the conditions that nurtured Western
intellectuals. It sustained and fostered civilization. Even though
repeatedly there were ignorant and debased priests and avari-
cious and power-hungry Bishops, and even though there were
cruel and misguided eruptions of clerical zealotry, the great majority of monks, priests, bishops, and popes were people of faith
and virtue, and they achieved these splendid things.

All the largess and sacred power and action of the Church is
largely forgotten in much of history. History for the most part is
the history of the aberrations of the Church, its failures. The inherent debilities of history have fed ideological predilections.
For three hundred years the bruiting of the Church's failures has
been the stock in trade of those elements of society hostile to the
Church—the Protestant revolt at first, and then, with mounting
vigor, the passion for radical secularization liberated by the Renaissance and the Enlightenment. The effect has been to
contaminate widely the image of the Church in the popular imagination.

Eventually liberalism has accommodated a conception of the
Church as a bastion of reactionism, as the enemy of progress,
and, in general, hardly other than an agency of evil. If we are to
perceive the freedom of the Church from the traces of the sins of
its children, we must have a general conception of what those
sins have been. We will see historical circumstances as partly
extenuating, and most of the evil actors will become quite human. The sinners within and for the Church were guilty, indeed,
but not at all the monsters lurking in the shadows of popular
prejudice. We will understand that the power of the Church for
sanctifying and giving meaning to life stands free of the human
stains of history.

My purpose is to attempt to dispel some confusion and to

ity. Inevitably Christianity is identified with Christendom. In the Middle Ages, the Church became indistinguishable from Christendom. Unhappily, but necessarily, although the Church is a divinely inspired institution, Christianity and the Church can never be quite the same thing. The Church, then and now, is constituted by human beings in a material world. Because liberal critics adopt the role of passive, and therefore innocent, observation, they do not acknowledge a fundamental principle of life, which is: Every commitment involves a compromise.

To see fairly the sins within the Church it is necessary to observe briefly the process by which Christianity became a part of the world of general human affairs.[217] We must be aware of the process by which the Papacy became "the Imperial Papacy." The Church by divine mission attempts to embody, propagate, and sustain Christianity. In all other respects, the character of the Church results from the fact that it emerged and flourished in the Roman Empire. It was first shaped by the cauldron of political expediency requiring the Crucifixion of Christ. It began to be shaped again by that fiery matrix precisely because of its astonishing success. By the fourth century, there were, by informed modern estimates, more than six million Christians in the Roman Empire and Christian communities flourished everywhere.

What now shaped the Church and would fundamentally shape much of its history was the recognition—by secular powers, first of all–of a fundamental political principle. That principle is that religion is an essential element in melding the social uniformity and cohesion necessary for peace and effective political administration. Unquestionably, recognition of this practical principle mixed with classical piety motivated the early persecution of the Christians. From Christ onward there were at least sporadic persecutions of Christians by the Roman state. Persecution became systematic and empire-wide under the Emperor Decius in 250 A.D. and reached horrendous culmination under Diocletian in 303. The end of Christian persecution was motivated by a mix-

ture of piety and political expedience comparable to that with which it began.

A fusion of elemental piety and a realization of the importance of religion as a political tool were dramatically present in the conversion of Constantine. As we have seen in Chapter 10, Constantine, previously a sun-worshiper, was convinced that a sign from the Christian God had assured his crucial victory at Milvian bridge, north of Rome. Although Christianity was not declared the official religion of the Roman empire until 380, by the Emperor Theodosius, Constantine in all practical respects established that condition, beginning with his Edict of Milan in 313, which restored to the Church its legal rights and all its confiscated property. In effect, the Church was eventually inseparable from and identifiable with the Empire, and, for all intents and purposes, the Church, like the Empire, now had Constantine at its head. In effect, Constantine was the Pope. For instance, he called and financed the Council of Nicaea in 325. He attended the Council, quite conspicuously, and controlled its deliberations and the decision by which it attempted to end once and for all the heresy of Arianism, excluding it from acceptability by the Catholic Church. The bishop of Rome was not present at this Council.

The Church verged now on its centuries-long tension with imperial power. One can hardly quarrel with the motivation of the Papacy in this contest. By this time the bishopric of Rome was in the process of assuming primacy among bishoprics. In other words it was becoming the Papacy, the head of the Christian Church. The inheritance of the Pope was the authority bestowed upon the Apostle Peter by Christ. The Pope had every reason to assume that the divine purposes of the Church would be subverted and corrupted in service to secular power and to assume the authority and responsibility of the Pope for spiritual direction in the world. (It would seem clear that Constantine conceived himself as endowed with the same authority and responsibility.) The Papacy cannot be blamed for its resistance

to secular power over the conditions, forms, and practices of spiritual life. But during the reign of Constantine that resistance was not very effective.

An opening for the reestablishment of Papal authority came eventually as the result of Constantine's having moved his capital from Rome to Constantinople. It resulted eventually in the division of the Roman Empire into the eastern realm that continued to be called the Roman Empire and the western realm that came, much later, under the Frankish kingdom established by Charlemagne, to be called, the Holy Roman Empire. The Roman Emperor at a great distance in Constantinople, was not able to protect Rome against the Germanic tribes whose onslaught brought about the Roman Empire"s disintegration in the West. Furthermore, due to political tensions with the Papacy, the Emperor was not always willing to provide the protection that was within his power.

Governmental administration of the city of Rome itself fell into disrepair. By default, Popes found themselves assuming imperial authority as the Emperor had once usurped religious authority. For example, on separate occasions Pope Leo I (440–461), called by the Church Leo the Great, undertook to save Rome by negotiating with Barbarian kings who had invaded Italy.[218] (In the first case, in 452, he saved Rome from the Huns of Attila. In the second instance, in 455, he failed, and the Vandals sacked Rome.) At this time the Church, especially under Leo I, was insisting on its independence of secular power and the Papacy's assumption of secular responsibilities served its inevitable function of supplanting the deteriorating Roman state in the West. It was thus that the Church became the central institution of the Western world.

Meanwhile the wealth and land holdings of the Papacy were increasing. From the first there were large bequests from wealthy Christians. Constantine lavished his personal wealth on the Church, building great churches all the way from Rome to Jerusalem. Pope Gregory the Great brought with him an enormous family

fortune and made it part of Papal wealth. The Papacy thus became the owner of vast estates in Rome and in Sicily. The Papal States came into being in 756 when the French King Pepin, who had come to the Pope's aid by defeating the Lombards who had invaded northern Italy, gave to Pope Stephen II various provinces including Rome and the Exarchate of Ravenna. (The Exarchate had been claimed and ruled in the name of the Eastern Empire by the Exarch, or viceroy of the Byzantine Emperor. Pepin and the Papacy could, and did, simply ignore this fact.) Possession of the Papal States made the Pope a secular as well as a religious ruler. The Papal States were a source of wealth and a recurrent cause of contention for the Church for over a thousand years and well into the nineteenth century. The Church soon became the largest holder of land in Europe. Eventually, the Church in many areas held thirty percent of the land; in some areas it held sixty percent.[219]

The Emperor in the East (whom we will hereafter refer to as the Byzantine Emperor) was unable, and frequently unwilling, to protect Rome, The Pope was forced to seek support elsewhere. Pope Gregory II (669–731) sought help from the Normans who occupied southern Italy. Pope Gregory VII (1073–1085)—another great pope though not bearing the official title of "Great"—came to realize that the future of the Papacy lay in strength to be found, not in the East, but in the North, in the Carolinan empire.. The political history of the Papacy from this time and for centuries to come is the story of shifting alliances with European powers and conflicts with others.

As part of this historical process, the Papacy became itself a military power. A conspicuous example is in the wars in the thirteenth century, recurrent for decades, between the Papacy (and the party called the Guelphs)on one hand and, on the other, the German Emperor Frederick II (and the Party called the Ghibellines). (For more on Frederick II see the discussion of the crusades later in this chapter.) A spectacular example of papal belligerency is presented by Pope Julius II (1503–1513), whom

Bézier in 1209, though Albigensian resistance lingered on for another twenty years.

The military repression of the Cathars was referred to as a crusade. We cannot hope to grasp the nature of the Medieval world and the quality of Christianity in that world without attempting to understand the crusades, which are in some respects the most bizarre aspects of Christian history. Ironically, it must be kept in mind that what history must accomplish in and following the Middle ages is an advance in the spiritualization of faith. The faith of the Middle Ages had an intensity that we can never share, but in its very intensity the substance of faith, its content, had some of the simple obviousness and tangibility that we can associate only with matter. That is the nature of an absolute faith.

We must not think of medieval people as people just like us except that they did some strange and sometime evil things. The strange and sometimes evil things they did are part of what they were. We must accept the fact that during most of the Medieval centuries the practice of trial by ordeal was universal. In one form of the ordeal, the accused was required to grasp a red hot iron. If his hand began to be cured in a few days, he was considered innocent. Another form of trial by ordeal was trial by combat. Disputes were settled when the contestants fought until one of them killed the other. The one who killed in this case was considered the innocent party. It is staggering to realize that trial by ordeal continued into the thirteenth century, a time of the triumph of Christianity and of the finest flowering of Western art and thought. (See below, page 254.) It is only fair, and actually it is not more than facing the truth objectively, to acknowledge that medieval culture embodied and assimilated a paradox: devout and genuine Christianity coexisted in symbiotic harmony with the most primitive practice of violence. We have no right, and no intellectual sanction, for considering either as more fundamental to the culture than the other.

The ordeal was an extremely primitive practice surviving until late in the Medieval world. The ordeal shares something, further-

more, with the crusades, which arose from the heart of the medieval world. That world can become at all comprehensible only with some understanding of the crusades. Two important factors were at work. One was the reigning quality of literalist and absolute faith. The other was the pervasive political and social structure. The luxuriant flowering of faith overgrew the world, and as it did it became identical with the world. This, in turn, meant that while the world became like faith, faith also was shaped by the world. Its reality tended to take on the concreteness—indeed, the materiality—of the world. We are capable of imagining a world that assimilates faith, a faith that is present and pervasive in the activity and imagination of the world. What is difficult for us to imagine is a world that becomes faith so that there is no possibility of distinguishing between faith and the world in which it flourishes. (This makes it more likely that the desire to liberate the Holy Land, which motivated the crusades, was compatible with the desire to conquer and possess new fiefdoms, new kingdoms of this world.) A fundamental consolidation of power and faith occurs in the sacralizing of the feudal system.

There were two elements controlling the structure of society. In so far as there was stability, it was the counter-balancing of military powers and the constant potential of military violence. There was trade, of course, chiefly in agricultural products, but what created the possibility for production was violence. Whatever was accomplished in the affairs of groups of human beings was dependent on a foundation in violence. Military violence and its potentiality were the horizontal matrix of this society. The vertical matrix of this society was the system of alliances between military powers, large and small, that is called feudalism. In this vertical dimension of feudal society, faith both tempered and, by implication, condoned violence. Violence was the original and ultimately basic dynamism of this society.

The feudal system was developing from the ninth century onward and had come into its fullest development in the twelfth century. Land worked by serfs was the essential source of wealth.

of the wealthy alone, especially in their wills, constituted enormous income.

As bishops were conspicuous within the aristocratic hierarchy, so were lesser religious figures in the general population. It has been estimated that one person in fifty had some claim to belonging to a religious order. Entering a religious order was a way of getting an education for some who later entered the employment of non-clerical masters. In fact, literate personnel were produced almost exclusively by training within the Church. As a result, most of the clerical work on an increasingly bureaucratized society was done by clerics in lay service.

The success of the Church resulted in its activity in all aspects of human life. In feudalism it pervaded even the most practical political affairs. It saturated a fundamentally violent society and in doing so it developed a new dimension which was a deformation of the principle of love—a commitment to violence in the name of love. It was as though a limb of the Christianity had turned cancerous, its malignity generating explosive energy. Yet in some measure we can imagine how this occurred. Suppose that you believed absolutely in the truth of a religion of love and were authentically aware of all that love might accomplish. Then suppose that forces appeared that intended to obliterate this faith. Would not violence in the name of love become not only reasonable but urgently necessary. And would this be entirely remote from our motives for fighting two World Wars?

The amalgam of faith and violence as the modus operandi of society achieved its quintessential expression in the most astonishing phenomenon of medieval Western history, which was, without doubt, the crusades, to which we will now turn.

The crusades continued for a period of over three hundred and fifty years.[221] The total number of people involved must have been over a million (in an European population much smaller than today's).[222] They were usually led by the most powerful rulers and aristocrats of the day. Not more than ten percent of the people in a crusade were armored knights, but they, the aristo-

crats and retainers of the ruling class, determined where the crusaders went and were responsible to a large extent for what they
did. This meant that wherever a crusade went, it carried with it
the principle of feudal violence in the service of an absolute
faith. As one result—often, but not always, opposed and lamented
by Popes and other religious leaders—atrocities on a large scale
were commonplace. En route within Europe, some of the crusaders massacred Jewish communities, and in the East both Jewish
and Islamic communities.

The background of the crusades is significant. After Christianity became a legal and protected faith in the fourth century, Christians
regularly undertook pilgrimages to places made holy by association
with the saints and heroes of the faith. A pilgrimage was often a long
and arduous undertaking, even though pilgrims were often hosted
and protected by religious institutions along the way. Pilgrimages to
the Holy Land became increasingly popular. By the middle of the
eleventh century, however, Islam not only controlled the pilgrim
routes to the Holy Land but was in possession of the holy city of
Jerusalem as well. The crusades began in response to these conditions. And there was another motivation. No one doubts that the
desire to recover the Holy Land was often associated with movements of reform, with a desire for deepened faith and increased
integrity within the Church.

The beginning took place when Pope Urban II preached a
sermon in 1095 calling for a crusade to be supported by all of
Europe. The response to Urban's sermon was spectacular. An
estimated 150,000 people, including the women, the elderly,
and the poor, embraced the crusade by having sewn on their
garments the cross of cloth that was the badge of the crusader.
We know that actually in a single group some 40,000 men
marched the more than a thousand miles to the East, among
them some 4,000 knights, most of whom were lords of estates,
with much to lose.[223]

Different groups, however, came at different times and under
different leaders, men of contrasting characters and motivations..

an expert army for defense of the crusader states. On the land routes from Europe they built huge fortresses and dedicated themselves to protection of pilgrims to the Holy Land. Against the background of all the varied and complex amalgams of faith and ambition compelling different crusaders, it may be most easily said of these military monks that faith came first. They certainly were not saints—some of them very far from it—but when we look for redeeming aspects of the crusades, these religious knights most easily come to mind.

And yet, certainly, the Templars and the Hospitallers were not the only dedicated Christians among the crusaders. The range of motivation between piety and naked ambition was very great. It may best be illustrated by drawing attention to two of the most spectacular leaders of crusades, the German emperor Frederick II (1194–1250) and the king of France, Louis IX (1214–1270).

Frederick was brilliant, learned, and possessed of fastidious taste. He was famous for his sensual luxuries cultivated in oriental style. He was also a totally unscrupulous megalomaniac, who happens to have been idolized by the Nazis.[225] As the result of his effort to turn most of Italy including the Papal states into a part of the German empire, he was engaged in a decades long conflict with the Papacy famous as the wars of the Guelphs (the pro-Papacy partisans) and the Ghibellines (the pro-Emperor partisans). As a crusader Frederick's was a record of deceit, treachery, diplomatic skill, and success, of a disgraceful kind.

Upon Frederick's coronation as Holy Roman Emperor he also declared himself King of Jerusalem, on the basis of his wife's descent. He took a vow to undertake a crusade to recapture Jerusalem, which had recently be retaken by the Muslim conqueror Saladin. After six years, in which Frederick repeatedly renewed this vow and failed to fulfill it, the Pope excommunicated him. In 1228, ten years after the crusaders forces in the Holy Land had first expected him, he arrived in Acre. Shockingly for everyone who had placed their hope in him, it turned out that Frederick had been in diplomatic negotiation with the Muslim powers. Con-

sequently a substantial part of the crusader forces, including most of the barons of the crusader state, along with the Templars, the Hospitallers, and the clergy, refused to follow him.

Frederick actually proceeded to make a unilateral treaty with the Muslims. It was agreed that the crusaders would not attack Egypt. In return Frederick would receive Jerusalem, Bethlehem, and Nazareth and a thin strip of land connecting Jerusalem to the coast. Frederick agreed that henceforth Jerusalem would remain unfortified and defenseless. and that if Christians broke the truce, Frederick would join the Muslims against them. Frederick destroyed all the weapons and siege equipment of his crusader allies, including those of the religious orders, leaving them defenseless. Though with his retinue he attempted in 1229 to disembark in the secrecy of dawn from the city of Acre, the population stirred early to shout execrations and cover the passing emperor with missiles of garbage. In bitterness, those in the Papacy wished to obliterate Frederick's Hohenstaufen line, and ten of his descendants died in Papal prisons.

We turn now to the other end of the spectrum of character and motivation among crusaders. Louis IX (1214–1270) was one of the great kings of France. He was a person of deep piety and great wisdom and a superb administrator. He practiced his faith in the service of France. He controlled carefully the officials of his government throughout the country, requiring that they take an oath not to accept bribes or practice extortion. After their terms of office had ended they were to remain forty days in their districts to make it possible for them to be charged with any offense that they might have committed while in office. They were forbidden to frequent taverns or to gamble. Louis was dedicated to public order. Prostitution and gambling were forbidden and blasphemy was subject to severe penalties.

Louis sat personally in judgment on many of the disputes between his subjects, establishing such a reputation for wisdom and justice that foreigners came to submit their conflicts to his arbitration. A special mark of the quality of Louis's reign is that

the feminine, or as some would have it, a discovery of the feminine. In Christianity the shift was expressed in the new emotionalism of Saint Francis and in a impulse given to the cult of the Virgin. We must realize, nevertheless, that this was still a fundamentalist faith, and its deepening was one of the springs of motive for the crusades.

The inevitable historical wedding of violence and faith that compelled the crusades is expressed also in that other response to enemies of the faith, the Inquisition, which is the most infamous phenomenon in popular memory of the Middle Ages. It will suffice here to recall that Luther and Calvin also burned witches and, in addition, to quote a distinguished historian: "The Inquisition came to occupy such a role in [modern] European demonology that we must be careful to keep it in proportion. It was not an institution but a series of inquiries. In some countries these were so resented that they were not continued, and the surviving records show that the proportion of executions was not high."[228]

We have yet to sample all the Vatican's dirty laundry, and it is by no means the case that all the sins committed within the Church, and in the name of the Church, can be considered excesses of faith. We must witness also instances of raw ambition, naked greed, sexual abandonment, a shameless dedication to deceit and conspiracy, and a capacity for murder. The flowering of evil in the Papacy when it occurred was largely the work of the Renaissance Popes. The chief culprits had sought and obtained the Papacy without any religious motivation or purpose whatever. The historical explanation is that when the Papacy was neither threatened nor protected by powerful secular monarchs, it fell into the hands of a corrupt Roman aristocracy. Renaissance history is littered with Papal scandals.

Alexander VI (Rodrigo de Borja y Borja) (1492–1503) of the famed family of Spanish descent called Borgia in Italy, was the most notorious of the Popes. His uncle, Pope Callistus III (1455–1458), another Borgia. , named him a cardinal deacon and bishop

of a number of sees, giving him control also of a number of abbeys. Eventually his uncle appointed him vice-chancellor of the holy see, an office in which he was able to make himself the second richest of the cardinals. As a cardinal he was quite open in his licentious life. He fathered several children. His favorites, born to an aristocratic Roman mistress, were Juan, Cesare, Lucrezia, and Goffredo. He gained the Papacy largely by bribery. Among his major concerns was enrichment of his family. When his son Cesare was only eighteen, Alexander made him bishop of several sees, and a little later made cardinals of both Cesare and Alessandro Farnese, brother of Guilia, his then current mistress. Eventually he made Cesare duke of Romagna. Late in his reign he devoted himself to crushing the great Roman families who he saw as competing with his own. His program for this purpose involved a number of assassinations and ruthless seizures of property.

Appropriately, Alexander was offended by Girolamo Savonarola the Dominican puritan and reformer who denounced Papal corruption. In the end Savonarola was excommunicated, examined under torture, and executed. We look vainly for the virtues of Pope Alexander VI. Yet we may use this Pope Alexander to make a very Catholic point. The excellent writer J. N.D. Kelly speaks of him as "Devout and a stickler for orthodoxy despite his personal profligacy . . ."[229] It hardly redeems this villainous man to point out that he shares some credit with better Popes for promoting the arts and embellishing the beauty of the Vatican in a number of ways.

It is possible, in tabloid like fashion, to chronicle other sins of popes. It has been claimed that Pope Boniface VIII (1294–1303) ordered the poisoning of his predecessor, Pope Celestine V. Pope Sixtus IV (11471–1484) connived at a plot which was intended to murder Lorenzo and Giuliano de Medici and which succeeded in murdering Guiliano. Leo X (1513–1521), son of Lorenzo the Magnificent, was made a cleric at seven years of age and a cardinal at thirteen, devoted much of his effort to further

enrichment of the Medici family. He also issued the specified Indulgences to finance the building of Saint Peters, which brought on Luther's Ninety-Five Theses and the Protestant Reformation. Discovering a plot against him among the cardinals, he executed the ring-leader. Julius III (15450–1553), who was otherwise a fairly effective Pope, was a cause of scandal. He was infatuated by a thirteen year old boy he picked up on the street, having his brother adopt the boy and, almost incredibly, making him a cardinal. Celestine III (1191–1198) is said to have conspired to murder Emperor Henry VI, and Innocent IV has been accused of conniving at a plot to kill Frederick II.[230] A few others could be added to this infamous list. However, it should be kept in mind that these few are among a total of 262 popes, most of whom were genuinely pious and devoted men.

A Pope of a very different kind embodies another kind of violation of our expectation of the Papacy. Pope Julius II (Guiliano della Rovere) (1503–1513) fathered three daughters during his time as a cardinal, but as a Pope he was famous for something else. A ruthless administrator, he was called "Il terrible." He was a skillful diplomat and an effective military strategist. He was also an avid practitioner of war. Personally leading his troops in full armor, he conquered large parts of Italy to bring them into the Papal state. By adroit alliances he was able to expel the French from Italian soil. These military and diplomatic goals were his chief concerns. It was said that there was nothing of the priest about him but the dress and the name.[231] But while strengthening the Papacy, Julian restored to it certain elements of integrity.

In a way almost unheard of among Renaissance popes, Julian refrained from using the papacy to enrich his family. In fact he published a bull declaring that simony would invalidate papal elections. He had inherited an empty treasury and when he died he left it abundantly rich. He was a dedicated patron of the arts, inspiring and promoting the careers of Raphael and Michelangelo. It was he who commissioned Michelangelo to draw up plans for the new Saint Peters, and initiated the selling of Indulgences to

finance it. He was honored for liberating Italy from foreign domination and supporting its unification.

Many of the Renaissance popes were certainly reprehensible, in one way or another. None of them meets the standards of liberal virtue. Yet we may not find it easy to judge them. Paul III (Alessandro Farnese) (1534–1549) was made cardinal by the infamous Alexander VI. He came to be called "cardinal petticoat" because his sister was Alexander's mistress. Even before he was ordained as a priest, he held many bishoprics. He kept a mistress who was a member of the Roman nobility and who bore him three sons and a daughter.

Eventually, however, Cardinal Farnese began to take his work as a bishop quite seriously. It seems to have brought about a crucial change. In 1513 he ended his liaison with his mistress, transformed his life, and gave support to the party of church reform within the curia. In 1519 he was ordained as a priest. In 1534 at the age 67 he was elected Pope by unanimous vote. He undertook to renew the popularity of the Papacy, giving brilliant feasts and masked balls in the Vatican and reviving the carnival. He also undertook to make the Farnese family one of the most powerful in Italy, practicing extravagant nepotism, which was an almost invariable practice of the Renaissance popes.[232] When two of his grandsons were only 14 and 16 years old, he made them cardinals and gave them important offices.

He was equally concerned to protect and sustain Catholicism. He was the first pope to realize the gravity of the Protestant challenge, and it was he who initiated the basic act of resistance. He called the Council of Trent (1545–1563) and thus established the Catholic Counter-Reformation. He contributed to reform in various other ways. He reduced the expenses of the College of Cardinal and improved its quality by a number of brilliant appointments. He encouraged reforms in religious orders and the establishment of new ones, including the Society of Jesus. He also established the Congregation of the Roman Inquisition, called the Holy Office. He excommunicated Henry VIII. He also re-

stored Rome university, built-up the Vatican library, and commissioned Michelangelo to paint "The Last Judgment" in the Sistine Chapel and to supervise work on the building of Saint Peters. It seems impossible to deny that, given his time and his place, Paul III was a first class human being.

We can hardly fail to contrast Paul III, virtues and sins as well, with some quite conventionally proper Popes. Benedict XIII (1724–1730) had resigned a dukedom to become a Dominican friar. Devout and learned, he devoted his time as Pope to priestlike attendance to the diocese of Rome. Apparently devoid of practical judgment and basic human insight, he turned over the more important Papal affairs to a thoroughly corrupt assistant under whose administration the Papacy and the administration of the Papal States became a public scandal. Another pope who contrasts with Paul III, and in yet another way, was Clement XIV (1769–1774). Clement's sin was a failure of nerve that betrayed the Counter-Reformation. Under the pressure of secular monarchs, he dissolved the Jesuit order, which constituted the finest and most effective creation of the Counter-Reformation. Clement thus brought the Papacy to what has been called "its most shameful hour."[233]

In crossing the wasteland, we must not be waylaid by righteous liberalism celebrating the sins of the Papacy. We must be forewarned that they do exist. We cannot deal with them on the basis of that inheritance of pristine purity that is a puritan inheritance of liberalism in dealing with things religious. This liberal ethic is extravagantly tolerant of all kinds of sins, but insists that religious people who are not saints are scoundrels. This is part of a puritan mind-set which leaves no room for a mixture of virtues and vices. It is realized in certain populations with Protestant backgrounds.

Protestantism has produced genuine saints. On the other hand anyone who has observed the behavior of industrial and agricultural red-necks in the southern and southwestern United States knows that no one can be more brutally degraded than lower-

class Protestants fallen from grace. (I recommend Lionel Garcia's novel *Hardscrub* as demonstrating this point.) Theirs is a culture totally alien to that, for instance, of prostitutes in Catholic countries who wear crucifixes while at work and attend Mass on Sunday. These quaint practices are a tribute to Christianity, which does not dream of eradicating sin but knows that it may be forgiven.

Chapter Thirteen

THE "ANGELIC DOCTOR"

For many secular minds, embracing religion may seem like
intellectual suicide. It is true that even in modern society there
are those for whom faith is based on rote learning and stained-
glass windows. It is part of the majesty of the Catholic faith that
these are authentic children of God included in the Church's
embrace which nourishes spiritual development at all levels of
human capacity. In contrast with the simplest believers are the
inherently intellectual, who can move toward Christianity only
on intellectual paths. The truth is that if they attempt to live within
an orthodox faith, they will find an intellectual life more widely
comprehensive, richer, and certainly more complex than they
have ever known before. So it is important to evoke now an ample
suggestion of the temper of the intellectual tradition they will
enter.

For all the Popes—the saints, the sinners, and the ineffectual
among them—there were great and distinguished minds within
their flocks—often within their retinues and often as their intellectual companions. The development of Christianity has been
graced by intellectual distinction throughout its history. Its culminating development was an awesome achievement the scope
and energy of which have never been exceeded. This was the
work of Saint Thomas Aquinas in the thirteenth century. One of
the few Doctors of the Church, he was dubbed "The Angelic

Doctor."[234] Despite some recent shifts in intellectual fashion, nothing can more fully represent Catholicism and its capacity for cultivating the human mind than the work of Saint Thomas. If we attempt to retrieve value from the past, much of it will come from this source.

The Christianity that came to Saint Thomas, embodied in scripture, custom, and Church doctrines, was now given a massive rational elaboration which achieved a special coherence with the world. The Church as an institution had structured, and meshed with, the world of affairs—diplomatic, military, economic, political. Now the world was structured intellectually in a way that made it an extension of Christian reality. Greek thought had in some measure shaped Christianity almost from the first, especially in the writing of Saint Paul, but also in the Epistle to the Hebrews, which probably was not written by Saint Paul, and in the Fourth Gospel. From the fifth century on, the major intellectual influence on the Church was the powerful mind of Saint Augustine, deeply influenced by the otherworldly bias of Plato. But now for the first time there was a massive system of thought in which Christianity exhaustively pervaded the world, identifying the relationships of all its parts. In this sense, the work of Saint Thomas, profoundly influenced by Aristotle, was a consummation of the Christianizing of the West. It occupied the intellectual center of Catholicism for six centuries and, despite a number of defections in the twentieth century, remains fundamental to Catholic thought. Knowledge of the status of St. Thomas in Catholicism is a corrective to some popular conceptions of the Church. The Church has been seen as a bulwark of unreasoning dogmatism, as a capricious claimant to infallibility, as the spontaneous and unthinking ally of wealth, power, and suppression, and a major support of political status quo. The Church has had such a character only when it betrayed the principles of Christ and of its greatest thinker.

What follows in this chapter will not attempt to summarize the enormous range of Saint Thomas's thought, but only to cover

will.[247] And "believing is the act of understanding assenting under the will's command."[248] It has been acknowledged that faith is always in some sense qualified, that every commitment entails a compromise. The assumption has been that one may accept a whole body of faith and affirm its authority without being able to fully accept particular articles of that faith. Saint Thomas's discussion of modes of faith distinguishes between belief "in" and "about" God from "believing for the sake of God."[249] That, of course, is inherent in the central proposal of this book.

Saint Thomas's thought is in harmony with most modern thought on a crucial point. His was the basic empiricist assumption: all knowledge begins with the senses as they respond to the natural world. This, I think, made him especially sensitive to the conflict between faith and secular knowledge that was beginning to emerge in his time.

The empiricist assumption underlies a formulation that is of fundamental importance to moderns who wish to maintain religious faith: The knowledge that we have of God is our most important knowledge, but it is extremely limited. We know that God exists, and we know his effects in this world, but we do not know the nature of God.[250] The nature of God transcends the reach of the mind limited to its capacity for knowledge of the forms that constitute the world. It is perhaps accordingly that we find good sense in Saint Thomas' doctrines as well as in his morality and politics. For instance, he condemned excesses in the cult of relics.[251]

The limits of our knowledge of the nature of God define a rule that must be basic for modern efforts of faith: theology is profoundly important but it is a science of limited possibilities. We betray the nature of God when we attempt to say too much about Him. Here is a guideline saving us from absolutist fundamentalism and excessive literalism of every kind. It acknowledges the vast intellectual uncertainty that must attend modern faith. We come to understand that although art is not religion, there is a fundamentally artistic element in the activity of faith.

It would seem clear that if we are to get any nearer than most of us are to the truth, we must find a way to exercise our religious imaginations without committing an outright desecration of modern knowledge. Saint Thomas provides a way of doing that. If we give the briefest attention to the notion of a divinely created world, we seem to confront an immediate, powerful denial implicit in modern science. The sciences of biological evolution and astronomy present us a world created in all its details by natural causes.

The existence of the millions upon millions of causes controlling development and function everywhere we look cannot be denied. How are we to think about them? What we generally call causes, Saint Thomas calls "second causes." The first cause is God. The Act of Being which causes all things to be by conferring on them an act of being confers on each also a power of causation. Saint Thomas was rigorously opposed to any line of thought tending to deny the omnipresence and power of natural causes. In other words, he was opposed to any effort to deny the authority of science so long as it did not attempt to be philosophy.[252]

We are not constrained, however, to believe that the potency of God is present only in the sustaining of "second causes." Spiritual reality transcends the material world. Although we must not exaggerate our ability to understand this realm of reality, our imaginations need help here. That may be provided by imagining another kind of causation different from the empiricist version. (For the empiricist version see Appendix B.) This other kind of cause, let us say, is not a kind of impingement of one thing on another. Rather an effect is one thing that grows out of another thing as an oak tree grows out of an acorn. The effect that grows out of a cause is, in a sense, the same as that cause. Or let us imagine cause as a kind of radiation that congeals into a simulacrum of its source. In another sense it propagates its source. In the end, for present purposes, we, as laymen and non-philosophers, must take metaphysical statements as poetry,

remembering that it is only poetry that communicates profound truth.

Saint Thomas's protection of the integrity of "second causes" has two important and related implications. 1)There is an important implication for the nature of prayer, which Gilson expresses in this way: "And although man cannot expect God to alter the order of His providence to answer his prayers, he can and should pray that God's Will be done. Thus through prayer will man become deserving of what God has decided from eternity to grant him." The emphasis is on prayer as adoration rather than petition. 2) As created beings capable of choosing the ends of our acts, we share with God the wielding of causality in the world. We are His assistants ["coadjutors"] in the direction of the world. If we take the two implications together, human action is strengthened in a claim to compete with prayer as a spiritual activity.[253]

Saint Thomas' position preserves the integrity of science as its function is generally conceived in the modern world. Yet there is a crucial difference. The entities conceived as causes and effects are not simply material things for Saint Thomas. The entities involved are substances. The concept of substances has been discredited from the scientific revolution of the seventeenth century onward, and from the point of view of the *science-world* substances do not exist. The great thinker Kenneth Burke insists, however, that we cannot get along without the concept of substance. It is part of reality as we can know it. If we are to believe in the reality of the life-world (See Chapter 6), we cannot disdain the conception of Saint Thomas. For Saint Thomas, substances are matter plus form, and form is an immaterial element. The form is an act of being resulting from and striving to emulate the Act of Being that is God Who is the act of creation. This is a sacred world. God is everywhere present in it.[254]

We can afford to neglect areas of Saint Thomas's work that are and will remain unacceptable to modern minds, whatever their religious inclination. Saint Thomas would seem to violate his restriction upon our understanding of the supernatural. He

elaborates on the realm of supernatural beings, and the modern reader will be startled by his treatment of the angels.[255]

We must remember that Saint Thomas conceived the universe as totally unified in a constant gradation from natural to supernatural beings. Given our natural knowledge of man as a natural being and our knowledge, both natural and Scriptural, of the existence of God, reason and the idea of unity required that there be a precise gradation of existence between man and God. The angels, their existence affirmed by scripture and tradition, could be rationally analyzed as filling these grades in creation. So there are three hierarchies of angels, each containing three different orders. Saint Thomas' treatment of the angels is governed by logical necessity.

In all fairness we may compare this with a belief of many contemporary scientists and other educated people. Let us concentrate on this point. By current estimates there are 40 billion galaxies. Our own galaxy is said to contain 100 billion stars. The belief of true angelic magnitude is that before the Big Bang, which is astronomy's version of creation, all the material of the present universe, all the material of 40 billion galaxies each with something like 100 billion stars, was concentrated in an area the size of a pin point. Still further concentration resulted in the original explosion or Big Bang.[256] In this case the logic connecting contemporary data with the event must reach across a distance of 15 billion years. Modern conceptions of the stars are governed by the necessity of mathematical logic, quite as Saint Thomas's conception of Angels was governed by verbal logic.

The area of Saint Thomas' thought presenting the most significant obstacle to modern minds is his treatment of sex. The central proposition is that sexual pleasure, though not essentially evil in itself, is profoundly evil if it does not have procreation as its purpose.[257] There does not seem to have occurred to Saint Thomas the idea that there could exist between husband and wife a mutuality in which the spiritual attraction between persons grades imperceptibly into the physical union of male and

female. The pleasure of a union of persons becomes a pleasure of the union of bodies. Something of this sort would seem to characterize truly human sexuality. In such sexuality, procreation becomes a beautiful potentiality, not necessarily a deliberate goal. The absence of this notion in Saint Thomas suggests that he had not participated in a spiritual revolution under way in his time (which was described in Chapter 12).

The change began in the previous century.[258] It was an intensification and a personalization of religious passion and it involved a new emphasis upon the feminine, or as some would have it, a discovery of the feminine. In Christianity the shift was expressed in the new emotionalism of Saint Francis and in a impulse given to the cult of the Virgin. Saint Thomas was a major influence in the development of the cult of the Virgin, but his rationalism might seem to have insulated him from the emotional flowering initiated by Saint Francis.

In any event, it is the spiritual revolution of Saint Thomas's century which the Church must at long last fully assimilate. We may also hope that this assimilation when it does occur will draw from Saint Thomas the element of discipline which this revolution thus far has sadly lacked. It must also be added that while the spiritual revolution was an enrichment of the notion of love, it was chiefly Saint Thomas in whom love and the idea that God is love became an intellectually manageable conception. Aspects of his towering conception may be briefly suggested as follows.

Every form is incomplete because it is a part—a part of creation as a whole. In its incompleteness there is an implication of the complete, which is a potency for action. This potency is a power of causation. In the natural form of every thing there is an impulse to emulate the act of being by which it came into being. Hence God's causality is at work in all of creation. "Love," says Gilson, is the unfathomable source of all causality." Ours is a sacred world. Saint Thomas' appraisal of the world is, as Gilson says, a radical optimism.[259]

God is Love. That fundamental idea has resulted in much

sentimentalism and insipidity in popular notions of Christ and Christianity. In Saint Thomas Love becomes an awesome principle, a principle capable of equation with a mature and rational conception of God. Love, as the source of all causality, is a universal force at work everywhere in the universe. Whatever moves is moved by some kind of love. It is the principle that holds the universe together. Divine love is the divine willing of the good, which is being, coherence, unity. Hence, love is the act of creation. That act reverberates in all things. In all things there is a desire to imitate the creative power of God. In inanimate and unknowing creatures, this desire is unconscious. But it is "that same straining toward God which, with intelligence and will, blossoms forth into human morality."[260]

There are different kinds of love, one kind in inanimate things, another in knowing creatures. Ironically, the relevance of Saint Thomas is reflected when, at first blush, he may seem to have thrust us into the analytic cynicism of the twentieth century. He says that the first love is love of the self. Are we then fundamentally and correctly selfish, fundamentally unloving? Then we are told that love underlies all the other passions. We may seem to hear Sigmund Freud in this—love as eros, sex, unfolding in everything we do and feel. And there is this: There is a bent of all things to follow their nature, to permit that which they essentially are to flower into actual being; in inanimate things this is called *natural love*. In human beings, it means that, in a sense, Saint Thomas can share the highest law of Nietzsche, who declared the death of God and whose last published work during his life was subtitled *A Curse on Christianity*. This highest law is: Become what you are.[261]

In partial parallels with modern thought there are reflections of the complexity and subtlety of Saint Thomas's analyses. His meanings, however, are profoundly different. For Aquinas man must become what he is, he must realize his essential nature, because it is the essential nature of a reasoning being and reason is the token of the divine in man. Nietzsche's essential point

was that reason is totally illusionary and invariably erroneous. Man must become the basically intuitive and instinctive being that he is, the essential animal that he is.

For Saint Thomas, the love of our reasoning self for itself is the first love. It is this love that will develop in all other passions, but it will not do so as an animality sublimated in human illusions. It is love to begin with and it will grow in diverse forms, some of them resplendent. Charity and friendship are only variations of love.[262] In its full realization, the love of reason, the element of the divine in the self, will grow into the love of God.

Love is the movement of appetite toward a good. Love brings together. It is the agent of unity in the universe. Knowledge is also a bringing together, but the power of uniting is greater in love than in knowledge. It brings about a union between the lover and the loved. In love between persons there is a transference of personalities. Consequently we delight in the unity of resemblance, which is the product of love. Love is a taking pleasure in the good, but there is another object of love. This is the beautiful.[263]

Both the good and the beautiful are inseparable from being. They differ only in our response. In our experience of the good, the will comes to rest. It is satisfied. In the beautiful, it is the intellectual or sensible apprehension that comes to rest. Hearing or seeing are fulfilled in themselves. They do not create a further need and are not a step in the fulfillment of a further need. Yet, they are always a foretaste of an ultimate repose. By the act of love that is Charity, we come to repose in God. There is a transference. He is transported into us and we into Him. May we not say that in the love of God for man there is a transference of God into man, which is the Incarnation? In the Incarnation from the beginning we share the divine nature.[264]

In yet another way Saint Thomas provides support for the intellectual integrity of religion in the modern world. Reasoning in the modern world has no place for the concept of evil, which is taken to be irrational. In an extremely important way, Saint Tho-

mas agrees. The conception of evil that we find in his thought dispels ancient contradictions and puzzles; it redeems the world for rationality. For Saint Thomas, as for Saint Augustine before him, evil is an absence. All being is good. Man and the universe are touched with evil because as beings they are not complete, they are imperfect. The total creation as the act of being—which is God—is perfect. The parts of this creation do not share in the perfection of the whole. But all being strives for that perfection.[265]

Before moving to the heart of the thought of Saint Thomas we must make some careful preparations. Despite the wide area of common ground that Saint Thomas shares with modernity, we must be prepared eventually to enter with him into an intellectual realm totally foreign to the secular mind. We will be following an intellectual pathway toward, and almost arriving at, a miracle. We may begin by confronting two statements that will seem very strange:

Being is an act.

God is the Act of Being

These statements are not understandable—at least, not entirely or even largely so. Yet we will have to use them to reconstruct part of the edifice of Saint Thomas and we must not be confused about their nature. These are not statements that Saint Thomas pretends fully to understand. They involve a mystery. Remember that what Saint Thomas can say about God is restricted to evidence presented by what He has produced in the objectively observable universe. We know the Being of God only to the extent that He has acted in the creation and governance of this world. We can know His Being only in its Act. The beings created in this world emulate the nature of their creator and are thus mysterious except insofar as we can say that they involve an act.[266]

All being involves mystery and act. That being involves a mystery is the fundamental conception of what is fashionably called "deconstructionism," except that its proponents assume that the mystery is an error and can be eliminated. We cannot

proceed unless we are reconciled to what secular thought does not permit, the recognition of the authenticity of mystery. Note that the statements above are so abstract as to border on complete meaninglessness. They are statements of minimum intelligibility about the maximum possibility of knowing about God. The intellectual edifice of Saint Thomas is largely clear and understandable. But fundamental to it are these statements of minimum intelligibility.

Saint Thomas's thought can often be impressive to modern minds, but at first it seems to be profoundly alien. The projects and basic purposes of Saint Thomas and modernists are entirely different. For the secular world, knowledge is science; the purpose of science is to manipulate the physical world in service to the physical needs and appetites of men. For Saint Thomas, knowledge is theology and philosophy; its purpose is to serve the spiritual need of men. The purpose of modern science is to explain movement, the impinging on physical entities of other physical entities or the transformation of one condition of an entity into another condition. For Saint Thomas, as for Aristotle, thought has a prior and more important purpose; it strives, not primarily to explain things that happen in this world, but to explain existence, to explain our having being in the first place. Science explains happening, basic philosophy explains why there is something rather than nothing.

In the twentieth century the question of "being," after a long disappearance, moved once again to the center of philosophical thought. Modern existentialists were aware of the inherent human dependence upon the concept of being. They were concerned, nevertheless, to deny the validity of the concept. There was only becoming: we do not step in the same river twice. (With this conclusion philosophy foundered, at the beginning of its history, in the thought of Heraclitus five hundred years before Christ.) Heidegger, the most influential of twentieth century philosophers, took the restoration of the concept of being as his controlling concern. No one denies that, despite the richness of

this thought, in his central objective, he failed. His failure leaves the vacuum celebrated by "deconstructionists" and by contemporary nihilism generally. It would seem clear that in Saint Thomas we will find the only possible concept of being. Being is a mystery. In so far as we can understand it at all, it is an act.

All things are created and sustained in their existence by the divine Act-of-Being which is God. Hence ours is a world in which God is continuously present in His effects.

All creatures pre-exist in God, as a part of God, in the form of Ideas (of Platonic origin). In the created world the Ideas are the formative acts represented in concepts and universals that give intelligibility to the amorphous foundations of existence. So in the realm of existence, God is the supreme principle of intelligibility. God is both the creator and the principle. Things are, and we comprehend them, through a divine agency. We do not have a better explanation of being than this. This is the only explanation that we have.[267]

If we are seriously to entertain, though not to understand, the idea of being as act, the best we can do is to consider rationalizations that can help. There is a sense in which things come into being when they become a part of our world, or in other words, when we perceive them. Such perception is an act; it is not a passive response but involves an action. We may say, furthermore, that things—*as we perceive them to be*—do not come into being until we have perceived them. In this sense, what we are calling "the world" is created by an act. Aquinas conceives our perception in accord with this idea. Without pretending to understand a great deal about Being or God, Saint Thomas concludes that God is an act. But God is not simply Being, he is the Act of Being that creates and sustains all being.[268] In order to think, there must be something to think about. In order to think, we must begin with being. Thus the God of Saint Thomas sustains meaning and reality against all nihilistic logic. Nihilism is the conception of a universe and all language about it as totally meaningless. The basic nihilist argument is that the meaning of

language always assumes—erroneously—the existence of God. Saint Thomas would agree as to the role of language, insisting, however, that the assumption as to the role of God is wholly justified.

There is yet a more particular way in which God, in the thought of Saint Thomas, sustains reality against nihilistic despair. Let us recall for a moment the way we see things. There is first of all the naked physical object as it exists simply in itself. It is a shape, a color, a texture—these meaningless in themselves. In this phase of perception the mind is purely passive. Color and shape simply impinge upon our visual faculty. But to this basic event something is added. We never see only color, shape, and texture; we know that what we are seeing *is*, for instance, a bird.

Our minds have added something to the impressions received by our eyes. The mind has added the universal concept *bird*. Consequently the particular color, shape, and texture becomes *this bird*. We may add that in an opinion that is very wide-spread, the concept, the universal, is essential to human seeing; without it we could not see "this bird" at all. (See the description of the origin of consciousness proposed in Chapter 6.) Light from the shape and color of the bird would impinge upon our eyes as light detectors and the resulting impulse in our nervous system would be conducted to whatever centers of instinctive action might be relevant to this particular image. But we would not "see." All seeing is human seeing.

This conception of seeing, informed by the understanding of language, provides a useful approach to the way Saint Thomas conceived our seeing and our knowing. In both cases what we experience is a universal existing in conjunction with, melded with, the image of an object. By virtue of the universal we "know" what the object is. This object is not only colors and shapes. We recognize it as a bird because we have the concept of a bird.

For Saint Thomas, too, we recognize the object—the bird—because we have the concept of it. The great difference is that for him the concept, or the universal existing as a definition—of the

bird—exists both in our minds and–here is his fundamental idea–
in the bird. The universal, or the essence as definition, exists in
the bird. It is the *substance* of the bird, its most fundamental
reality. It exists also in our observing mind because the mind has
no form of its own. We simply become what we see. (I do not
think we can seriously deny that there is a measure of truth in
that.) Despite the differences, there is in the idea of substance a
rapprochement between Saint Thomas and linguistically informed
modern thought. Any probable spiritualization of our outlook will
move toward Saint Thomas. He maintains that the universal is
abstracted by the human intellect from the particular and concrete object. However, the power that abstracts the universal and
effects all human thought is not of a material nature.[269] Neither is
the form or the concept, the universal, that is abstracted from the
concrete form. These are elements of the divine in the human
and are part of our participation in divinity.

For modernist thought substance is solely a product of the
mind, a creation by language and therefore unreal. From the
point of view of scientific analysis, substance does not exist. We
are compelled to reject that position by insisting upon a shift in
the nature of reality. According to that shift (See Chapter 6), substance is all the reality we can truly know. In our conception
substances constitute the life-world, which exists, not "out there"
as part of existence independent of us, but as the realm of reality
arising between our conceptual power and external existence.

Here again we meet Saint Thomas. In his conception, substance is the heart of the being of the object itself.[270] Substance,
as he conceives it, is known only by the intellect: "Understanding penetrates to the essence of the thing, for the object of intellect
is 'what is.' He says, "For the substantial nature of things lies
hidden under the accident "[271] Substance, indeed, is the "proper
object" of the intellect.[272] And he makes a distinction crucial for
the Catholic faith. In the words of a distinguished commentator:
"Substance describes the core reality known to intellect, accidents [describe] whatever touches the senses."[273]

The accidents, as in the previous example, are the color and the shape of the bird; the substance is the conception and realization of "the bird."

We come within reach, then, of the basic doctrine of the Catholic faith, which was most meaningfully defined by Saint Thomas. The doctrine is that in the Eucharist the bread and wine become the body and blood of Christ. There has occurred, in the words of Saint Thomas, a *transubstantiation*. The *substance* of the bread and wine have become the *substance* of the body and blood of Christ. One may embrace with fervor the transformation of reality that has been insisted upon. Concepts, and the substances which constitute our reality, take their meaning from, and are part of, massive webs of connections in human memory.

The trivial conceptions of bread and wine are supplanted by a conceptual structure of great magnitude. Here is an enormous convergence of historical forces. The words of transformation spoken by the priest were uttered first by Christ on the eve his crucifixion, the bread broken, the wine taken in commemoration of his crucifixion on the morrow. They have been uttered daily throughout the world since the time of Christ. We commemorate here the most influential being in all of history and his bringing into the world a new way of being. The commemoration occurs in coherence with a place shaped by centuries of spiritual realization. At the altar where the priest presides, an ignominious death has been charged with victory. It stands firmly at the center of historical physical and intellectual ordeal during two thousand years. In memory, and in tacit memory, there is a gathering and pouring into the objects of bread and wine from endless centuries and from a centered and structured community co-extensive with the universe. We remember Christ. We commune with Christ's victory and become one with him. The Church, which we constitute, becomes the Body of Christ. The bread and the wine, at the center of the Church, become the Body and the Blood of Christ. By an intellectual movement we draw near to the miracle, which we can now believe and live.

Parts of Saint Thomas's conception of the natural world have been invalidated by modern science. A few aspects of his moral teaching we may find unpalatable. They correspond to those aspects of the Church that we hope to see transformed in time. On the other hand, we will inevitably be attracted by the close observation and the sustained brilliance of most of Saint Thomas' analysis. And none of our objections can obscure his abundant riches—the practical good sense, the generosity, the noble conception of humanity, the resplendent vision of human government and of the world, the certainty of the existence of God. These are part of the great civilization implicit in the religion of Saint Thomas and of the Church.

Chapter Fourteen

AT THE EDGE OF THE DESERT

We remain in the desert, approaching its limits, moving around the distant margins of the garden–for which we have as yet no adequate words. We will not be able to evoke spiritual reality. We will not know peace. Ours is a striving–peace the goal—but one to be achieved only by the individual when he, alone and on his own, has crossed the horizon to be envisioned. Our project has been to get a glimpse of the horizon. We must look again at the ground we have covered.

What is proposed is the ordeal of submission to a great but imperfect institution, which within our limited power we will attempt to change while acquiescing in the possibility that the change we wish for may not occur.

Faith, we come to realize, is not something that just happens to us. It is something that we do, but something for which we have lost the technique. We face a secular-sacred barrier. The barrier seems insuperable, but the far side of the barrier seems compelling. On this secular side ones sense of identity is weak and diffused, morality drifts into the nebulous. Truly basic questions are never defined. Yet there is a sense of virtue superior to the authority of any institution, and an illusory assumption of the possibility of moral perfection. On the spiritual side of the barrier goals are defined and there is a foundation from which to grow. There is the promise of answers. Right and wrong are based

on settled principles, and you must decide only the details. There is a strange sense of imperfection and yet an awareness of hope. And there is something unique; it is unimaginable as part of the secular condition. There is a warmth sustaining life.

The question is how to cross the barrier, how to enter another condition of being. How to leave behind the tedium, the sense of fatality, the monotony, the sterility of the physical and moral violence of modern culture.

Once the possibility of faith seems real, you recoil as from violence, appalled by the passing thought of sainthood, cringing from a perhaps overwhelming power. Then you are reassured by recognizing your self-flattery. At best, much less than sainthood will be achieved. And, as in nothing else, you will act in total freedom. And we can take heart because the crucial moment, the moment of acceptance if it occurs, will take place within the serenity, order, sanity, and security that is the achievement and meaning of Christianity and the Church.

We do not abandon the genuine gifts of modern history. Our positivistic habits of mind are very dear to us and bring us great benefits. In these habits of mind we share in the large intellectual enterprise of our time. It has achieved, through science, technology, and rational government, the amelioration of the human condition that has been the product of the heritage of seventeenth-century Enlightenment flourishing in the mind of the twentieth century. We must not sacrifice these habits of mind. We must not refuse to use them in every instance where we may perceive a real possibility of their fruitfulness. On the other hand we must recognize not only the limitations of these habits of thought, but also the devastation of the world resulting when they are adopted as a metaphysical system. They become such a system when they are assumed to be the exclusive key to existence. That assumption is an illusion.

In all the directions of which it is capable, the secular mind reaches limitations that are intellectually catastrophic. The analysis of philosophical logic ends inevitably in nihilism—a total

meaninglessness and the evanescence of reality. Pursuit of the inner nature of matter dispels reality by arriving where reason cannot follow. Truzn says of the electron, "It is pointless to speak of an electron's 'objective' reality, that is, of some reality that exists regardless of whether it is observed or not, because that reality can never be seized."[274] Outwardly, exploration of the astronomical universe arrives by superb mathematical processes at conclusions more absurd than the existence of angels as resident in the stars. We must be aware that this is the ultimate nature and fate of the secular mind if we are to find our way out of the darkness. Against the most stern prohibitions of modernity, we must believe that there are other than objective sources of knowledge. We know now that centuries of accumulated reasons against faith have lost their authority.

There are two secret truths—Nihilism and God. The processes that eliminate God lead inevitably to nihilism. On the way to nihilism, these processes eliminate not only God but everything else. The theological antithesis of nothing is being. In the light of the power of analytic reason, only God can warrant being. The fact is that analytic reason cannot get us to God or to being. Being without God does not exist. All reason is analytic and, left to itself, eventually eliminates being. Nihilism means that the processes that eliminate God eventually eliminate themselves. In order to reason we begin with being, and that requires the assumption that God exists. With that understanding, we stand on a new foundation for the comprehension of ancient truths.

Even in the play of nothingness, we recognize that spiritual revelation was not completed by the prophets of the Old and New Testaments and that all of history is process of spiritual revelation. We recognize, as a very special point, that the Protestant revolt and Modernism contribute to the revelation. The understanding of history as revelation is necessary for at least two basic realizations. The faith that history has delivered to us is at its heart what it has always been, but that central truth exists in a mode different from that which flourished in early centuries. It is

more fragile. It must be cultivated by different methods. It exists more exclusively in the registers of spiritual exaltation of which it has always been capable. It escapes from inevitably primitive ethnocentrism and embraces a conception of mankind that is totally comprehensive and totally generous. It achieves more fully and uncompromisingly the fullness of love as the foundation of the world.

The second crucially different characteristic of the faith that history has delivered to us is that it is uniquely difficult. In the earliest centuries faith was spontaneous. With extremely few exceptions, all human beings believed in God. They differed only in their conceptions of the divine. Faith, furthermore, was absolute. Men of faith were often more capable than we of the forgetfulness that secularized their world, but when they turned back to faith they turned to an unrelievedly literal and absolute faith. Faith in the modern world is more difficult. It is achieved only by an act of will, and the realization that we are co-creators of the world with God.

During the infancy of human history we conceived ourselves as totally free intellectual and moral agents. Our freedom was our primary reality. Then in the brief adolescence of our history—lasting only two centuries or so, while we assimilated science and technology—we conceived ourselves as captives and slaves, totally determined—all phenomena controlled by material causation, every moment of our lives governed by forces beyond our control. This was the conviction of all presumably educated people. The material universe lying outside of us and conceived as machine-like, a giant automaton, was our reality. Now we have come of age and understand the awesome result of our divine natures and our participation in God: we share responsibility for reality. In so far as we can know reality, it is not the reality that exists within us nor a reality outside, in our environment. The reality that we can know occurs between our inner being and the circumambient universe. The magic scrim that encircles us and evokes the totality of being is language. In the intermingling of language with the universe and with our souls lies reality.

Secular spirits confront the wasteland because they are intellectually alive, and they can cross it, but only by achieving first some basic intellectual changes. These are accomplishments for which our educations provide us no preparation whatsoever. Perhaps the first necessity is that we assimilate a proposition basic to truly vital philosophy from the eighteenth century onward and prevailing among the most significant thinkers of this and the last century. That proposition leads eventually to the realization that language is sacred.

In language we have discovered a primary tool of God in the creation of humanity, of the world, since in so far as we know, there is no world without the perception that language makes possible for humanity. From language we have a fundamental aspect of our world. A part of our basic knowledge is that there are realms and conditions in which the wheels of process are stilled and that these are the realms and conditions in which reality exists. The stillness here is inherent in consciousness. It is the condition that brought us and our world into being. Our knowledge of this stillness is part of our knowledge concerning our subjective nature and is inseparable from the grounds of our belief in God.

Despite all kinds of theological sophistication and the power of thought to delineate a world sustained by God, you cannot ever free yourself entirely of the modernist nightmare of a world totally controlled by material determinism. We must now achieve deliberately what for more than twenty thousand years of human consciousness we achieved intuitively. And we will be successful in only a limited way. After all intellectual effort, faith requires of you a leap of faith, an impassioned act of the will to believe. Having compelled your consciousness across the abyss of modernism, you will eventually discover the grace of God that led you to that leap of faith. You will discover that, as Kierkegaard told us, the desire for faith is faith.

The essential intellectual transformation is the relinquishment of the intellectual autonomy of the individual mind, thus

coming to the obeisance of the spirit essential to faith. This is an act of humility which is also an act of sacrifice. And yet this is the way of restoring to humanity the dignity with which we were created, the only way of sustaining faith in reality, in moral truth, and in reason. Beginning in the desert, we seek for God in fidelity to the human race.

One comes to the imagining and the embrace of the order of love. Love is the principle of unity. It holds all things together and sustains the being of all things in eternal fruitfulness. At the nuclear level, we must say, love is the "strong force," which binds quarks into protons and neutrons, and protons and neutrons together to form atomic nuclei."[275] At another level, love is gravity. In animal life it drives the sexual impulse uniting organisms for reproduction. Love is the principle unifying the elements of human sensory response—sound and light—to generate consciousness. Love informs every perception and invests the realm of human knowledge, making it possible. Then with the development of consciousness, love endows the moral and psychological individual—the individual as a spiritual being—with unity in which freedom is inherent and in which love is capable of being apprehended. The individual unified and free is not the prisoner of love. He is free to choose and choosing is always choosing for or against love. Love investing the world of all reality that we do not control, is capable of reigning, at our will, in human relationships. (How sad, how revolting, a culture that perceives sex as the limit and summation of love.) Love is the possibility of the redemption of humanity that we first fully knew in Christ. Evil is the absence of love.

We come to a crucial issue. One begins by cultivating an acquaintance with death. This is essential because you cannot proceed without achieving a cultural and historical negotiation of the conception of immortality. Because we are human and uniquely have the knowledge of death, we must think death. The secular alternative is a neurotic mindlessness, which is far more inconsistent with our sense of integrity than is a deliberate em-

brace of faith. But thinking death poisons life. To be faithful to
life we must somehow think, not death, but life, to the very end.
The belief in the immortality of the soul is what makes that possible. It is another belief that we do not understand and which
we must consign to the fringes of the mind. But there on the
fringes, deposited there by sacred words to be summonsed again
by words, the belief in life after death sustains the belief of life
during life.

It it quite possible, indeed, that you will be unable to believe
emphatically in the immortality of your soul. Andre Malraux said,
"The art of a living religion is not an insurance against death but
man's defense against the iron hand of destiny by means of a
vast communion."[276]And certainly such a vast communion is the
achievement of Christianity. It has been remarked how little the
founding thinkers of Christianity were concerned with immortality.

What you can and must believe is that the world and life are
good. What you can and must believe is that the Incarnation of
Christ is implicit in creation and that all existence is sustained
by God. If you are to believe in the divinity of Christ you do not
permit yourself to entertain that horrible nothingness that saturates the empirically conceived world and that is the metaphysical
expression of death. This death is in no way distinguishable from
your death as you can know it. **You cannot know your own death.
Your death is always the result of a logical projection, just as
is the nothingness of the empirically conceived world.**

The fundamental function of the image of the crucifixion is
to make familiar to you the paradox: **I both live and die.** This is
possible because life and death do not exist in the same realm of
being. So, without believing–that is to say, imagining literally–
that I will live forever, my affirmation of life and the world occurs
within a penumbra of immortality. Faith in immortality is not an
intellectual affirmation but a psychological regeneration. A fundamental move is to exorcize from your consciousness the basic
Protestant horror of the crucifixion, the image omnipresent in

Catholicism. This image saying that death is swallowed up in victory but that death comes first and is real is an image that you learn to love. It is the central image of the Christian faith.

Once the existence of God becomes really plausible, we arrive at three necessary propositions. First, the existence of God abolishes all logical limitations on what can happen in the universe. Second, we must exercise extreme caution and restraint concerning claims as to what has actually happened. Third, we cannot as individuals establish and maintain the caution and restraint necessary for social and intellectual order and are dependent upon an authoritative institution to fulfill that function. Both the health of society and the temper of the intellectuality by which we find God requires the arrival at an orthodoxy, which in the Christianity of the West only Catholicism maintains.

What must be envisioned is not a transformation that can be achieved by the violence of a rush of emotion. Nothing so orgiastic as a sudden conversion under the fire of evangelical zeal. Nothing quite so bloody as being born again. That is unquestionably possible in the realm of fundamentalism, but we must not pretend that as spiritual beings we live in democracy. The violent transformation that may occur in fundamentalism need not be questioned as to its spiritual authenticity, but neither may it be emulated by the intellectually mature. Something far more subtle is in the offing, a spirituality that invests an awesome world of great complexity. To sanction the explosive passion of revivalistic faith—to accept as real the experience of simple vulgarity—and not to be contaminated by it is part of the achievement of the quality of faith, fragile but intense, that is the only faith possible for modern spirits in the modern world. Spiritual realization for them cannot be an explosive escape from the darkness of individualism. A way that is led and monitored by the energy and discretion of deliberate thought must arrive at a serenity of worship and intellectual completeness. The spiritual goal achieved must have a history and amplitude of vision com-

We long for an enchantment of the world that will come to us without our asking and establish its reality by the passivity of our response to it. Our passivity, however, falsifies the world. Faith is the desire of faith, and such faith and desire are to be sustained by deliberate action. The deliberate verbal practice must be planned, organized, and continually executed. This is what occurs in prayer, which constitutes the practice of faith.

There is a certain absurdity in talking about spiritual things in psychological or political terms. Yet these are terms that we understand, and if we are to make progress toward spiritual realization, it is necessary that we begin here. We know that we cannot speak clearly about the ultimate effects of prayer. What we can say is that in prayer we come to a unique experience of wholeness and freedom. (We need only dare ourselves to try.) The wholeness and the freedom are part and parcel of each other. The worldly world—its demands, frustrations, shackles–all this drops away. We experience the only freedom we have ever truly known.

Prayer and thought are the same thing–a bringing together, a unifying, an effort for order. Thought denies God, and eventually it becomes clear that thought has lost is foundation. Thought is an extension of prayer; technological thought is a lower and relatively trivial range of prayer. In prayer we organize the material (language) that creates (through which God creates) the world to focus in the organization of the spirit.

One is soon aware that this form of speaking is like no other. All other speaking is accompanied by a quiet rage of personalities against personalities, a deep offense at the necessity of appropriateness, of tact, of adjusting to occasion, to place, and to the uncertainties of social relationships–a fear of refusal to hear, of misunderstanding, of failure to negotiate intended meaning, of danger–an ache of uncertainty and hope. All this has dropped away. The least that can be said about this–while standing only on the border of faith–is that you are speaking to the totality of things mirrored in your being.

In more primitive conditions this is done spontaneously. Our more elaborate consciousness makes it possible, and necessary, that we do this deliberately. History has put at our disposal the cultural tools for doing this. In our expanded creative powers we are more clearly now the children of God. The conception opens to us the possibility of prayer. Christ and the Church become available to us through prayer.

The primary form of prayer is ritual. Among the Western religious bodies, it is the Catholic Church that has fully preserved and perpetuated Christian ritual. This is not a distinction of style or taste. It is a fact of absolutely fundamental importance. This is worthy of great emphasis, for in the lives of most of us ritual has disappeared. A fundamental psychological and communal process has vanished. Even if we are immune to the lure of faith, most of us are capable of a certain nostalgia for ritual. In this we certainly learn something about ourselves.

When we look closely we discover that the relationship between ritual and religion is profoundly intimate. Religion is not a simple, straight-line sequence of inner processes and cannot be the secret, private experience of isolated individuals. Religion is a synthesis of multi-layered meaning. Ritual, too, is a synthesis of multi-layered meaning. We must attempt to discuss ritual, but we must do so with constant caution and an awareness of the inadequacy of the discussion. Any discussion of ritual is necessarily incomplete. Furthermore it must limit itself to dealing, one at a time, with its separate levels of meaning, and cannot hope to capture, or even clearly to suggest, the totality that is achieved by ritual. The Catholic Church is a total program of prayer.

The articulation of separate effects of ritual in the discussion which follows is deeply indebted to what is perhaps the most impressive exploration and analysis of ritual ever written. This is Roy A. Rappaport's *Ritual and Religion in the Making of Humanity*.[281]

Ritual, says Rappaport, is the basic social act.[282] It is, he argues, the activity giving rise to those characteristics of human-

ity that are not the product of exclusively biological evolution and that distinguish humans from animals–the characteristics of consciousness and culture, and eventually of the history and the civilization that is implicit and inherently potential in consciousness. Rappaport's thesis is spectacular as anthropology and of profound importance for the project being undertaken here, the engagement of religion as necessary, not only for our personal destinies, but to the regeneration and preservation of civilization. Rappaport says, "Religion . . . has been the ground upon which human life has stood since humans first became human, that is, since they first spoke words and sentences."[283] And, "humanity is a species that lives and can only live in terms of meanings it itself must fabricate in a world devoid of intrinsic meaning but subject to natural law."[284]

Ritual is not something that we listen to or observe. It is something in which we participate. It has fundamental consequences for faith. Belief is almost never complete or constant. Always there is at least a faint wavering, a seductive call of secularism. Ritual participation is an action that quiets that call, a commitment that confirms belief. The act is not hypocrisy; it expresses the desire for faith. It also signals ones solidarity with a community and enforces the effect of faith in ones self and in the community.

Ritual is an embodiment of what Rappaport calls "eternal sacred postulates." These are the values and the ethical principles and rules of conduct that hold society together. Thus ritual is a function of integration, cohesion, unity. In all human beings there are anarchic tendencies. This is inevitable because we are given multiple and sometimes conflicting selves by the differences in our kinds of experience. We live at different time and in different ways in different realms, for instance, in private, familial, or sexual realms, in a professional or occupational realm, and in public realms of shared experience. The participant "reaches out of his private self" into a public order.[285] What Rappaport calls the Ultimate Sacred Postulates, or the articles of

the religious creed, define the place of the private order within the social order. Thus ritual is a bridge between private and public realms.

We may describe the effect of ritual in psychological and physiological terms. Ritual reorganizes the individual's psychic structure. The left hemisphere of the brain, the "dominant" hemisphere, controls the linear processes of speech, discursive thought, and mathematics. It is concerned with movement. The right, "non-dominant," hemisphere is specialized for recognition of visual patterns, for images. It is specialized for space and stillness. It is sensitive to atmospheric and holistic embodiments of meaning; it is responsive to emotion, registering by unconscious processes, for instance, the meaning of facial expression. The effect of ritual is to bring the function of the right hemisphere into dominance, with its emphasis on stillness and wholeness. Within the entire nervous system there is an effect of the unification of opposites. Within the autonomic (non-volitional) nervous system there is a balancing of the sympathetic (contracting) system with the parasympathetic (expanding) system. The effect reaches into the viscera and the striated muscles creating an experience of unity and wholeness. There is a sense of harmony with the universe, of Oneness, of unity of the self with God. "The numinous and the holy," says Rappaport, "are thus rooted in the organic depths of the individual."[286]

Some might consider the foregoing introduction of psychological and neurological principles into sacred phenomena and experience to be a desecration, an emphatic denial of the holiness of the spirit. But not if they consider that as moderns we must first approach faith through byways laid down in secular thought. And not if they recall that the special faith first available to us insists that spirit arises from matter and that ultimate spiritual realization is the goal toward which the entire universe evolves.

The effect of ritual, says Rappaport, is what has been called "higher-order meaning."[287] It is distinguished from "lower-order

meaning," which simply observes distinctions and prefers one thing to another, for instance: *He was noble in his courage in battle.* There is also "middle-order meaning," which is achieved by metaphor: *He was a lion in battle.* In higher-order meaning one becomes identified with that which is other than oneself. This is achieved by an act of participation, either psychological or actual participation. Ritual is always more than symbolism. If we are mindful of the conception of reality inherent in the nature of language, then we may say something quite extraordinary. That which is symbolized in ritual becomes a reality in the course of the ritual. This is a psychological inevitability. Rappaport puts it this way: "The distance between signs, significata and those for whom they are meaningful may be greatly reduced, if not annihilated. . . . Meaning stops being referential, becomes a state of being. . . ."[288]

Ritual in its primal development always constitutes a cycle of rituals that occur throughout the year. This involves distinctions between sacred times and ordinary times. In the quickened tempos of ritual activity in sacred times, the participant loses himself in oneness with the community and escapes from the secular time in which he ordinarily lives.[289] There is rhythmic recurrence and repetition from one performance to the next, and the participant comes to know experience as never changing. In the repeated period of never changing experience, in recurrence, there is an implication of changelessness. There is an implication of eternity. Through ritual we come into spiritual knowledge. Ritual is religion.

The gift of consciousness as a twin-birth with language was attended by a deep discord, a disruption of animal unity. Ritual as rhythmic repetition of movement may have been the first essentially spontaneous effort to quiet this discord.[290] Ritual in generating the notion of the eternal may have been the basis for the discovery of the conception of God. Whether or not this is so, during most of the totality of human millennia the conception of God would be integrated through ritual with the limitless activity

of desire, ameliorating the pain of discord and directing and shaping the energy it generated as the source of all human achievement. Religion is inherent in the means by which we became human. Faith retains its power to assuage and to direct. It remains the only conclusive antidote to the particular pain inherent, not just in the human organism, but in the condition of human life.

Ritual organizes a total environment. A part of ritual is the place provided for its occurrence. In the Catholic Church we come into the center of a realm of total communication. This is dramatically true of the great Gothic cathedrals, and in greater or lesser extent, of all Catholic churches. The interior is covered with stone images of sacred persons and spiritual beings. The floor plan is laid out in the form of a cross. Holy beings are represented on inner walls and ceiling. Episodes of Sacred history are presented in stained glass windows in all the walls. The general proportions of architectural form and space are based on the intervals of Gregorian chant.[291] The enactment of the basic Sacred event occurs within the representation all at once of a Sacred cosmos.

Within that sacred realm you become part of a community. Here you do not find a group of people representing the solidarity of a class or a profession. Few of them are from the country club. Some of them may be your economic or intellectual superiors. In the pew in front there may be a nuclear physicist and, five isles forward, a professor of philosophy. The portly man adjusting the microphone at the pulpit may be a banker, the brilliantly dressed woman entering the sacristy a famous lawyer. You may also find that a great many here are in some sense your inferiors, economically, intellectually, socially. The man across the aisle may be a janitor or a shoe salesman rapt in the devout adoration of an extremely simple and literal faith. Sitting near him, in guardedly chaste dress, may be a fitfully repentant prostitute. Then there enters a frail girl of Mediterranean beauty with a gorgeous one-year old on her arm, and whenever she looks at the child she smiles. Behold Madonna!

Chapter Fifteen

A DESERT CATECHISM

The discussions throughout this book have been based on the hope for two kinds of transformation. One is social. The other is individual. The first is intellectual. The second is spiritual. Given the nature of the wasteland, the intellectual transformation is assumed to be essential to the spiritual transformation. However, the two possibilities are profoundly different. They exist in distinct ontological realms. For a number of fundamental reasons, the engendering of the spiritual transformation cannot be undertaken here. It cannot result from discursive, intellectual processes. A spiritual transformation can result only from an act and a practice. This means that an authentic spiritual transformation must occur under the tutelage of the Church. It lies essentially beyond my authority. It is unquestionably true that in a larger sense the intellect is a part of spiritual reality, and I will presume to express a single spiritual truth in religious language. The essence of the meaning of Jesus Christ is contained in the prayer of Pierre Teilhard de Chardin: "Grant us to recognize in others, Lord God, the radiance of your own face." In anything more than this, concrete evangelization is necessarily beyond the purview of the effort here.

What may be achieved here is a desert catechism. It may be compiled from the chapters that have gone before. It is about organizing possibilities that exist within the desert. It does not

attempt to achieve religious redemption but only what can be accomplished toward redemption within our condition of desolation. The effort is necessary only because we are denizens of the desert and marked by the desert. The process envisioned does not become faith. It is concerned with the discovery of a movement specifically antecedent to and propaedeutic to the embrace of faith.

The secular process moving toward faith begins when you affirm and take to heart the following:

++ Despite the prevalence of luxury, comfort, and physical well-being, Western culture undergoes a degeneration which moves toward putting to sleep all that is distinctively human.

++ You are implicated in the prevailing cultural degeneration.

++ The despair you feel at the condition of the culture results from a fundamental identification with humankind which is a part of the sense of decency inherent in your nature and is the basis for the expectation that you will act.

++ Regeneration of the culture cannot begin with social programs. Regeneration of the culture must begin with regeneration of individuals.

++ It follows that any hope you entertain for the culture requires that you undergo a transformation of yourself of the kind that is necessary for the transformation of the culture.

Redemption of any kind begins with recognition of the forces definitively shaping our culture:

++ The flourishing of scientific knowledge and technological development has brought enor-

mous physical benefits but has fostered and
made virtually to prevail materialistic assumptions that despoil the spiritual and ethical foundations of civilization.

++ In the absence of spiritual and ethical values
sustaining democracy, purely political influences
have prevailed. Competition of interests has made
of equality the single value at work in society.

Due to our cultural desolation, the first basis for hope depends upon challenging the ultimate authority of reigning cultural
assumptions:

++ The mode of knowledge peculiar to science and
technology is a very great human achievement,
but a very late development and entirely inadequate to maintaining cultural vigor. This mode
of knowledge depends upon the cultivation of
passive reception of the impress of the physical universe. The inevitable goal of such knowledge is the illusionary possibility of total understanding.

++ Science within its own domain has revealed
areas in which its limitations become apparent, in nuclear mechanics, in mathematics, in
the principle of non-locality, in Foucault's pendulum, and in the obvious extravagance of some
of the aspects of the scientific theory of the
origin on the universe.

++ Scientific reports about the nature of the universe are abstract and therefore necessarily incomplete.

++ The hope of total explanation is based on the
illusion that we can stand apart from the universe in order to observe it.

++ If science could present what it would consider a total explanation, an explanation of everything, there would remain the fundamental
question, "Why is there something rather than
nothing?"

Once aware of the limitations of the explanatory power of
science, we become aware of the mistake of confusing science
with metaphysics and find necessary a more inclusive conception of human knowledge:

++ While science is defined by the effort to exclude the influence of human subjectivity from
knowledge, all the meanings associated with
science are in fact imposed upon its findings
by subjective knowledge.

++ The aspiration of science to total explanation of
the universe assumes the unity of the universe,
an assumption which underlies the basic impulse
of all distinctly human effort and of all science
and is a component of human subjectivity.

++ All meaning is subjective knowledge.

++ Consciousness is the uniquely human condition
of knowing. When we realize that it is language
that generates consciousness, we understand
that, both in ways of which we are unaware and
in other ways of which we are aware, we create,
not only scientific knowledge, but all knowledge
that is not simply the instinctive recording of
animal experience. All human knowledge is ultimately subjective knowledge.

++ To deny the authenticity of values and meaning because of their purely subjective source
would be to embrace nihilism and to repudiate
civilization.

++ We maintain a primitive expectation that reality is something certain and permanent. We realize, however, that neither in the science-world reported to us in the mathematical abstractions of science, nor in the life-world which is brought into being by language, do we find reality so conceived. Reality as habitually and almost universally conceived within a secular frame of references does not exist.

The life-world, however, is not only the world that science must observe before its abstract operations can begin. It is the world in which all meaning is derived and which all meaning is about. A transformation of life that proceeds from nihilism to meaning requires an imagination trained to turn to the life-world as its basis of reality. Thus science relinquishes its domination of the human intellect.

++ Fully aware of our basic human function in the creation of all knowledge and all meaning, and deeply committed to our identification and alliance with humanity, we necessarily assume responsibility for creating the meaning that sustains civilization.

We must assume that the secular mind, except when idle and absent-minded, begins in the dead center of nihilism. The movement away from that deathly nothingness begins, not with an idea but an act. It begins in need and an act of will. It is an act of audacity and rebellion. Violating the most severe strictures of secular dogma, it is prepared to look into the relationship of religion to human life:

++ The impulse to unity basic to the human mind and compelling all rational processes is fundamentally a religious element inherent in our nature.

++ For the human animal, unlike other animals, instinct is inadequate for survival.

++ The survival of human beings requires that rational and mythic processes augment the resources of instinct. Meaning is part of the survival equipment of human life.

++ The images and motifs that are the building blocks of religions are the universal product of human subjectivity and basic mythic formulations persist across the gamut of human cultures.

++ In the absence of formal religions, human beings inveterately invent faiths, which, in the absence of institutional controls, take the form of cultural deformities which have pernicious effects on civilization.

++ All thinkers seriously concerned about the direction of modern culture see religion as the only force capable of stemming the drift toward the dissolution of Western civilization.

++ The embrace of religion becomes a fundamental social responsibility.

++ Astronomical knowledge encourages a speculation propitious for faith: The mythic formulations that are universal in human cultures reflect the impress of the universe as a whole on the human organism and psyche. Affirmation of this proposition is a key to the possibility of faith. It is the fundamental goal of the leap of faith that Kierkegaard saw as necessary for religion in the modern world. It is the appropri-

ate subject of Pascal's wager. Granted this leap
and this wager, the embrace of specific religious faith follows easily.

Once the modern mind finds that religion conceived in a
general way is intellectually permissible, there remains the question of the specific religion that is to be embraced:

++ A number of the major religions can prove re-
warding for the individual, but a religion representing an exotic culture can only contribute further to the atomization of the West. Only
a religion integral with the culture can generate the unifying effect necessary for general
cultural regeneration.

++ Whether we consider the fact from a secular
perspective or a spiritual perspective, Christianity is the anti-entropic element of the
West.

Once Christianity is seen as the only religion likely to serve
the stability of Western culture, there remains the question of the
form of Christianity to be embraced:

++ There is a single center of permanence in Western civilization, and while all else has been in
constant change, this center has not changed
in the two thousand years of its history.

++ In the Western world a single institution has
survived without essential dissolution and for
two thousand years this institution in so far as
its influence has not been opposed has been
the surety of all other institutions.

++ The Roman Catholic Church is the institution
which has most effectively resisted the divi-

sive and centrifugal forces inherent in Western civilization.

++ While Christianity is alive for many individuals in any number of the twenty-five thousand Protestant denominations, the Roman Catholic Church is uniquely the institution in which Christianity is sustained unequivocally and without reservation.

++ The Church is uniquely capable of constituting a counter-culture in a postmodern world. In its world-wide magnitude and in its spiritual integrity the Church is the institution most obviously capable both of sustaining the principles of the sacredness of the individual and of rationality underlying democracy and, at the same time, resisting the forces of deterioration inherent in democracy.

++ The social programs of the Church make it clear that cultural conservatism does not require political individualism and the fostering and protection of greed and special interests.

++ Current controversy concerning extremely important aspects of the Church constitutes an ordeal the resolution of which can be greatly facilitated by the enlistment of superior intellects within the powerful ranks of the creative spirits already within the Church.

Modern culture is contaminated by an attitude associating the Church with evil of almost mystical intensity. This illusion is dispelled in the light of certain realistic considerations:

++ When culpable actions within the Church are frankly described, they emerge as the kind of

tianity. What you are capable of at this point is the embrace of a new history of the universe, one based on the "special faith" with which this book began, a faith consistent with modern knowledge:

Stardust, in pilgrimage through eons, gave rise to the earth and a flourishing of organic energy. The sacred gift of language to the most sentient of animals generated the twin birth of the world and man. The deployment of the world and the awakening of man in consciousness created in humanity a profound unease. There existed not only what is present in the here and now. For a single organic purpose, there existed all at once a wild multiplicity. No longer was the animal organism free to organize itself in response, one at a time, to a few things attuned to basic animal appetites. In the clustering of all things in the essential contemporaneousness of consciousness, human appetite was fragmented, directed to all things, and satisfied by none. There was born what we call desire. It is the impulse to unity, born in the stars, that drives all human effort, all thought. It leads us imperatively to the total unity that is God.

The necessity of unity is the necessity of being, which is implicit in stardust and which transcends the processes of brute reality and requires a fulfillment beyond them. Thus in the earliest sacred powers of history we discovered conceptions of God. These conceptions were elementary at first, but also divine in a way proportioned to the stage of the advance of history. God was first the God of a people. Within the collectivity the practices restraining the otherwise chaotic energy of humanity and serving their survival were sanctified and sustained by the deity. The interests of peoples came into conflict and their diverse God-centered cultures invested them with enmity to each other. War became the substance of history, and God became a hope of protection demanding harsh disciplines and anguished loyalties amidst menacing catastrophes, human and natural. God was then

fearful and remote, the God of a dangerous world, a God of emergencies and war and a God competing with other Gods.

With the growth of cities and civilizations, there was a multiplying of intellectual energies. The divine drive to unity in the human soul arrived, in different cultures, among different people, at the necessary singleness of God. And yet this single God remained, in each case, the God of a people, remote and fearful. Then distinct and different peoples disappeared and were diffused with each other under the canopy of a single great power. In the revelation of Christ, God became the God of all people as they became part of the great unity of Empire. Such a God, ceasing to be a God of war, became a God of love. The divine process of history revealed a God for all humanity, and a God nourishing the inward and separate spirituality of individuals. This God of love was understood as an incarnation of the principles structuring all existence.

The souls of men–their intellects and imaginations—were drawn to a God of love.

Their love was allowed to grow in a hunger of knowledge, which is desire and the universal impulse to unity, which is a correlative of the principle of love uniting all things in themselves and with all things. Assured in the unity of God, minds turned to seek that unity in the world. They incorporated with the God of love the visions, first one and then the other, of the unity of all of the created world. These visions had been achieved by divine personalities in a spiritual reign of the impulse to reason. The first of these visions, that of Plato, saw the key to the universe focused in the internal nature of human beings. The second vision, that of Aristotle, saw the all inclusive unity in the assemblage of the totality of external things. The subjectivity of Plato and the objectivity of Aristotle became the polarity of the dialectic movement of mind. The divine revelations in Plato, Aristotle, and Christ joined in the soul of Western civilization.

Knowledge and its pursuit—which are forms of love–were, in the Renaissance, accompanied by the glorification of man.

Then in the Enlightenment, the pursuit of knowledge became the deification of reason and of man. Thus reason, prior to brief Romantic interludes, was poised for the destruction of itself and the denial of man in the nineteenth and twentieth centuries. The march of science was accompanied philosophically by a rising bacchanalia of positivistic negation. Reason spiraled into the abyss of nihilism. Abetted by science, reason despoiled its foundation and revealed its dependence, for its very content, upon God. Finally we arrive intellectually empty handed—with many things but with no knowledge whatsoever.

The nadir of our intellectual failure is simultaneous with social catastrophe. In society as in the intellect, materialism ravages all value, and profit-taking usurps the ancient function of cultural formation and direction. In the centrifuge of social organization, all differences are dissolved. The structures engendering discipline and aspiration give way to universal autonomy and total equality. Physical beings are nourished and given cures and prophylactic protection while the conditions essential to mind and to human effort disappear. We contrive to sustain the species in conditions of comfort and deadening satisfaction prejudicial to the continuity of man. Our direction is toward sleep.

Bearing with us a cargo of political baubles and technological conveniences, we come, in spiritual poverty, at long last prepared to throw ourselves upon the mercy of God–if there is a God. We begin to look more curiously at ourselves. Then we discover something quite startling. Each of these human beings is, indeed, authentically individual and unique, but in their very vividness and in the power of their clamor, each for recognition of his individuality, they conceal something. They belie the awesome and invisible matrixes of which each is a product and inextricably a part, the matrixes, the enveloping and generating continuities, first of all, of galaxies and language.

Discovery that we are not autonomous observers of everything else, but that like everything else we are embedded in an

infinite universe of being and that the whole presses upon us, engendering the chemistry of our organisms, coloring our passions, populating our souls—this is the beginning of the realization that we are a part of God.

This is the first necessary movement of the psyche. The universe of which we are a part is not dead. It is limitlessly creative. We participate in that creativity. The universe that created us speaks through us in terms and figures attuned to our being and endowing existence with meaning. We are embodiments of the word, the logos, the principle of the structure of all being. We discover that the purest and most absolute incarnation of that universal principle occurred two thousand years ago. In that incarnation we understand the necessity for our souls of incarnation, that they cannot survive on abstractions, for abstractions can never be more than partly true. As we are an embodiment of the principle of the totality of being, we can survive spiritually only by the response of our whole being. Our souls are not only intellectual. They must see and hear and feel.

In Christ subjective and objective reality came uniquely together. The truth of Christ is an infinite complexity that is invariably betrayed by individuals and separatist groups practicing the authority of God in their usurpation of his autonomy. The effect is the endless division, fragmentation, and eventual vitiation of spiritual reality. Only an institution integral with society, and thus with the spiritual whole, can sustain with fidelity the revelation of Christ. The Roman Catholic Church filled that role for sixteen centuries and in its character confirmed by the sacred processes of history prefigures the possibility of a society restored to wholeness.

Of such a society we have at least a Platonic memory and can articulate a hope. In so far as influence of Christianity and the Church are effective in society, their purpose and effect, will be a decency which, in the presence of contemporary popular culture, is almost beyond imagination. The aim will be

> at raising the intellectual tone of society, at cultivating the
> public mind, at purifying the national taste, at supplying true
> principles to popular enthusiasm and fixed aims to popular aspi-
> ration, at giving enlargement and sobriety to the ideas of the age,
> at facilitating the exercise of political power, and refining the
> intercourse of private life.[292]

Implicit in such a hope is the possibility of prayer—and a profound need. As a turning point in ones life, one decides, in silence, with much tentativeness, to speak, while attempting to entertain as reality, the possibility that there is a hearer. What you will come to know, privately, and in the solemnity of the ritual of Christ, is not to be touched by discursive language. Evangelical passion and missionary rhetoric can do nothing for you. You are not to expect a sudden transformation, a conversion of orgasmic intensity. But knowledge sets you free. Modernity, after ravishing the world of meaning has arrived at unquestionable authentication of faith. On the edge of the desert, knowledge and reason can do no more. The need must do the rest. The faith needed now proceeds, not by thought, but beyond thought and into an act.

APPENDICES

APPENDIX A

The Arguments for "A Special Conception of God"

The articles of faith for which arguments are presented here are to be found in Chapter 1, pages 21 through 27. The arguments are numbered here to correspond to the articles of faith as they appear in the text.

Let us begin with a statement of **"What we know."** For the most part, we will use generally accepted scientific findings alongside formulations drawn from and coherent with the best of modern philosophy and modern psychology. None of the statements of what we know is inherently at discord with science or the scientific assumptions of secular philosophy. They are products of the rational intellect and are based on the assumption that the rational intellect is the only and sufficient source of all the knowledge that we may affirm. Eventually, however, it must be assumed that knowledge resulting purely from the rational intellect may be entirely valid but incomplete.

Following each statement of "What we know" will be a statement under the heading, **"What we may believe."** It is not assumed that what we may believe is implied by what we know, only that it is consistent with this particular part of what we know. We must assume that knowledge that is complete is the result of the rational intellect but only as it is informed by the totality of our being. It follows, therefore, that while adhering as faithfully

as possible to the statements of what we know, we will adopt an assumption of which they are oblivious. Our analysis assumes that there is a God. Any discussion of religion that does not begin with this assumption is either intended to deny the authenticity of religion or it is inane. Therefore it must not be assumed that anything that follows is intended as a proof of the existence of God, which is impossible.

[1] THE NOTHINGNESS WHERE WE FIND GOD

What we know: Death is an endowment of life with various meanings, but they are never enough; they do not justify death. Indeed, its wild irrationality produces our demand of an ultimate meaning. Yet in its ravenous oblivion it underlies all our inquiry. We dig continuously toward it. In our omnivorous analyses, the reality of every entity abdicates to the entities making it up, and these in turn disappear into the entities making them up, all ending eventually in disappearance—an ultimate nothingness, which seems the inevitable goal of peculiarly human knowledge.

What we may believe:—The limit of our knowledge in nothingness is an uncrossable border within the incomprehensible immensity and power from which we are derived. Having arrived at this immensity, we realize that this too is given us. The nothingness we face is the frightening denial of our omnipotence. What we really face are our limitations and the immensity that lies beyond them—the unutterable, the incomprehensible, from which we come. Acknowledging this monstrous ambiguity as our origin, we come—in our ultimate capacity for acceptance—into a new transcendence. We draw upon something in us that eternally affirms, saying always finally "Yes." And reconciliation to the abyss beyond our reach is a movement in the love of God. (Here and in all that follows the word "transcendence" we will be used to designate a function, or realm, or characteristic lying beyond the reach of knowledge that assumes that human beings can be explained in purely animal terms.)

[2] MATTER AND SPIRIT

What we know: Consciousness arises from matter and is a product of both cosmic and organic evolution.

What we may believe: With the noble pagan philosopher, George Santayana, we can say, "It is a prejudice to suppose that spirit is contaminated by flesh; it is generated there."[293] Man is the transcendence toward which cosmic and organic evolution of the past has moved, and, as an instance of a higher transcendence, we represent the goal toward which the universe evolves.

[3] SPIRIT IN MAN

What we know: Man comes into being when the dawn of consciousness occurs in the evolutionary process. Before that there existed, not man, but his predecessor, an extraordinarily adaptable animal. Consciousness is the revelation of the existence of things and the relationships between them that constitute the world. Consciousness driven by language builds the noosphere—the enormous structures of knowledge overlaying the meaningless body of physical existence and constituting the realm of man and spirit. These structures are science, art, morality, values, government, religion. They are all institutions, all meaning. Consciousness is life as human beings know it. Man is consciousness.

At the turn of the century intense scientific effort to explain consciousness has totally failed. The study of consciousness presents one extreme and most unusual difficulty. Whatever may be the explanation that we propose, we are envisioning a causal mechanism that lies outside consciousness, but we can know consciousness only from within it. So we can never have a perspective in which we witness the conjunction of cause and effect. Everyone is agreed that it has another most unusual characteris-

tic, which is that it is not like anything else. Unlike everything else, there is no category of which it is a part. Science cannot deal with such a characteristic. For this reason, certain scientists, although dedicated to explaining consciousness, have declared that its failure to fit a category is a "trivial" fact and can be ignored. A few "cognitive scientists" have resorted to the extreme measure of declaring that consciousness does not exist.[294]

What we may believe: Man is consciousness. Beginning with the assumption that there is a God, we are free from the obligation to observe certain scientific discretions, which, in fact, we may interpret as evasions. The impossibility of the conjunction of a conceivable cause with the effect of consciousness, we will recognize as a mystery. In this, as in the other most unusual characteristic of consciousness—its failure to fit any category—we will not hesitate to see that which is unique. Human beings are unique and every individual is unique. Only human beings have and are produced by history. Every individual is the result of a unique history. Furthermore, every consciousness exists only once and is utterly irreplaceable. It is known only by one being. Later we will see another measure of the uniqueness of the individual. And, indeed, the notion of the unique is the notion of a miracle. The basic assumption of science is that there is nothing unique.

Assuming that there is a God of some kind, we will conclude that consciousness is spirit. Spirit in man is as described by Santayana: "By spirit I understand the light of discrimination that marks . . . differences of essence, of time, of place, of value; a living light ready to fall upon things as they spread out in their weight and motion and variety, ready to be lighted up. Spirit is a fountain of clearness."[295] Consciousness is a freedom. In consciousness, we stand outside the brute imperatives of *this time* and *this place:* other times and other places supply us with programs for possibilities of escaping the power of this time and this place. Every freedom is a transcendence. Consciousness is the first human transcendence and basic to all other human transcendence.

[4] OUR INHERENCE IN THE WHOLE

What we know: Modern philosophy and its conception of science begin with Descartes in the early seventeenth century. Without putting it in so many words, Descartes thought of the scientist as enjoying the eye-view of God. The scientist stood entirely apart from the universe and was capable of viewing the whole of it. Capable of viewing the whole, he could eventually explain it all. This was the hope of the autonomy of science, that hope that science could in effect become God by explaining everything. The Cartesian assumption prevailed for almost three hundred years. The trouble with the assumption was that it omitted something terribly important, as we now belatedly understand. In its perspective on the universe it omitted the observer.

Most people of secular mind continue in Cartesian complacency, quite confident that everything can be explained and oblivious of the fact that in the twentieth century science has discovered radical limitations on human knowledge. A number of things lead to this conclusion. For instance, when the Faustian, God-pretending project of total explanation would seem to have pressed nearest to its goal, it fails. This occurs in the field of quantum mechanics, in which physics attempts to deal with ultimate particles of matter. In quantum mechanics, there occurs this strange phenomenon.[296] Two photons are emitted from the same material in such a way as to assure that they exist in entire separation from each other. One of the photons is polarized. Then, despite the total absence of any means of communication between the two photons, the second changes to reflect the polarization of the first. This phenomenon is known as "nonlocality," meaning that an effect has occurred in absence of the conditions for causation required in the terms of Newtonian physics. It is a violation of common-sense, the common sense with

[6] THE SEARCH FOR GOD

What we know: Consciousness is a disruption of the unity of the organism with that from which it emerges, and it is permanently stricken with a memory of unity which becomes an imperative. The impulse to unity drives all consciousness, shaping all things seen and making possible every conception. It is essential to the principle sustaining all reality.

What we may believe: Our unceasing and inherent drive for unity is essential to sustaining the reality of the world and is eventually a search for, and an expression of a need for, God.

[7] THE SPIRIT IN HISTORY

What we know: At the very beginning of human experience, as knowing and awareness begin more and more to overlay intuitive patterns of animal life, consciousness is engaged in two kinds of activities, each at first very limited. On one hand there is a small area of partial control. Here rudimentary tools are produced by elementary technique combined with ritual, which primitive man does not distinguish from technique. There is a much larger area where control is essentially problematic; it hardly exists at all. Here another kind of production occurs, propagating images and narratives which objectify human response to an obscure but powerful sense of awesome powers. History accomplishes the development and elaboration of these areas. The area of technology is expanded and, eventually, becomes independent of ritual and presumed supernatural power. The area made up of myth and ritual is incorporated with an expanding and diversified range of community affairs. Within history evolution continues to produce an ever expanding world increasingly subject to rational understanding and direction, or, in other words, a world of increasing freedom.

What we may believe: The growth of human knowledge from the beginning of consciousness onward is a growth of freedom, which is to say, an expansion of humanity and transcendence. Development both in technology and in the realm of meaning is an expansion of the human spirit.

[8] DEEPENING OF THE HUMAN SPIRIT

What we know: The unceasing impulse to realize unity is the human effort to make sense of things. Every expansion of freedom and humanity makes possible an amplification and intensification of the conception of the principles at work in the world. The drive to unity succeeds again and again—only to have its imaginative achievements denigrated, yet giving rise always to ever more complex, more inclusive, and more nearly adequate conceptions of the universe.

What we may believe: Every expansion of secular knowledge throws into question accepted conceptions of God, makes possible an expanded and more complex conception of the creative principles at work in the world, and results in an enriched and intensified knowledge of God. Though we achieve increased subtlety and sophistication, there remains inherent in our nature an expectation of an ultimate unity and a cosmic consummation.

[9] THE SOURCE OF MEANING

What we know: The history of science was inspired from the beginning with a notion of arriving eventually at some fundamental truth. That hope came very gradually to complete disappointment. We now recognize that science and objective knowledge generally produce only facts. The march of science and empirical philosophy finally reveals to us, if only by default, that all meaning has subjective origins, which is to say, it emerges from sources within the organism.

What we may believe: All meaning emerges as forces internal to the human organism shape the character and value of objective knowledge. All essential knowledge is subjective knowledge. In so far as our minds permit of the conception of God, we find the evidence of His existence within ourselves.

[10] JUSTIFICATION OF GOD

What we know: Being and nothingness are inseparable conceptions and except for the existence of both being and nothingness consciousness could not have come into being.

What we may believe:—The inseparability of being and nothingness does not prevent our attempting to combat the existence of evil in the world, but it provides a basis for ultimate acceptance of the will of God.

[11] MEANING AND DEATH

What we know: Every consciousness within cultures later than the most primitive comes into the realization that at some point it will no longer be. This is knowledge of a most uncommon sort. In all other reliable knowledge there is a comprehension in which both intellectual and intuitive factors are at work. We comprehend both with our intellect and with our senses. In the knowing of an object there is at work both a conceptual and a physical recording of a kind that is called a "representation," and in all our abstract ideas there are present both intellectual and, to a lesser degree, sensuous elements. The knowledge of our death is unusual in that there is a conception and no image whatever. We can imagine dead bodies; we can imagine dying, but we cannot imagine death. The conception is totally conceptual and totally negative. It is the conception of the absence of our consciousness, a condition for which we have a logical con-

struct—we can formulate it verbally—but we cannot imagine it. To imagine it would be not to imagine; it would be to die. To this we have an intuitive response, indeed, but it is not an intuitive comprehension. It is a rejection, a revolt. In the absence of immediate danger, a purely conceptual experience. This conceptual experience is possible only in the condition of consciousness separating the organism from its animal nature and yet it elicits the most basic of organic responses, the stirring of the instinct for survival. In human experience, this now distinctly human instinct organizes life as it does for no other being. It shapes all conscious planning of our lives. It creates time—and limits it, giving rise to all our urgencies, giving meanings to each of our affairs. Most importantly, we come to perceive also that the death of each of us is peculiarly ones own. Death, as Martin Heidegger says, "individualizes." "Death is Dasein's *ownmost* possibility. . . . Here it can become manifest to Dasein that in this distinctive possibility of its own self, it has been wrenched away from the "they."[298] (For Heidegger' s *"Dasein,"* read *"the individual"* or *"consciousness."*)

What we may believe: From consciousness there emerges an experience unique within the universe that we know about. It is another measure of transcendence. Our distinctive knowledge of death is the incontestable guaranty of our individuality, that is to say, the absolute uniqueness of each of us. We begin to realize that death is part of the gift.

[12] TRANSCENDENCE AND DEATH

What we know: I will now string together a number of statements paraphrasing passages in Heidegger, who is the most influential philosopher of the century and who insists that his is not a religious philosophy.

I can observe dead bodies, but I cannot experience the death of others. I can experience my own death only in the knowledge,

while I live, that I will die. Consciousness becomes a whole only by coming to an end, but there is no way of knowing the end. Consciousness can never know death; it can know only that it is dying. In all other conditions I am related to other people and other things. Confronting death I am in utter solitude. Whatever possibility exists in this confrontation is peculiarly my own. The common attitude toward death is a condition of denial, but this is a denial that never quite succeeds. It involves the debilitating compromise of a lie. But there is a different possibility. The individual becomes an individual and achieves his authenticity as an individual in the "resolute anticipation," the unwavering acceptance, in effect, the approval of his death. The affirmation of our death achieves an ultimate freedom and is attended by a deeply felt joy.[299]

What we may believe: Thus we may come to a singularly human achievement. We come into the power of consent—and something more than consent—the power of willing our death as part of the abundance of life. In this transcendence we free ourselves of the prison of animality. We have a foretaste of total freedom.

[13] LOVE AND OUR ORIGIN

We falsify and betray our majestic origin unless we live in awareness of it. Forgetfulness is abandonment to oblivion in the midst of being. Confronted with the incommensurability and power that are our origin, we must choose between forgetfulness or an embrace which is part of the coherence of the whole of things that is called love.

APPENDIX B

Modern Knowledge and the Loss of Meaning

All knowledge is attended by certain assumptions. Modern secular knowledge—most of the knowledge constituting university courses, for instance—attempts to be as scientific as possible and carries with it the assumptions of science. There is nothing wrong with science in itself; it has brought us innumerable benefits. The harm that is done by science is the result of mistaking its working assumptions for ultimate truths, as constituting a metaphysics. Even without formulating those assumptions, good students assimilate them. It is therefore of extreme importance that students be made aware of those assumptions. This is the first step necessary to avoid imprisoning young minds by destructive and unintended metaphysics.

Central to science is the idea of causation, and the practical and virtually spontaneous conception of cause is that inherited from David Hume and elaborated and defined by John Stuart Mill. The assumptions associated with this conception of cause are empiricism, materialism, and determinism. These assumptions are the form in which the state in refusing to provide essential philosophical correctives to the implications of secular knowledge invades the realm of faith. I will elaborate these assumptions in a series of simple propositions, numbering them for reference as we go. The argument will show how a few simple ideas can

APPENDIX C

NICENE CREED

We believe in one God
the Father, the Almighty,
maker of heaven and earth,
of all that is seen and unseen.
We believe in one Lord, Jesus Christ
the only Son of God,
eternally begotten of the Father,
God from God, Light from Light,
true God from true God,
begotten, not made,
one in Being with the Father.
Through him all things were made.
For us men and for our salvation
he came down from heaven: *All bow*
by the power of the Holy Spirit
he was born of the Virgin Mary,
and became man.
For our sake he was crucified under Pontius Pilate;
he suffered, died, and was buried.
On the third day he rose again
in fulfillment of the Scriptures;
he ascended into heaven
and is seated at the right hand of the Father.

He will come again in glory to judge the living and the dead,
and his kingdom will have no end.
We believe in the Holy Spirit, the Lord, the giver of life,
who proceeds from the Father and the Son.
With the Father and the Son he is worshiped
and glorified.
He has spoken through the prophets.
We believe in one holy catholic and apostolic Church.
We acknowledge one baptism for the forgiveness of sins.
We look for the resurrection of the dead,
and the life of the world to come. Amen.

Notes

Chapter 1 Where We Begin and Why
Pages 12-28

1 Friedrich Nietzsche, the superman; Karl Marx, the humanization of society; W. B. Yeats, the romance of aristocratic passion; James Joyce, literary art, realized as objectification of the human psyche; D. H. Lawrence (and William Carols Williams), truth derived from the ungarnished immediacy of the moment; Ernest Hemingway, physical courage; William Faulkner, the remnants of a lost local nobility; Wallace Stevens, imagery, meditation, and groundless hints of meaning for the sake of poetry as an end in itself. T. S. Eliot and W. H. Auden explored the Wasteland before turning in nostalgia to traditional faith, and in doing so they moved beyond modernism.

2 Mikhail Bakhtin, *Rabelais and His World,* trans. Hélène Iswolsky (Bloomington, Indiana: Indiana University Press, 1984),14.

3 Ibid., 18.

4 Ibid.,26, 27.20-21, 27.

5 Ibid.,11, 22, 11.

6 The term "cultural mass" comes from Daniel Bell, *The Cultural Contradictions of Capitalism* (New York: Basic Books, 1976; Paper 1978), 20n21.

7 Karl Rahner, *The Foundations of Christian Faith: An Introduction to the Idea of Christianity,* trans. William V. Dych

(New York: Crossroad, 1998). Both Father Rahner and the present author are deeply indebted to Pierre Teilhard de Chardin and to Martin Heidegger. See my *Kenneth Burke and Martin Heidegger: With A Note Against Deconstructionism* (Gainesville: University of Florida Press, 1980.) The indebtedness of the discussion to Hegel is obvious. I am also indebted to Hans Küng, especially for his *Does God Exist? An Answer for Today,* trans. Edward Quinn (New York: Crossroad, 1991.)

Chapter 2 The Wasteland
Pages 29-48

8   The other greatest masterpiece was the *Ulysses* of James Joyce, which, like *The Wasteland*, was published in 1922. For Joyce, the ending of the civilization of the past is the cause of celebration , which is the function of *Ulysses.*

9   Friedrich Nietzsche,*The Gay Science*, ed., trans. Walter Kaufmann (New York: Random House, 1974), 167.

10   Friedrich Nietzsche, *The Birth of Tragedy* in *The Birth of Tragedy and the Genealogy of Morals,* trans. Francis Golffing (Garden City, New York: Doubleday & Company, 1956), (Section 23) 135-6.

11   "The Second Coming,." *The Collected Poems of William Butler Yeats* (Definitive Edition;New York: Macmillan, 1956),184.

12   Martin Heidegger, "The Turning," (1962), in *The Question Concerning Technology and Other Essays*, trans. William Lovitt (New York: Harper & Row, 1977), 41-2.

13. In this chapter no effort will be made to discuss the contemporary knowledge of modern physics that is most relevant to religious thought. The effort here will be only to discuss the knowledge that in the past has in fact seemed most to influence thought on religion.

14. See John Horgan, *The End of Science: Facing the Limits of*

Knowledge in the Twilight of the Scientific Age (New York: Addison-Wesley Publishing Company. 1996).

15   By Timothy Egan, NYT, Monday, October 23, 2000, A1, A20.

16   John Henry Cardinal Newman, *Apologia Pro Vita Sua*, C. F. Harrold, ed.,(New York, 1949), Chapter 5.

17   Jean Baudrillard, *Illusion of the End,* trans. Chris Turner (Stanford, California: Stanford University Press,1994), 104-105.

Chapter 3 The Spiritual Imperative
Pages 49-65

18   "'Only a God Can Save Us': The *Spiegel* Interview (1966)," in Thomas Sheehan, ed. *Heidegger: The Man and the Thinker* (Chicago: Precedent Publishing, Inc., 1981), 57.

19   Pitrim A. Sorokin, *Crisis of Our Age*, 2n ed. (Oxford: One World Publications, Ltd.,1992), 219, 251, 256, 261.

20   Arnold Toynbee, *Civilization on Trial,* in *Civilization on Trial and The World and the West* (New York: The World Publishing Company, 1958), 143.

21   Jürgen Habermas, "Gershom Scholem: The Torah in Disguise (1978)," in *Philosophical- Political Profiles.* Frederick G. Lawrence, trans. (Cambridge: The MIT Press, 1983), p. 210.

22   Daniel Bell, *The Cultural Contradictions of Capitalism* (New York: Basic Books, 1978), 169, 170.

23   Giambattista Vico,*The New Science*, trans. Thomas Goddard Bergin and Max Harold Fisch (Ithaca: Cornell University Press, 1968), 424.

24   "A society is to its members what a god is to its faithful." "Since the universe exists only insofar as it is thought of and since it is thought of in its totality only by society, it takes its place within society; it becomes an element of

society's inner life, and thus is itself the total genus out-side of which nothing exists. The concept of totality is but the concept of society in abstract form." Emile Durkheim, *The Elementary Forms of Religious Life*, trans. Karen E. Fields (New York: The Free Press, 1995), 208,443.

25   Immanuel Kant, *Fundamental Principle of the Metaphysics of Morals*,   trans. T. K. Abbott (Buffalo, New York: Prometheus Books, 1988), 49.

26   "Along the way I have established that the fundamental categories of thought, and thus science itself, have religious origins" Durkheim, "Conclusion" of *Elementary Forms of Religious Life*, 421.

27   This interpretation of the Incarnation is partly indebted to Marcel Gauchet, *The Disenchantment of the World: A Political History of Religion*, trans. Oscar Burge (Princeton, New Jersey: Princeton University Press, 1997). See especially pages 74-79. This is a brilliant book developing extremely important insights, but I think its basic thesis is mistaken. Gauchet argues that the monotheism in the major religions and especially in Christianty is a religious development eventually assuring the demise of religion. I believe that both monotheism and Christianity were part of religious growth and that the contradictions, the mystery, in Christianity is a key to the continuing development of a deeper spirituality.

Chapter 4 The Inward Change
Pages 66-80

28   Martin Heidegger, *An Introduction to Metaphysics*, trans. Ralph Manheim (New Haven and London, 1959), 45.

29   "The Turning," (1962), in *The Question Concerning Technology and Other Essays*, trans. William Lovitt (New York: Harper & Row, 1977), 41-2.

30   Postmodernists may object to the inclusion of Heidegger
      in this list. After all, Derrida claims him as his closest
      progenitor. Heidegger anticipated a completion of the
      modern, which we may identify with postmodernism. See
      Heidegger's *Nietzsche*, volume IV, trans. Frank A. Capuzzi
      (New York: Harper and Row, 1982), 28. It is also true
      however, that he looked forward to our going beyond the
      modern (postmodern) to a more authentic culture. He
      emphatically did not authorize the negation of being that
      is Derrida's central message. Heidegger's brief adherence
      to the National Socialist party is, of course, totally abhor-
      rent, but it may also be taken as a measure of his vision of
      the cultural crisis in European civilization, and it cannot
      diminish the fact that with the possible exception of
      Wittgenstein, he is the philosopher most influential in the
      second half of this century.

31   Harvey Cox, *Fire from Heaven: The Rise of Pentecostal Spiri-
      tuality and the Reshaping of Religion in the Twenty-first
      Century* (New York: Addison-Wesley Publishing Co., 1995).
      The discussion of pentecostalism that follows is based on
      this book.

32   Of pentecostals world wide 13 percent are affluent, but 87
      percent live below the world poverty line. Ibid.,119.

33   Robert Wuthnow, "Indices of Religious Resurgence in the
      United States," in *Reigious Resurgence: Contemporary Cases
      in Islam, Christianity, and Judaism*, ed. Richard T. Antoun
      and Mary Elaine Hegland (Syracuse, New York: Syracuse
      University Press, 1987). Much of the data that follows on
      resurgence is from this book.

34   Doreen Carvajal, "In Books, It's Boom Time for Spirits,"
      The New York Times, "The Arts/Cultural Desk," November
      11, 1997. (The *Times* is hereafter *NYT*.)

35   D.J.R. Bruckner, "Theater in Review," Cultural Section,
      NYT, June 18, 1997.

36   Peter Marks, "Next Wave Festival: Review/Theatre; Songs

of Martyred Nuns," "The Arts/Cultural Section," *The New York Times* November 6, 1997.

37 Steven Drukman, "Theatre: In the Shoes (Five Pairs) of Women Seeking Solace," "Arts and Leisure Section," *NYT,* March 8, 1998.

38 Laurie Goodstein, "Television; Has Television Found Religion? Not Exactly," Arts and Leisure Section, *NYT,* November 30, 1997.

39 Bishop Joseph A. Fiorenza (of the Galveston-Houston Diocese), "Quinquennial Report Summary," *The Texas Catholic Herald,* April 24, 1998, p. 3.

40 Michael Novak, "The Most Religious Century," *NYT,* OP-ED Section, May 24, 1998, page 11.

41 Gertrude Himmelfarb, *One Nation, Two Cultures* (New York: Alfred A. Knopf, 1999), 90-91. She cites the forthcoming Robert W. Fogel, *The Fourth Great Awakening and the Future of Egalitarianism* (Chicago, 2000).

42 Hans Küng, *Does God Exist? An Answer for Today,* trans. Edward Quinn (New York: Crossroad, 1991), 185. Küng is a great Swiss Catholic theologian regrettably but necessarily deprived by the Church of his canonical mission to Catholic theology as the result of his position on Infallibility.

43 Neale Donald Walsch, *Conversations with God, Book 1*(New York: G. P. Putnam's Sons, 1995).

Chapter 5 Subjective Knowledge and Truth
Pages 81-101

44 We may say that a concept is simply the devocalized memory of a sound, for instance, the sound of "cup." It has always associated with it an incomplete and thus generalized memory of the physical image of cups. This compound of generalized auditory and visual memories that we call the concept "cup" may be applied to any particu-

lar cup, in which case the immediate meaning of "cup" is that particular cup on the shelf.

45   Clifford Geertz, *The Interpretation of Cultures* (New York: Basic Books, 1973), 136.

46   Ibid., 127.

47   Ibid., 130.

48   Michael Polanyi, *Personal Knowledge: Towards a Post-Critical Philosophy,* Corrected Edition, (Chicago: The University of Chicago Press,1962),49.

49   Mircea Eliade, *A History of Religious Ideas,* Vol. 1, *From the Stone Age to the Eleusinian Mysteries*, trans. Willard R. Trask (Chicago: The University of Chicago Press, 1978), 25- 166.

50   Ibid.,xiii.

51   Mircea Eliade, *Patterns in Comparative Religion,* trans. Rosemary Sheed (A Meridian Book. New York: New American Library, 1974), 463.

52   Ibid., 464.

53   Trinh Xuan Thuan, *The Secret Melody: And Man Created the Universe* (New York: Oxford University Press, 1995), 121.

54   Ibid., 118-119.

55   Ibid., 166, 190.

56   Ibid., 199.

57   Ibid., 224.

58   Ibid., 232.

59   Ibid., 239.

60   Ibid.,122.

61   Ibid.,271.

62   Ibid., 271.

63   Ibid., 272.

64   Alain Aspect, Philippe Grangier, and Gérard Roger, "Experimental Tests of Realistic Local Theories via Bell's Theorem," *Physical Review Letters,* 47(1981): 460-463.

65   The more recent experimentation has been done by Nicolas

Gisin and colleagues at the University of Geneva. *The New York Times*, July 22:(1997),B7,B11.

66 Henry Stapp, "Quantum Theory and the Physicist's Conception of Nature: Philosophical Implications of Bell's Theorem," in *The World View of Contemporary Physics: Does It Need a New Metaphysics?* ed. Richard Kitchener (Albany: State University of New York Press, 1988), note 8, chap 3.

67 Thuan, *Secret Melody*, 273-274.

Chapter 6 Reality Anew
Pages 102-117

68 Some of the names are as follows: Johann Gottfried Herder, Wilhelm von Humboldt, F. H. Bradley, Charles Sanders Peirce, T. S. Eliot, Mikhail Bakhtin, Lev Semyonovich Vygotsky, Martin Heidegger, Émile Benveniste, Susanne K. Langer, Hans-Georg Gadamer, Paul Ricoeur, Roland Barthes, Kenneth, Burke, Jacques Lacan, Maurice Merleau-Ponty, Alexander Romanovich Luria, Walker Percy, Nelson Goodman, Derek Bickerton.

69 Daniel L. Schacter, *Searching for Memory: The Brain, the Mind, and the Past* (New York: Basic Books, 1996), 162-180.

70 The sequence here is in accord with the "spreading activation theory" of M. Ross Quillian. Cited by Charles J. Lumsden and Edward O. Wilson, *Promethean Fire: Reflections on the Origin of Mind* (Cambridge: Harvard University Press, 1983), 82.

71 Ferdinand de Saussure,*Course in General Linguistics*, trans. Wade Baskin (New York: McGraw-Hill, 1966), 66.

72 Edmund Husserl, *The Crisis of European Sciences and Transcendental Phenomenology: An Introduction to Phenom-*

enological Philosophy, trans. David Carr (Evanston: North-western University Press, 1970), 145.

73   Ibid., 48-49,209. It is the world that can be discussed in natural language: it can be "linguistically explicated."

74   Martin Heidegger, *An Introduction to Metaphysics*, trans. Ralph Manheim (New Haven and London: Yale University Press, 1959),105.

75   Edmund Husserl, *The Crisis of European Sciences and Transcendental Phenomenology: An Introduction to Phenomenological Philosophy*, trans. David Carr (Evanston: North-western University Press, 1970), 112-113, 124-125, 59.

76   Edmund Husserl,"The Crisis of European Man," in *Phenomenology and the Crisis of Philosophy*, trans, Quentin Lauer (New York: Harper & Row (Harper Torchbooks), 1965), 140.

77   Husserl, *Crisis of European Sciences*, 108. This idea appears in Husserl's later work, but it is not central to his philosophy, in which phenomena became a kind of absolute.

78   Stanley Rosen, *The Question of Being: A Reversal of Heidegger* (New Haven and London: Yale University Press,1993), 63. Because of Husserl's "phenomenological reduction," which tended to make phenomena an absolute, Rosen dislikes Husserl's phrase "the life-world," preferring "the everyday world." I also reject the "reduction" but I do not make this distinction.

79   William Blake, *Milton: Book the First,* Plate 29, lines 6-10,14-16.

80   George Santayana, *Skepticism and Animal Faith*(New York: Dover Publications, 1955), 63.

81   P. F. Strawson, *Skepticism and Naturalism: Some Varieties* (Methuen, 1985). Cited by J. Z. Young, *Philosophy and the Brain* (Oxford: Oxford University Press, 1987), 214.

82   Martin Heidegger, *On the Way to Language,* trans. Peter D. Hertz (San Francisco: Harper & Row 1971), 35.

83   Rosen, *Question of Being*, 87.

84   Ibid., 122.

85   See Michael Polanyi, *Personal Knowledge: Towards a Post-Critical Philosophy* (Chicago: The University of Chicago Press, 1958).

86   Santayana, *Animal Faith*, 110.

87   Hilary Putnam, *Reason, Truth and History* (Cambridge: Cambridge University Press, 1981), 134, 144.

88   Stanley Rosen, *The Ancients and the Moderns: Rethinking Modernity* (New Haven; Yale University Press, 1989), 20.

89   Iris Murdoch, *Metaphysics as a Guide to Morals* (New York: Penguin Books, 1992), 140, 293.

90   Charles Taylor, "Rationality," in *Philosophy and the Human Sciences*, vol. 2 of *Philo sophical Papers* (New York: Cambridge University Press, 1985), 142.

91   Rosen, *Question of Being*, 91.

92   Kenneth Burke, *Attitudes Toward History*, 2d ed. (Boston: Beacon Press, 1961), 323

93   Charles Taylor, "Self-Interpreting Animals," in *Human Agency and Language*, vol. 1 of *Philosophical Papers*, 57.

94   Antonio R. Damasio, *Descartes' Error: Emotion, Reason, and the Human Brain* (New York: G. P. Putnam's Sons, 1994), xiii.

95   Alasdair MacIntyre, *Whose Justice? Which Rationality?* (Notre Dame, Indiana: University of Notre Dame Press, 1988), 396.

96   Alain Finkielkraut, *The Defeat of the Mind*, trans, Judith Friedlander (New York: Columbia University Press, 1995), 117.

97   Martin Heidegger, "Letter on Humanism," *Basic Writings*, ed. David Farrell Krell (New York: Harper & Row, 1997), 235.

98   Murdoch, *Metaphysics as a Guide*, 51.

99   Charles Taylor,"Language and Human Nature," in *Human Agency and Language*, 247.

100   Damasio, *Descartes' Error*, 246.

Chapter 7 History and Adornments of the Spirit
Pages 118-132

101 Etienne Gilson, *The Spirit of Medieval Philosophy*, trans. A. H. C. Downes (Notre Dame: University of Notre Dame, 1991), 276.

102 Ibid., 219.

103 "Letter to Carondelet, 5 January 1523," in John C. Olin, editor, *Christian Humanism and the Reformation: Selected Writings of Erasmus* (New York: Fordham University Press, 1987), 188.

104 Robin Lane Fox, *Pagans and Christians* (New York: HarperCollins, 1988), 102-167.

105 Rodney Stark, *The Rise of Christianity: A Sociologist Reconsiders History* (Princeton: Princeton University Press,1996),147-162.

106 Arnold Toynbee, *Civilization on Trial*, in *"Civilization on Trial" and "The World of the West"* (Cleveland, Ohio: World Publishing, 1958), 143.

107 Quoted by Paul Johnson, *A History of Christianity* (A Touchstone Book. New York: Simon & Schuster, 1995), 162.

108 The noosphere crowns the other spheres of evolutionary development, such as the hydrosphere, the atmosphere, and the biosphere. The term and the conception is from the great Father Pierre Teilhard de Chardin, *The Phenomenon of Man*, trans. Bernard Wall (New York: Harper & Brothers, 1959), 180-184.

109 Quoted by Karen Armstrong, *A History of God: The 4000-Year Quest of Judaism, Christianity and Islam* (New York: Alfred A. Knopf, 1994) , 220n32.

110 Martin Heidegger, *Being and Time*, trans. John Macquarrie

and Edward Robinson (New York: Harper and Row, 1962),355, 356, 358.

111   The Vatican II document *Lumen Gentium,* quoted by *Catechism of the Catholic Church,* Article 847.

112   Gilson, *Medieval Philosophy,* 172.

113   The formal expression of the faith adumbrated here is The Nicene Creed, which is to be found in Appendix C.

Chapter 8 Whore of Babylon or Bride of Christ
Pages 133—157

114   As a contribution to lay discussion of these topics, and without intending to usurp the magisterium, or teaching function, of the Church, I will express here my opinion on these questions. It seems clear to me that contraception must be approved and that abortion must not. Clerical celibacy is essential to the Church's ability to stand apart and serve as a restraint on subversive developments in the general culture. Female ordination in the celibate priesthood is much needed. The policy on annulments must be changed. There must be Church sponsorship of scientific research concerning the relation of the order of nature to homosexuality. The conception of the order of nature must be revised to include the life-world, as described in Chapter 6, "Reality Anew," as part of the order of nature. I defend Papal Infallibility later in the present chapter.

115   Andrew M. Greeley, *The Catholic Myth: The Behavior and Beliefs of American Catholics* (New York: Simon and Schuster, 1990), 46-46.

116   See, for instance, the reforms of Joseph II of Austria (1765-1790) who "completed the liberation of the serfs begun by his mother, granted freedom of religion within his domains, and filled his kingdom with schools, orphanages,

hospitals." Many of his reforms, says Eamon Duffy, "would be realized two centuries later in the Second Vatican Council."Eamon Duffy, *Saints and Sinners: A History of the Popes* (New Haven: Yale University Press, 1997),195, 197.

117 In Book XI, Browning's villain and arch-materialist says, "'You never know what life means till you die:/ Even throughout life, 't is death that makes life live,/Gives it whatever the significance." (2378-2380) Browning was a resolute partisan of religion and he firmly believed that there was a God but he also felt certain that we know nothing about the nature of God. His was a Protestant heritage and his faith in the end was limited to the individualistic affirmation of Romanticism. He also perceived the unity of life, of which *The Ring and the Book* is an artistic embodiment, but as a nineteenth century English liberal, he could place no hope in any human institution, much less the Roman Church.

118 This official, actually called Promoter of the Faith, has the mission of bringing to bear rigorous standards of proof to assure the objective basis of Sainthood.

119 Father Greeley assures us that the Church is essentially a democracy. This does not mean that he would object to the statement made here.

120 This tendency is placed in perspective and made noble in Hans Küng, *On Being a Christian*, trans. Edward Quinn (New York: An Image Book, Doubleday, 1984. Original German edition, 1974).

121 Marcel Gauchet, *The Disenchantment of the World: A Political History of Religion*, trans. Oscar Burge (Princeton, New Jersey: Princeton University Press, 1997), 181ff.

122 Wilfred M. McClay, "Two Concepts of Secularism," *The Wilson Quarterly* (Summer 2000), 54-71.

123 This idea is developed by the Russian Christian philosopher and linguist, Mikail Bakhtin, *The Dialogic Imagina-*

tion, trans. Caryl Emerson and Michael Holquist (Austin: University of Texas Press, 1981), 262-263 and elsewhere.

124 Quoted in *Catechism of the Catholic Church* (English translation, 1994),28.

125 Garry Wills, *Papal Sins: Structures of Deceit* (New York: Doubleday, 2000).

126 Robert D. Kaplan, *The Coming Anarchy: Shattering the Dreams of the Post-Cold War* (New York: Random House, 2000),34. 46-47.

Chapter 9 The Garden of Heresies
Pages 158-172

127 Quoted by Jacques Barzun, *From Dawn to Decadence: 500 Years of Western Cultural Life* (New York: HarperCollins Publishers, 2000), 40.

128 The profile is based on the article "Gnosticism," by Hans Jonas in *The Encyclopedia of Philosophy*, ed. Paul Edwards (New York: Macmillan Publishing Co, Ind. and The Free Press, 1967) 3:336-342.

129 Elaine Pagels, in *The Gnostic Gospels* (New York: Vintage Books, 1979,1989) develops at length the many passages in Saint Paul corresponding to Gnostic thought. She does not feel the evidence make a Gnostic of Paul, and she points out that he was explicitly opposed to the doctrine in general.

130 Max Weber, *The Sociology of Religion*, trans. Ephraim Fischoff (1963; Boston: Beacon Press, 1964),105.

131 Mircea Eliade, *From Guatama Buddha to the Triumph of Christianity*, trans. Willard R. Trask, vol. 2 of: *A History of Religious Ideas* (Chicago: The University of Chicago Press, 1982), 277-281.

132 Ibid., 352-358.

133 Ibid.,355.

134 Ibid.,42-45.

135 Ibid., 45.

136 Ibid., 48.

137 Ibid., 48, 81.

Chapter 10 Agents of Faith:
Saint Paul and the Great Emperor
Pages 173-192

138 The wording is that of the Cambridge University anthro-
pologist Keith Hart in his foreword to Roy A Rappaport's
Ritual and Religion in the Making of Humanity (Cambridge: Cambridge University Press, 1999), xvi. Hart
points out that Rappaport, in a book of tremendous importance, rejects this assumption and finds religion necessary to sustain civilization.

139 This is the statement of the extremely learned ex-nun,
Karen Armstrong, *A History of God: The 4000-Year Quest
of Judaism,, Christianity and Islam* (New York: Alfred A.
Knopf, 1994), 86. Miss Armstrong's deep piety would seem
to have required a repudiation of Christianity to justify
abandoning her vows.

140 Acts of the Apostles 22:4.

141 Acts of the Apostles 9:3-19.

142 Paul Johnson, *A History of Christianity* (1976; A Touchstone Book. New York: Simon & Schuster, 1995),5.

143 Edward Gibbon, *The Decline and Fall of the Roman Empire*, 3 vols. First published 1776- 1781. (Modern Library.
New York: Random House, nd), I:491.

144 Harold J. Chadwick, *The New Fox's Book of Martyrs*. Based
on John Foxe, *Foxe's Book of Martyrs*, first published in
Latin in 1554, in English in 1563. (New Brunswick, N. J.:
Bridge-Logos, 1997). 19-20.

145 Gibbon, *Decline*, 1:561.

146 Ibid.,568,569.

147 Ibid.,562.

148 Rodney Stark, *The Rise of Christianity: A Sociologist Reconsiders History* (Princeton, N.J.:Princeton University Press, 1996), 166.

149 Quoted and approved by the Oxford scholar Robin Lane Fox , *Pagans and Christians* (New York: HarperCollins, 1986), 609.

150 Stark, *Rise of Christianity*, 185.

151 Gibbon, *Decline*, 1:436.

152 Stark, *Rise of Christianity*, 7.

153 Ibid., 7.

154 Harold Bloom, *The American Religion: The Emergence of the Post-Christian Nation* (New York: Simon & Schuster, 1992).

155 Gibbon, *Decline*, 1:441,405,643.

156 Chadwick, *New Foxe's Martyrs*, 612.

157 Gibbon defers, though with tongue in cheek, to the "primary" causes, which many assume to be spiritual. Gibbon, *Decline*, 383.

158 Rodney Stark lays it down as a rule: *"As societies become older, larger, and more cosmopolitan, they will worship fewer gods of greater scope."* *The Rise of Christianity*, 201.

159 Johnson, *A History of Christianity*, 8. This entire discussion has been influenced by Johnson's book.

160 Ibid., 9.

161 Gibbon, *Decline*, 1: 394.

162 Elaine Pagels, *The Gnostic Gospels* (1979; Vintage Books. New York: Random House, 1989), xxxii.

163 The question has been treated by many writers. I draw especially upon the following: Gibbon, *Decline*, 1:383-430;Johnson, *History*, 5-15;Mircea Eliade, *From Gautama Buddha to the Triumph of Christianity*, vol. 2 of *A History of Religious Ideas*, Trans. Willard R. Trask (Chicago: The University of Chicago Press, 1982), 413-414; Stark, *Rise of Christianity*, 167,198.

164 Eliade, *History of Religious Ideas*, 2:413.

165 Stark, *Rise of Christianity*, 167.

166 Peter Brown, *The Cult of the Saints* (Chicago, University of Chicago Press,1981), 79.

167 Fox, *Pagans and Christians*, 609.

168 Gibbon, *Decline*, 1:405.

169 Fox, *Pagans and Christians*, 610, 611, 612.

170 Gibbon, *Decline*, 1:637.

171 Eliade, *History of Religious Ideas*, 2:411.

172 Johnson, *History*, 67-8.

173 Gibbon, *Decline*, 1:638.

174 Fox, *Pagans and Christians*, 624.

175 Gibbon, *Decline*, 1:644.

176 Ibid., 642.

177 Fox, *Pagans and Christians*, 622-623.

178 Ibid., 628.

179 Eusebius, *Life*, ii,70. Cited by Will Durant, *Caesar and Christ: A History of Rroman Civilization and of Christianity from their beginning to A.D. 325* (New York: Simon and Schuster, 1944), 659.

180 A fateful fact in the life of the Church was that through at least the eighth century Emperors assumed and were conceded Papal functions, sometimes issuing pronouncements that were edicts of both treason and heresy. On the other hand, at least from the eighth century on imperial ceremonies and some imperial functions were adopted by the Papacy. Johnson, *History*, 170, 171.

181 Eusebius, *Historical View of the Council of Nice*, 6. Cited by Durant, *Caesar and Christ*, 649.

182 Fox, *Pagans and Christians*, 655.

183 Johnson, *History*, 88.

184 Fox, *Pagans and Christians*, 655.

185 Ibid., 656.

186 Johnson, *History*, 88.

187 Fox, *Pagans and Christians*,642-653.

188 Ibid., 662. See Fox, page 22, on the general significance
     of the discovery revealing the existence of the Council of
     Antioch.
189 Ibid., 658.

Chapter 11 Power in the World and the Spirit
Pages 193-214

190 Paul Johnson, *A History of Christianity* (A Touchstone Book.
     New York: Simon & Schuster,1995), 107-109.
191 See above, p. 201. See also my *Kenneth Burke and Mar-
     tin Heidegger: With a Note Against Deconstructionism* (Uni-
     versity of Florida Monographs: Humanities Number 60.
     Gainsville: University of Florida Press, 1987).
192 I owe most of this paragraph to Henry Chadwick, *August-
     ine* (New York: Oxford University Press, 1986).
193 Max Weber, *The Sociology of Religion*, trans. Ephraim
     Fischoff (1963; Boston: Beacon Press, 1964), 241.
194 Ibid., 42,49,52.
195 Norman F. Cantor, *The Civilization of the Middle Ages* (New
     York; HarperCollins, 1993), 76.
196 The rank of deacon, which fell into disuse for centuries,
     was restored by Vatican II. A deacon is a member of the
     diaconate, one of the three forms of the sacrament of Holy
     Orders, the others being the priesthood and the episco-
     pacy. A deacon is authorized to do virtually everything a
     priest can do except say the mass. Deacons may be mar-
     ried and generally earn their livelihoods outside the Church
     in secular occupations.
197 Johnson, *History*, 132-133.
198 Cantor, *Civilization*, 86.
199 Johnson, *History*, 139.
200 Quoted by Johnson, *History*, 132.
201 Ibid., 148.
202 Ibid., 181.

203 Except as otherwise indicated, the facts concerning Gregory the Great and his namesake, Gregory VII, are from the remarkable work by J. N. D. Kelly, *The Oxford Dictionary of Popes* (New York: Oxford University Press, 1986).

204 Quoted by Johnson, *History*, 162.

205 Cantor, *Civilization*, 244.

206 Ibid., 252.

207 Mircea Eliade, *From Mohammad to the Age of Reforms*, trans. Willard R. Trask vol. 2 of *A History of Religious Ideas* (Chicago: The University of Chicago Press, 1982), 413

208 There are thus recognized two kinds of monasticism: the "eremitic" form of religious hermits and the "cenobitic" form of religious communities.

209 Johnson, *History*, 141.

210 Ibid., 149.

211 Ibid., 156.

212 Ibid., 151.

213 Weber, *Sociology of Religion*, 132.

214 Talcott Parsons,"Introduction," in Weber, *Sociology of Religion*, lii.

Chapter 12 Sins in the Church: Imperial Papacy and Feudal Lords Pages 215-243

215 This mass took place on March 12. 2000. See Vatican documents "Universal Prayer: Confession of Sins and Asking of Forgiveness" and "Homily of the Holy Father Asking Pardon." An earlier, thirty-three page document produced by a Vatican International Theological Commission had developed the historical and theological foundations for this extraordinary act, "Memory and Reconciliation: The Church and the Faults of the Past" (December 1999).

216 See, for instance, Garry Wills, "The Vatican Regrets" *The New York Review of Books*, May 25, 2000, 19-20.

("*the light of nations*"), "The Dogmatic Constitution of the Church" for its authority.

278   Karl Rahner, *Foundations of Christian Faith: An Intro-duction to the Idea of Christianity*, trans. William V. Dych (New York: Crossroad, 1997), 392-393.

279   Ibid., 188.

280   Paul Ricoeur, *Figuring the Sacred: Reilgion, Narrative, and Imagination*, trans David Pellauer, ed. Mark I Wallace (Minneapolis: Fortrees Press,1995), 5-6.

281   Roy A. Rappaport, *Ritual and Religion in the Making of Humanity* (New York: Cambridge University Press, 1999). Rappaport taught at the University of Michigan until his death in1997. From 1987 to 1989 he was President of the American Anthropological Association.

282   Ibid.,138-139.

283   Ibid., 407.

284   Ibid.,406.

285   Ibid., 103-106.

286   Ibid., 226-230. The quotation is on 230.

287   Ibid.,72-73.

288   Ibid., 73.

289   Ibid., 221-225.

290   Ibid.,16.

291   Gregorian chant is also called *Plainsong* or *Plainchant*. It is the traditional ritual melody of the Catholic Church, which grew up in the first centuries of Christianity. Its rhythms are based on the natural tendency of a speaker (especially in a large auditorium) to utter his words on one note with a dropping of the voice at the end of the sentence. It is not the regular rhythm of poetry but that of speech. Its formal development began under the influence of Saint Ambrose, Bishop of Milan, (See page 198 above.) at the end of the fourth century and brought to full development by Pope Gregory (See page 208, above.) in the sixth century. In the Mass, the words of the priest at

the elevation of the host are uttered in plainsong. It is also heard in the responsorial psalm that is sung by the cantor at intervals in the reading of Scripture.

Chapter 15 A Desert Catechism
Pages 282-296

292   In these words, John Henry Cardinal Newman, addressing a Catholic university in his *The Idea of a University*, formulated the aims of liberal education. For Cardinal Newman in the last half of the nineteenth century, the hope for society could rest on the character of the aristocracy and upper bourgeoisie who were educated by the universities. In our very different society that is not enough. We must hope for the cultural redemption of society as a whole or we can hope for nothing.

Appendix A
Pages 299-310

293   George Santayana, *Skepticism and a Animal Faith* (New York: Dover Publications, 1955), 273.

294   See Paul M. Churchland, *The Engine of Reason, the Seat of the Soul: A Philosophical Journey into the Brain*, A Bradford Book (Cambridge; The MIT Press, 1988), 178, 180.15

295   Santayana, *Animal Faith*, 237.

296   Alain Aspect, Philippe Grangier, and Gérard Roger, "Experimental Tests of Realistic Local Theories via Bell's Theorem," *Physical Review Letters*, 47(1981):460-463.

297   Henry Stapp, "Quantum Theory and the Physicist's Conception of Nature: Philosophical Implications of Bell's Theorem," in *The World View of Contemporary Physics: Does it Need a New Metaphysics?* ed. Richard Kitchener

(Albany: State University of New York Press, 1988), note 8, chapter 3.

298   Martin Heidegger, *Being and Time*, trans. John Macquarrie and Edward Robinson (New York: Harper and Row, 1962), 309,307.

299   Ibid., 284, 284, 291, 294, 298, 398, 356, 357, 378, 359.

INDEX

To order additional copies of this book, contact:
Xlibris Corporation
1-888-7-XLIBRIS
www.Xlibris.com
Orders@Xlibris.com

Crossing the Wasteland

An Intellectual Quest for God

Samuel B. Southwell